NEW PROCLAMATION

NEW PROCLAMATION

Year A, 2005

Easter through Pentecost

Barbara R. Rossing

John J. Pilch

Deirdre J. Good

Robert Kysar

Harold W. Rast, editor

FORTRESS PRESS

Minneapolis

NEW PROCLAMATION
Year A, 2005
Easter through Pentecost

Scripture quotations are from the New Revised Standard Version Bible, copyright © 1989 by the Division of Christian Education of the National Council of the Churches of Christ in the USA and are used by permission.

Cover design: Kantor Group, Minneapolis.
Illustrations: Lucinda Naylor, *Icon Two: Visual Images for Every Sunday,* © 2004 Augsburg Fortress.

Except from "Two Tramps in Mud Time" on p. 148 is from *The Poetry of Robert Frost,* edited by Edward Connery Latham. Copyright 1936 by Robert Frost, © 1964 by Lesley Frost Ballantine, © 1969 by Henry Holt and Co. Reprinted by permission of Henry Holt and Company, LLC, and The Random House Group, UK.

The Library of Congress has catalogued this series as follows.
New proclamation year A, 2001–2002 : Advent through Holy Week / Francis J. Moloney . . . [et al.].
      p. cm.
    Includes bibliographical references.
    ISBN 0-8006-4245-7 (alk. paper)
      1. Church year. I. Moloney, Francis J.
    BV30 .N48 2001
    251'.6—dc21   2001023746

New Proclamation, Year A, 2005, Easter through Pentecost
ISBN 0-8006-4252-X

The paper used in this publication meets the minimum requirements of American National Standard for Information Sciences—Permanence of Paper for Printed Library Materials, ANSI Z329.48-1984. ∞

Manufactured in the U.S.A.
09   08   07   06   05   1   2   3   4   5   6   7   8   9   10

In memory of

Harold W. Rast,

colleague and friend,

1933–2004

CONTENTS

THE SEASON OF PENTECOST
DEIRDRE J. GOOD

THE SEASON OF PENTECOST
ROBERT KYSAR

PREFACE

New Proclamation continues the time-honored Fortress Press tradition of offering a lectionary preaching resource that provides first-rate biblical exegetical aids for a variety of lectionary traditions.

Thoroughly ecumenical and built around the three-year lectionary cycle, *New Proclamation* focuses on the biblical texts, based on the conviction that those who acquire a deeper understanding of the pericopes in both their historical and liturgical contexts will be motivated to preach engaging and effective sermons. For this reason, the most capable North American biblical scholars and homileticians are invited to contribute to *New Proclamation*.

We have asked the contributors to follow a similar pattern in their presentations but have allowed them to alter and improve that pattern in ways they think might be more helpful to the user. For example, one of the authors in a previous volume began each discussion of the Sunday lections with the Gospel rather than the First Reading, since it is assumed that most users preach on the Gospel reading for the day. In other instances, some authors have chosen to combine the interpretation and response to the texts into one section rather than separating them into two distinct sections.

In general, *New Proclamation* is planned and designed to be user-friendly in the following ways:

- *New Proclamation* is published in two volumes per year, designed for convenience. The present volume covers the lections for the second half of the church year, Easter through Pentecost, which culminates in Christ the King Sunday.

- The two-volume format offers a larger, workbook-style page with a lay-flat binding and space for making notes.

- Each season of the church year is prefaced by an introduction that provides insights into the background and spiritual significance of the period.
- The application of biblical texts to contemporary situations is an important concern of each contributor. Exegetical work is concise, and thoughts on how the texts address today's world and our personal situations have a prominent role.
- Although the psalms ("Responsive Reading") are infrequently used as preaching texts, brief comments on each assigned psalm are included so that the preacher can incorporate reflections also on these in the sermon. The psalms, for the most part, represent the congregation's response to the first reading and are not intended as another reading.
- Boxed quotations in the margins help signal important themes in the texts for the day.
- The material for Year A is here dated specifically for the year 2005 for easier coordination with other dated lectionary materials.
- These materials can be adapted for uses other than for corporate worship on the day indicated. They are well suited for adult discussion groups or personal meditation and reflection.

It is important to keep in mind that the Gospel is the formative principle of the lectionary and that most sermons are based on it. From the First Sunday of Advent to Trinity Sunday of each year, the Old Testament reading is closely related to the Gospel reading for the day. However, from the first Sunday after Trinity Sunday to the end of the year (Christ the King), provision has been made for two patterns of reading the Old Testament in the RCL: (1) paired readings in which the Old Testament and Gospel readings are closely related, and (2) semi-continuous Old Testament readings that are not necessarily related to the Gospel.

We thank Barbara R. Rossing, John J. Pilch, Deirdre J. Good, and Robert Kysar for sharing their insights and experiences from years of committed Christian preaching. We hope that you find in this volume ideas, stimulation, and encouragement for your ministry of proclamation.

HAROLD W. RAST

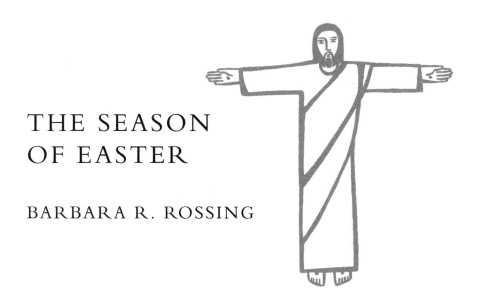

THE SEASON OF EASTER

BARBARA R. ROSSING

The Easter celebration at the tomb of Jesus in Jerusalem begins with the Holy Fire. In a ritual that dates back more than twelve hundred years, the Greek Orthodox Patriarch stoops to enter the darkened stone shrine in the center of the Church of the Holy Sepulchre. The crowd waits expectantly with bundles of thirty-three slender candles in their hands (to mark the years of Christ's life on earth) that will be lit from the Holy Fire. A small flicker of light miraculously appears in the ancient tomb where Jesus' body was buried so long ago. When the patriarch emerges, flame lit from Jesus' sepulchre is raucously passed from outstretched hand to outstretched hand, extending the light of the risen Christ throughout the community and throughout the city.

Resurrection dawns again in our midst this year, beginning at the tomb. Whether as a flickering candle in a sepulchre or the flicker of hope in war-torn Iraq, Easter proclaims that God brings life out of death—right in the midst of our most hopeless or violent situations. All the Easter Scripture texts underscore this new life of faith and hope. Resurrection hope transforms communities of beleaguered followers into courageous witnesses to Jesus' presence. Resurrection calls on believers to "give account for the hope that is within you" (1 Peter 3:15).

The Emmaus story, assigned for the Third Sunday of Easter, has become for me a paradigmatic model of how to experience resurrection in daily life. I return to this wonderful story in Luke 24 again and again. Only in Year A does this story get top billing on Sunday morning, although it is assigned for Easter Eve in every year of the lectionary. We need to lift up the Emmaus text for people. Like those two dejected disciples walking the wrong direction, away from Jerusalem, we so often fail to see glimpses of resurrection even when they are right beside us. We get stuck in rehashing our own dejected stories of "we had hoped" over and over. We miss the luminous presence of Christ in our midst.

And then something breaks through— some "Aha" moments of seeing God's risen presence on the roads of our world, as Jesus breaks bread and opens the scriptures to us. In the midst of shattered dreams, in the midst of all that "we had hoped," Jesus falls in walking with us and renews our hope.

The fifty days of Easter are a time to see and celebrate the presence of the risen Christ alive in the world today—overturning the forces of death. We find Christ in the Scriptures and breaking bread. We find Christ in the scars and wounds that he shows to us, reminders of torture and execution. We find him in shattered hopes and deep fears, coming through locked doors and meeting us when we flee. Our hearts are set on fire with the "Aha" of recognizing Christ's presence with us on all our Emmaus journeys. The task of the preacher is to give voice to the resurrection, to name the living Christ who accompanies us.

Resurrection is a lively topic of study these days, and I seek to bring some of those recent scholarly resources to preachers. Most of all, however, the questions that drive this commentary are not so much what happened two thousand years ago, but what difference Jesus' resurrection makes in the world. How is Jesus alive and loose in the world today? On what roads is he walking with us? These are the questions that biblical writers address in the texts assigned for this season.

The Epistle of 1 Peter shows how people who have no home or story become God's own people, chosen and precious. The sense of living hope and "home" at the heart of 1 Peter can transform us today, just as it transformed communities of displaced exiles living under Roman imperial violence in the first century. The Acts of the Apostles take us back to the early church, back to our beginnings, to learn the power of resurrection for our daily life together. With the apostles we enter into the joy of the early Christian community's breadbreaking and economic sharing; we witness their courageous testimony in the face of empire and hardship. Most of all, in the gospel stories for the Easter season, we hear the assurance that God is with us always. The risen Christ has already gone ahead of us to Galilee, to meet us again and again in the world.

THE RESURRECTION OF OUR LORD (EASTER DAY)

MARCH 27, 2005

REVISED COMMON	EPISCOPAL (BCP)	ROMAN CATHOLIC
Acts 10:34-43	Acts 10:34-43	Acts 10:34a, 37-43
or Jer. 31:1-6	or Exod. 14:10-14, 21-25; 15:20-21	
Ps. 118:1-2, 14-24	Ps. 118:14-29 or 118:14-17, 22-24	Ps. 118:1-2, 16-17, 22-23
Col. 3:1-4	Col. 3:1-4	Col. 3:1-4 or 1 Cor. 5:6b-8
or Acts 10:34-43	or Acts 10:34-43	
John 20:1-18	John 20:1-10 (11-18)	John 20:1-9
or Matt. 28:1-10	or Matt. 28:1-10	

FIRST READING

ACTS 10:34-43 (RCL, BCP);
ACTS 10:34a, 37-43 (RC)

Interpreting the Text

In many traditions during the Easter season, the First Lesson is taken from the Acts of the Apostles instead of the Old Testament. The goal is to see and proclaim Christ as alive in the world and the church today, just as in the immediate post-Easter period of Acts. The message of Acts is that the risen Jesus lives on in the stories and the life of the community. "Jesus did not wear a shroud for long," reminds activist-poet Daniel Berrigan is his commentary on the book of Acts. The preacher can invite people to see the book of Acts as "our Acts, as well as the Apostles."[1]

Peter's speech from Acts 10 comes from the larger story of Peter's and Cornelius's mutual "conversions"—Peter's conversion to the gospel's inclusion of Gentiles and Cornelius's conversion to faith in Christ. Peter could not understand the radical meaning of his vision of the sheet full of unclean animals until he was sent to the house of the God-fearing Roman military officer Cornelius. Now "I truly understand," says Peter of his newfound conversion, that God "does not discriminate." Table fellowship between Jews and Gentiles symbolizes the radical boundary-crossing embrace of Jesus, the Jesus who himself "ate and drank" with sinners and Gentiles.

The narrative context of the encounter is what makes Peter's speech so dramatic. Even though the narrative is not included in this Easter pericope, the preacher can bring it in. Today's text gives us the very first words that Cornelius and his household hear about Jesus, the very first sermon to a Gentile audience in the book of Acts. It is this context of conversion as well as ethnic boundary-crossing that makes this speech so powerful as a resurrection text. Resurrection changes the social structures of our world.

Reflecting the radical inclusiveness of the gospel, Peter teaches Cornelius the essence of Christianity in a short creedal summary about Jesus. Like all the speeches in Acts, it shows Luke's careful shaping: God came "preaching peace by Jesus Christ" (v. 36). The core summary of the ministry of Jesus is that he was anointed with the Holy Spirit and "went about doing good and healing all who were oppressed by the devil" (v. 38); they put Jesus to death "on a tree," but God raised him up on the third day. We are witnesses to the fact that Jesus "ate and drank" with people (a probable reference to the issue of table fellowship with Gentiles, v. 41). In Jesus' name, God grants forgiveness to everyone who believes.

Responding to the Text

Both the narrative context and the specifics of Peter's sermon make for great Easter proclamation. Cornelius, a soldier, represented the hated, occupying Roman military empire—yet God gave him a vision that Peter needed to hear. The entire story reminds of how we need one another's experiences and visions of resurrection—even those of our enemies—in order to grasp God's big picture. Peter had to learn his own sermon message: that God shows no partiality.

Peter still had to go back to the Jewish Christian community to persuade them of the legitimacy of Cornelius's conversion, much as the church today must test appeals to the Peter/Cornelius story regarding specific debates about inclusiveness on issues such as sexuality.[2] But Peter's conversion, followed by his moving sermon and conversion of the whole household of Cornelius, reminds us that God's

THE ENTIRE STORY REMINDS OF HOW WE NEED ONE ANOTHER'S EXPERIENCES AND VISIONS OF RESURRECTION—EVEN THOSE OF OUR ENEMIES—IN ORDER TO GRASP GOD'S BIG PICTURE.

bigger vision often includes those whom we exclude—whether pacifists, military officers, or those whose sexuality we question, or those of a different ethnicity. Resurrection life brings about radical, boundary-crossing consequences for the church and for individual Christians!

Set in the middle of Baruch's (Jeremiah's scribe and student) memoirs, chapters 30–33 offer a word of hope and promise to a people scattered and torn apart by invading empires, war, and exile. These verses resonate with images of the exodus. Not only does God promise "grace in the wilderness" (vv. 2-3), but the assurance that Israel will celebrate with "the dance of the merrymakers" alludes to Miriam's dance of victory by the waters of the Red Sea, following the exodus (Exod. 15:21). Just as the Israelites celebrated with abandon at their release from the hands of Pharaoh, so once again God promises to bring rest to the wanderers (v. 2), to restore, renew, and rebuild Israel's abundance (vv. 4-5), and to restore the worshiping community (v. 6). The joy of such prophetic vision on Easter Sunday is the assurance that God restores, renews, and rebuilds our lives and communities again and again in a cycle of resurrection, a cycle that continues with our own encounter of the risen Christ today and comes to fulfillment in the promise to make all things new.[3]

EXODUS 14:10-14, 21-25;
15:20-21 (BCP, alt.)

The parting of the Red Sea waters tells of rescue, deliverance, fulfillment, and witness to God's liberating presence, a story read also at the Easter Vigil. The familiar larger-than-life details—walls of water (v. 22), the Egyptians tripping over their own equipment (v. 25)—make for a melodramatic scene of victory for the good side and doom for the evil side. Yet v. 18, which is left out in the lection, tempers this decisive split between good and evil with the proclamation that even "the Egyptians shall know that I am the LORD." Easter celebration is about the extremes of reversals. Slaves are set free. Those in bondage triumph over their captors. The crucified one lives again. We identify ourselves with those who experience such reversals. We are the slaves, the ones in captivity. And we have triumphed! But we are also the Egyptians who chase after those whom we oppress. Verse 18 gets at the heart of the matter in proclaiming that even the Egyptians know God's power in their lives. Easter reversals bring the presence, knowledge, and transformational power of God's revelation into every aspect of our identity. And as a result, we celebrate victory! Miriam's song and the celebration of the women on the shores of the Red Sea (Exod. 15:20-21) proclaim God's victory in a sensual feast of poetry,

> EASTER CELEBRATION IS ABOUT THE EXTREMES OF REVERSALS. SLAVES ARE SET FREE. THOSE IN BONDAGE TRIUMPH OVER THEIR CAPTORS. THE CRUCIFIED ONE LIVES AGAIN.

dancing, singing, rhythm, and music. The song itself is one of the oldest surviving pieces of Hebrew poetry. Also reflective of the ancient tradition is the designation of Miriam as a "prophet" (15:20), an attestation to her importance within the life of Israel.

RESPONSIVE READING

PSALM 118:1-2, 14-24 (RCL);
PSALM 118:14-29 or 118:14-17, 22-24 (BCP);
PSALM 118:1-2, 16-17, 22-23 (RC)

Psalm 118, a community song of thanks sung by Jews at the Passover seder, is also "the Church's Easter psalm par excellence," sung at the Easter Vigil and the Easter morning liturgy in all three years of the lectionary.[4] Martin Luther said that he "fell in love with this Psalm" and prized it above all others.[5] Repetition gives the psalm its power, with the ever-intensifying declaration that God's "steadfast love (*hesed*) endures forever!" Verses 10-13 (omitted here, sung during Holy Week) describe the trauma of torture and death. But God has triumphed over death, leading the psalmist to proclaim, "I shall not die, but I shall live, and recount the deeds of the LORD" (v. 17). For Christians, Jesus Christ is the stone rejected by builders who has become the cornerstone (v. 22), and he is marvelous in our sight.

SECOND READING

COLOSSIANS 3:1-4 (RCL, BCP, RC)

Interpreting the Text

Easter invites us to turn our minds to the "things that are above," and to order our lives in light of the resurrection. This passage from Colossians sets the context for the lengthy ethical exhortation that will occupy the second half of this epistle. Since we are Easter people, and since we have been raised with Christ, this fact must transform every structure of our lives.

Colossians was probably not written by Paul, as evidenced in this very statement that "you have been raised with Christ" (v. 1), which conflicts with Paul's own careful formulations in Romans 6 that we have been "buried with Christ" but, presumably, not yet raised. Yet the soaring "realized eschatology" perspective on resurrection that permeates this letter offers a wonderful basis for a transformed ethic for Easter Christians. The entire letter of Colossians proclaims an expansive Christology and soteriology—the vision of a cosmic Christ in whom "all things" were created, and in whom all things hold together.[6] The letter's cosmic vision reminds us that resurrection means new creation. The declaration that our lives are "hidden with Christ in God" gives us a new geography. Christ's resurrection now locates our lives in the very heart of God.

ACTS 10:34-43 (BCP, alt.)

See the comments on today's First Reading.

1 CORINTHIANS 5:6b-8 (RC, alt.)

See the comments for Easter Evening, Second Reading, below.

THE GOSPEL

JOHN 20:1-18 (RCL);
JOHN 20:1-10 (11-18) (BCP);
JOHN 20:1-9 (RC)

Interpreting the Text

The Gospel of John narrates vivid stories of Jesus' Easter appearances to individual disciples as models of faith for the entire community. They are written "so that you may come to believe that Jesus is the Christ . . . and that through believing you may have life in his name" (20:31). Familiar phrases from the Synoptic Gospels, such as "He is risen," do not appear in this text. Rather, the Johannine focus is on "seeing" and "believing." Mary Magdalene is the disciple whose story frames this episode (vv. 1-2, 11-18). Having stood with the other women and the beloved disciple at the foot of the cross (19:25), Mary is now the first person at the tomb.

THE JOHANNINE FOCUS IS ON "SEEING" AND "BELIEVING."

Sandwiched into Mary Magdalene's story is the narrative of Peter and the beloved disciple running to the tomb. Shifts in the verbs used for "seeing" may reflect stages on the way toward faith in John 20.[7] Initially, Mary "sees" (*blepei*, v. 1) that the tomb is empty and fears that grave robbers have taken Jesus' body. The same verb describes the beloved disciple's "seeing" the grave cloths in v. 5— sight that is not yet faith. Peter also "sees" (*theōrei*) the grave cloths, just as Mary "sees" the two angels in v. 12, but even this seeing is still not faith. Only the "seeing" marked by the verb *horan* is perfect sight that leads to faith—and in keeping with this Gospel's preference for the beloved disciple, this sight is first achieved by the beloved disciple upon entrance into the tomb: "he saw (*eiden*) and believed" (v. 8). Mary also comes to this same kind of sight, as evidenced in her testimony to the disciples, "I have seen the Lord" (v. 18).

The "garden" setting for Jesus' tomb (*kēpos*, 19:41) and for the Lord's appearance to Mary Magdalene is unique to the Fourth Gospel. Paradise traditions may lie behind this garden encounter if the irony in Mary's identification of Jesus as the "gardener" is a deliberate allusion to God as gardener in Gen. 3:8. The garden of the sepulchre now restores what was lost in the first garden. Some ancient commentators and feminist scholars hear echoes also of the garden of the Song of Solomon in vv. 11-18, as Mary searches for her beloved ("Have you seen him whom my soul loves?" Song of Sol. 3:3); Mary "peers into" the tomb (*parakyptō*, v. 11—the same word as the Greek text for Song of Sol. 2:9); her beloved has "gone to the garden" (Song of Sol. 6:2); and when Mary finds Jesus there, she "holds him and would not let him go" (Song of Sol. 3:4). In her desire to hold on to the Lord, Mary may be a representative for the Johannine community that feels "orphaned" (14:18) and longs for an ongoing intimate relationship with Jesus.

Jane Schaberg suggests that the appearance of Jesus to Mary Magdalene also echoes the story of Elijah's ascent into heaven in 2 Kings 2, a prophetic succession narrative.[8] The word "ascending" furnishes the link: Jesus says, "I am ascending to my Father" (present tense, v. 17). In Schaberg's view, John portrays Jesus as in the actual process of ascending when he meets Mary in the garden. Mary now witnesses his ascension, much as Elisha witnessed Elijah's ascent into heaven. If such a parallel to Elijah's ascension is intended, it means that in some sense Jesus is commissioning Mary Magdalene to be his successor, just as Elijah commissioned Elisha.

The command not to cling to Jesus (v. 17) is not necessarily a rebuke of Mary but an indication that Jesus' resurrected body is now transformed—understandable especially if Jesus is in the process of his ascension. From now on, Mary's relationship to her beloved is to be expressed not through touch but through testimony.

Jesus commissions Mary to go to the disciples with news of his appearance. He also tells her of his new familial relationship with them: For the first time in the Gospel Jesus refers to his followers as "brothers and sisters" (v. 7; the Greek *adelphoi* includes the feminine). Mary is to proclaim that Jesus' God is now "my God and your God."

Responding to the Text

Whether or not the 2 Kings 2 link to a prophetic succession narrative is convincing, John 20 is certainly an occasion for highlighting the apostolic witness of Mary Magdalene, an "apostle to the apostles," as early exegetes described her. The popularity of the novel *The DaVinci Code* has generated a great deal of interest in the historical figure of Mary Magdalene. While Dan Brown's novel sexualizes the relationships between Mary and Jesus, in my view it is more liberating to highlight instead her apostolic relationship. Gnostic texts such as the *Gospel of Mary Magdalene* help us appreciate the antiquity and richness of the tradition of Mary's apostolic role, but we can also see that role in canonical texts such as John 20.

Christianity owes its existence to Mary's witness, to her model of faith that responds to Jesus speaking her name and goes out from the garden into the world in public proclamation. Mary does not hold on to Jesus but goes forth in faith to proclaim to the disciples, who had returned to their homes, "I have seen the Lord."

Other characters in John 20 remind us that not all Christians can expect such intimate and personal encounters as Mary's in the garden as a basis for faith. The beloved disciple is the first person to "believe," although he himself does not meet the risen Jesus. Peter models a faithfulness that heeds the words of Mary and runs to accompany the beloved disciple to the tomb yet does not fully understand the scriptures.

John's Gospel, like all the Easter Gospels, acknowledges the difficulty of faith in the risen Jesus. In the combining of these different experiences of resurrection—Mary's, Peter's, and the beloved disciple's—the text places value on each one. Understanding of the Easter event builds piece by piece in John 20, progressively for the individual characters and progressively for the community of faith. This valuing of

> JOHN 20 IS CERTAINLY AN OCCASION FOR HIGHLIGHTING THE APOSTOLIC WITNESS OF MARY MAGDALENE, AN "APOSTLE TO THE APOSTLES," AS EARLY EXEGETES DESCRIBED HER.

different experiences and ways of coming to faith can be a source of strength for us, both as individuals and as the community of faith. The task of the preacher is to tell the resurrection story in such a way that each person hears the risen Jesus calling him or her by name.

MATTHEW 28:1-10 (BCP, alt.)

Interpreting the Text

Matthew's empty tomb story proclaims the glory, wonder, and majesty of Jesus' resurrection. The women go the tomb not as mourners to anoint a dead body with spices, as in Mark's Gospel, but rather with the confidence of disciples going to "see." What they see is an apocalyptic scene, a life and death drama that shakes even the earth itself.

Matthew strengthens Mark's focus on the faithfulness of the women as model disciples. Whether the preacher chooses this Gospel or the John 20 text, the central role of Mary Magdalene is important to emphasize in both scenes—as attested in the Easter Proper Preface for Holy Communion: "Therefore with Mary Magdalene and Peter, with all the witnesses of the resurrection, with earth and sea and all their creatures, we praise your name and join their unending hymn." Unlike Mary's intimate, solitary encounter with Jesus in John's garden, in Matthew's Gospel Mary goes to the tomb together with the other Mary.

As in Mark's Gospel, all the male disciples flee before Jesus' crucifixion (Matt. 26:56). Meanwhile, the "many women" who had followed Jesus from Galilee and "ministered" to him (*diakoneo*) stand by him through his crucifixion, looking on from afar. Among these many women the text names Mary Magdalene, Mary the mother of James and Joseph, and the mother of the sons of Zebedee (Matt. 27:55-56). Mary Magdalene and the other Mary also witnessed Joseph of Arimathea's burial of Jesus' body and the sealing of the tomb with a large stone (Matt. 27:62).

> WHETHER THE PREACHER CHOOSES THIS GOSPEL OR THE JOHN 20 TEXT, THE CENTRAL ROLE OF MARY MAGDALENE IS IMPORTANT TO EMPHASIZE IN BOTH SCENES.

These two women keep vigil opposite the sepulchre, unwavering in their faithfulness to Jesus even in his death.

The same two Marys go again to Jesus' sepulchre two days later, in continuity with their previous faithfulness. They go to "see," presumably in anticipation of his resurrection—perhaps recalling Jesus' predictions that he would go to Jerusalem to be killed and that he would be raised on the third day (16:21; 17:22-23; 20:18-19). Matthew's Gospel is ambiguous as to whether the women's predawn visit to the tomb means that they know and believe the promises of resurrection.

A great earthquake accentuates the supernatural, spectacular dimension of Jesus' resurrection—an echo of the earthquake at Jesus' crucifixion two days earlier that split rocks and opened tombs (Matt. 27:51-52). Both crucifixion and resurrection shake the foundations of heaven and earth, fulfilling Old Testament prophecies such as Ezek. 37:12-13: "I will open your graves and lead you out of your graves."[9] Crucifixion and resurrection also shake the imperial regime's political grip, as symbolized by the terrified Roman guards who are like dead men. Resurrection is a profoundly political event in Matthew, proclaiming that the Roman imperial rule of death did not have the last word.[10]

A mighty angel rolls back the stone and invites the women to see the empty tomb where Jesus had lain. Jesus has risen, he is not here! It may be appealing to preach the supernatural elements of resurrection in Matthew—the earthquakes, the dazzling angel with a face like lightning who rolls away the stone, the zombie-like state of the Roman guards. If so, the preacher should include the anti-imperial political dimension of this apocalyptic portrait. But I find equally liberating for today the angel's promise that Jesus has "gone ahead" (*proagei*) into Galilee. The angel commissions the women to tell the disciples that Jesus has "gone ahead" to Galilee. The Greek verb for "going ahead" (*proagei*) conveys the sense of "leading," the same word Matthew uses to describe the star that would "go ahead" of the magi and led them to the infant Jesus (Matt. 2:9).

No sooner do the women set off running in obedience to the angel's command than Jesus himself meets them on the road. We are told nothing about Jesus' physical appearance, only that he greets the women and they immediately recognize him. He gives them the same charge as the angel: They must proclaim to the disciples that he has gone to Galilee. The women "worship" Jesus (v. 9), an action echoed later in the eleven disciples' "worshiping" of him on the mountain in Galilee (28:17)—evidence that the women did indeed go and testify to the disciples.

Responding to the Text

Jesus promised his disciples before his death (Matt. 26:32) that he would "go ahead" of them to Galilee, even though the twelve disciples would all fall away. For us today, as for the women at the tomb, this means that Jesus goes ahead of us to lead us into the world—into a transformative way of life that testifies to the power of resurrection wherever we live. "Jesus is going ahead—not going away," notes Elisabeth Schüssler Fiorenza, underscoring the horizontal dimension of the angel's words.[11] The "empty tomb does not signify absence but presence: it announces the Resurrected One's presence on the road ahead, in a particular space of struggle and recognition."[12]

Where does Jesus "go ahead" of us into Galilee, into the world, in this Easter season? Marianne Sawicki argues that the disciples are commanded specifically to go to Galilee because Galilee is the location of "the mountain to which Jesus had directed them. . . . In effect, the Christian who wants to see the risen Lord is being directed to the Beatitudes and the Sermon on the Mount—or rather, to *obedience* to these teachings."[13] The commissioning of the Eleven on the mountain in Galilee in Matt. 28:16-20 confirms obedience to Jesus' teachings in the Sermon on the Mount as the Matthean goal.

But if Schüssler Fiorenza is right that Matthew's emphasis (like Mark's) is that Jesus is "going ahead" in a horizontal sense—rather than going up into heaven—then Matthew is teaching us to look for experiences of resurrection presence not only in Galilee but also in Galveston, Galesburg, or Grand Forks—on all the roads of our lives. "Resurrection means that Jesus, the Living One, goes ahead of us. . . . The Living One can be found only when we experience that 'he is ahead of us' and that he opens up a future for us." Like the women, we can run to meet that liberating future. The stone has been rolled away.

The command to go to Galilee does not whitewash the experience of death and violence. Resurrection comes to us first of all in our most broken and unexpected places, breaking the structures of the Roman occupation regime in Jerusalem and the structures of every regime of death in our lives today. The story of Mary Magdalene and the women at the empty tomb can help us develop "our own christological meaning-making in the face of violence and killing today."[14]

Notes

1. So Daniel Berrigan, *Whereon to Stand: The Acts of the Apostles and Ourselves* (Baltimore: Fortcamp Publishing, 1991), xxi, 169. Berrigan repeats the refrain, "Our Acts as well as the Apostles'" throughout his commentary.

2. See, for example, Luke Timothy Johnson, *Decision Making in the Church* (Philadelphia: Fortress Press, 1983), as well as recent church study materials on homosexuality.

3. I am grateful to Katherine Shaner, my research assistant, for writing this explication and comments on other psalms and alternate readings for the Second, Third, Fourth, and Fifth Sundays of Easter.

4. Irene Nowell, *Sing a New Song: The Psalms in the Sunday Lectionary* (Collegeville, Minn.: Liturgical Press, 1993), 116.

5. *Luther's Works,* American Edition, 14:45.

6. See Elaine Siemsen, "*Ta Panta!* All Things Restored!" *The Lutheran* (April 2004), 20–22 (http://www.thelutheran.org/0404/page20.html)

7. This is not the case in John's Gospel as a whole, however, which employs verbs for "seeing" interchangeably. See Raymond Brown, *The Gospel according to John,* 2 vols., Anchor Bible 29 (New York: Doubleday, 1970), 1:501–2.

8. Jane Schaberg, *The Resurrection of Mary Magdalene: Legends, Apocrypha, and the Christian Testament* (New York: Continuum, 2003), 304–51.

9. So N. T. Wright, *The Resurrection of the Son of God* (Minneapolis: Fortress Press, 2003), 633. Wright also cites Isaiah 26; Zechariah 14; and Daniel 12.

10. For a political reading of Matthew 28 see especially Warren Carter, *Matthew and the Margins: A Socio-Political and Religious Reading* (Maryknoll, N.Y.: Orbis, 2000).

11. Elisabeth Schüssler Fiorenza, *Jesus: Miriam's Child, Sophia's Prophet* (New York: Continuum, 1995), 126.

12. Ibid., 126.

13. Marianne Sawicki, "Recognizing the Risen Lord," *Theology Today* 44 (1988): 446 (http://theologytoday.ptsem.edu/jan1988/v44-4-article2.htm).

14. Schüssler Fiorenza, *Jesus,* 125.

THE RESURRECTION OF OUR LORD (EASTER EVENING)

MARCH 27, 2005

REVISED COMMON	EPISCOPAL (BCP)	ROMAN CATHOLIC
Isa. 25:6-9	Acts 5:29a, 30-32 or Dan. 12:1-3	
Psalm 114	Psalm 114 or Psalm 136 or Ps. 118:14-17, 22-24	Ps. 118:1-2, 16-17, 22-24
1 Cor. 5:6b-8	1 Cor. 5:6b-8 or Acts 5:29a, 30-32	
Luke 24:13-49	Luke 24:13-35	Luke 24:13-35

Easter Eve emphasizes food as a sign of resurrection, culminating in the wonderful story of breaking bread at Emmaus—a favorite resurrection appearance story for many. In a world of hunger, meals with God underscore the joy of abundance. Meals also prove the tangible dimension of resurrection: Jesus is risen in the flesh! He can eat and so can we!

FIRST READING
ISAIAH 25:6-9 (RCL)

The banquet of abundant food links this text to the meal setting of the Emmaus encounter (Luke 24). God sets for us a rich table on Mount Zion and then, in a final course of the meal, God "swallows up death forever." Such an Old Testament reference to the end to death is very rare. Tenderly, God will wipe away all tears and will destroy the shroud of death that was cast over us. Easter celebrates that "this is our God," who invites us to the great eschatological feast and destroys our death.

ACTS 5:29a, 30-32 (BCP)

Peter's speech before the Sanhedrin after the escape from prison enrages the audience. Only the intervention of Gamaliel will save the disciples this time. Characteristic Lukan themes in this speech include the Holy Spirit and allusions to scripture. The reference to "hanging on a tree" draws on Deut. 21:22-23, the curse on anyone who hangs on a tree. The reference to God's "right hand" where Jesus is exalted alludes to Psalm 110 (see the comments for Ascension Day).

DANIEL 12:1-3 (BCP, alt.)

Daniel 12 formulates the first biblical glimpse of the idea of resurrection that will come to full development in the New Testament. God will raise the martyrs from the dead as vindication of their righteous cause. Daniel was written not at the time of Nebuchadnezzar, as it purports, but during the Seleucid period (167 B.C.E.). In the apocalyptic scenario, the battle against the evil emperor Antiochus Epiphanes is also viewed as God's cosmic battle against the powers of evil. After the battle, a person's fate will be determined by whose name is in the book of life. In this dualistic resurrection scenario, the "wise ones" (*mashkilim*) will be raised to shine like bright stars, while the wicked will awake to everlasting shame.

RESPONSIVE READING
PSALM 114 (RCL, BCP);
PSALM 136 or 118:14-17, 22-24 (BCP, alt.);
PSALM 118:1-2, 16-17, 22-24 (RC)

The Easter Eve psalms celebrate the exodus story. Psalm 114, one of the Hallel psalms sung at Passover (Psalms 113–18), praises God for redemption from Egypt. Water imagery roots the people's liberation in creation motifs. In personified metaphors, the sea "looks" around and then flees in terror, the Jordan River reverses its direction, the mountains and hills skip for joy, and the psalmist taunts them all with the wonderful rhetorical question, "Why?" God's victory not only liberates the people from Egypt but also reshapes the entire cosmos.

Psalm 136 moves through each step of the exodus with the refrain, "for his steadfast love endures forever."

SECOND LESSON
1 CORINTHIANS 5:6b-8 (RCL, BCP)

The "paschal lamb" imagery for Christ is the reason for this text's selection for Easter Eve. In its original narrative context the passage fits less well with the Easter theme, however, since Paul is using the imagery of a lump of dough to express outrage at incest in the community. Paul images the man who has sinned as "old leaven" who must be excised because he poses a danger to the community, which is imaged as the "new lump." (Paul cites the same parable about the danger of a little leaven leavening the whole lump also in Gal. 5:9, again warning the community about associating with evildoers.)

The Gospel
LUKE 24:13-49 (RCL);
LUKE 24:13-35 (BCP, RC)

See the comments on the Gospel for the Third Sunday of Easter.

SECOND SUNDAY OF EASTER

APRIL 3, 2005

REVISED COMMON	EPISCOPAL (BCP)	ROMAN CATHOLIC
Acts 2:14a, 22-32	Acts 2:14a, 22-32 or Gen. 8:6-16; 9:8-16	Acts 2:42-47
Psalm 16	Psalm 111 or 118:19-24	Ps. 118:2-4, 13-15, 22-24
1 Pet. 1:3-9	1 Pet. 1:3-9 or Acts 2:14a, 22-32	1 Pet. 1:3-9
John 20:19-31	John 20:19-31	John 20:19-31

Whereas last week's Easter Sunday texts proclaimed our experiences of "seeing" the risen Jesus, today's texts proclaim grace and hope especially for those who have *not* seen. Thomas's story and the refrain of 1 Peter that "you have not seen him" guide Christians to live in light of the resurrection, even though we have not physically experienced seeing Jesus. How do we learn to follow and love the risen Jesus? And what does the "living hope" of his resurrection presence look like in our world today?

> WHEREAS LAST WEEK'S EASTER SUNDAY TEXTS PROCLAIMED OUR EXPERIENCES OF "SEEING" THE RISEN JESUS, TODAY'S TEXTS PROCLAIM GRACE AND HOPE ESPECIALLY FOR THOSE WHO HAVE *NOT* SEEN.

FIRST READING

ACTS 2:14a, 22-32 (RCL, BCP); ACTS 2:42-47 (RC)

Interpreting the Text

For the next three Sundays, the sequential readings from Acts 2 will take hearers back to Peter's first Christian sermon at Pentecost. Today's lection shows how early Christians opened their Bibles to interpret Jesus' fate in light of scripture, especially the Psalms. Next week's lection narrates the amazing effects of the sermon, leading to repentance and baptism for thousands of converts. The Fourth Sunday of Easter will tell of the even more amazing *koinonia* and joyful sharing of possessions that marked the Jerusalem community's life together.

Peter rises to address the crowds of Diaspora Jews. Filled with Pentecostal spirit, his tone is urgent and fiery, appealing to scripture and to his hearers' own experience. His careful argumentation shows how early Christians grappled to make sense of Jesus' death by interpreting it in terms of God's biblical "plan" (*boulē*, v. 23; see also Luke 7:30; Acts 4:28; 13:36; 20:27). Peter proclaims the story of Jesus by drawing on Israel's ancestral stories and sacred psalms.

Some twenty-eight speeches occupy almost one-third of the book of Acts. These speeches and their exegetical arguments can be difficult for the preachers who are more comfortable with narratives than discourse. Yet the key is to see how in Acts' long speeches of Peter, Paul, and Stephen "there is a constant drawing of water from a literally bottomless wellspring of tradition." We can explore the speeches as narratives in the way they situate Jesus in a long line of biblical Israel's story. "The force, the drawing power of the tradition are evoked in the telling of the ancestral stories, again and again. . . . It is as though the story of Jesus were drawn from their (Israel's) very entrails, an event renewed, made vivid, made present in liturgy and Scripture reading and instruction."[1]

God "raised Jesus up," Peter tells his hearers. It was impossible for death to hold him. The verb "raise up" (*anistēmi*) in vv. 24 and 32 drives Peter's proclamation. Even David, called a prophet, foresaw and wrote about "resurrection," as evidenced in a lengthy quote from Psalm 16 (the psalm assigned for today in the lectionary; quoted in Acts 2:25-28) and in v. 31. Jesus' earthly deeds—his signs and wonders and miraculous healings—all prove God's appointment of him, in continuity with the marvelous deeds of God throughout Israel's history.

The "you" of Peter's speech is very broad ("as you yourselves know," v. 22), since most of the audience in Jerusalem for the festival had not personally witnessed Jesus' wonders or signs. Peter faced the task of convincing these hearers of the presence of Jesus both in the scriptures and in their midst—even though they had not been eyewitnesses to any events other than Pentecost. As part of that persuasive effort, Peter calls his hearers "brothers" and identifies with them as fellow Israelites. Finally, the "you" of Peter's speech shifts to "we" in v. 32: *we* are all of us witnesses that God has raised Jesus up.

Responding to the Text

Where do we see God's "plan"? In our day when fundamentalists argue that God's plan requires a specific set of end-time events to happen, we must protest that this is not the view of Luke-Acts. Acts sees God's "plan" (*boulē*) in the events of Jesus' life, death, and resurrection and the ways those events transform our lives. Acts invites us to go back to the wellspring of subversive biblical stories, to tell and re-tell how God's plan brings life out of death. And Acts invites all of us to see ourselves as part of Peter's all-embracing "we"—as witnesses to Jesus' resurrection and to the wonders he has done "in our midst" even if we ourselves were not eyewitnesses.

The preacher may need to deal with the issue of who killed Jesus, either this week or next week—especially in light of concerns about anti-Judaism raised last year by Mel Gibson's film *The Passion of the Christ*.[2] Peter first blames "lawless people" for Jesus' death—clearly the Roman political leaders. (Herod and Pontius Pilate will be specifically named as responsible for Jesus' death in 4:27.) Yet because Peter also accuses the Israelites as "you" (the main verb of the sentence in v. 23 is the second person plural *aneilate*, "you took away," along with the participle "you affixed"), the preacher may need to deal with issue of why Luke blames the Israelites collectively for Jesus' death. Luke's primary purpose is not to affix blame, but rather to contrast God's raising of Jesus with human sin. At the very least, as Fitzmyer reminds, "the early church recognized that Jesus' death was the result of a conspiracy of different elements: a disciple (Judas), Jews (Jerusalem leaders), and pagans (Romans)."[3]

> ACTS INVITES US TO GO BACK TO THE WELLSPRING OF SUBVERSIVE BIBLICAL STORIES, TO TELL AND RE-TELL HOW GOD'S PLAN BRINGS LIFE OUT OF DEATH. AND ACTS INVITES ALL OF US TO SEE OURSELVES AS PART OF PETER'S ALL-EMBRACING "WE"—AS WITNESSES TO JESUS' RESURRECTION AND TO THE WONDERS HE HAS DONE "IN OUR MIDST" EVEN IF WE OURSELVES WERE NOT EYEWITNESSES.

GENESIS 8:6-16; 9:8-16 (BCP, alt.)

This reading encompasses two events—the end of watery wanderings, and the making of God's covenant with Noah. The first section tells the story of the flood's end, through the colliding of several textual traditions, including the Babylonian flood epic (Gen. 8:6-12) and the priestly tradition (Gen. 8:13-19). Noah sends out the dove until it does not return, signifying that it has found a dwelling place on the newly renewed earth. Noah's persistence in sending and patience in waiting are models for our relationship with God.

> NOAH'S PERSISTENCE IN SENDING AND PATIENCE IN WAITING ARE MODELS FOR OUR RELATIONSHIP WITH GOD.

In the second section of this reading (Gen. 9:8-17), the language and style model a kind of ancient Near Eastern treaty that scholars call a royal grant. God, the sovereign protector and sustainer, promises to never again destroy the earth but asks for nothing in return. Unlike the covenant with Abraham in Genesis 17, which requires circumcision as a sign of faithfulness on the part of men of the community, God's covenant with Noah comes unconditionally. As a sign, or rather as the signature on the treaty, God sends a rainbow in the clouds, a sign that recurs again and again throughout the ages.

ACTS 2:42-47 (RC)

See the comments for the Fourth Sunday of Easter, below.

RESPONSIVE READING
PSALM 16 (RCL)

Acts 2:25b-28 quotes Ps. 16:8-11 within its larger theme of witness to Jesus' work in the world. The entirety of Psalm 16 is a personal testimony of trust in God, trust that reaches through the psalmist's entire being, heart, soul, and body (v. 9). Tapping into the power of this responsive reading begins with tapping into the personal nature of the confession so that the psalmist's words become our words, our own experience of trust in God. Spoken as such in community, we hear that we are not alone in our testimony, but instead unified in our witness.

PSALM 111 (BCP)

As your community gathers on the Second Sunday of Easter, the celebration of Jesus' resurrection continues—even if the tenor of praise and worship that soared on Easter Sunday can feel muted just a week later. Psalm 111 begins with the ritual call, "Praise the LORD!" just like the call and response often heard during the Easter season, "Christ is risen! Christ is risen indeed, Alleluia!" The psalmist then recounts the great works of God, emphasizing faithfulness, justness, and unceasing nature of God's fidelity. Praise, worship, and prayer in community become the practice of collective wisdom (v. 10)—a practice that enlivens "Sunday after" celebrations.

PSALM 118:2-4, 13-15, 22-24 (RC);
PSALM 118:19-24 (BCP, alt.)

See the comments on the Responsive Reading for Easter Day.

SECOND READING
1 PETER 1:3-9 (RCL, BCP, RC)

Interpreting the Text

For the next six Sundays, the Second Readings will be from 1 Peter, a wonderful letter of hope and identity—giving us a "home" in God. Martin

Luther loved this letter, with its imagery of the royal priesthood from which he developed his crucial doctrine of the priesthood of all believers. "Which are the true and noblest books of the New Testament?" Luther asked. "John's Gospel and St. Paul's epistles, especially that to the Romans, and St. Peter's first epistle are the true kernel and marrow of all books. . . . It would be advisable for every Christian to read them first and most, and by daily reading to make them your daily bread."[4] The goal of these six Sundays' commentary will be to help preachers make these lessons come alive as "daily bread" for their congregations.

First Peter addresses Diaspora communities in Asia Minor, disenfranchised "exiles" and aliens. In this letter we come face to face with Christians vulnerable to local harassment, struggling to claim a sense of hope and identity amid the pressures of empire, poverty, slavery, and displacement. Several recent commentaries on 1 Peter have brought to life the social dimension of the letter. As Don Senior makes clear, 1 Peter is by no means as submissive a letter as it first appears.[5] Even its directives to "suffer" and "submit" may reveal more of a careful subaltern strategy of resistance than passive submission. In our time, when we once again live under the claims of a dominant global "empire," this Christian letter of hope holds great relevance. Its rich store of images can speak to multicultural communities, to people in our congregations who have experienced dislocation or displacement. The letter can help Christians today to navigate the claims of empire while also living as a hope-filled counter-community or Diaspora in the face of the dominant culture.

> IN OUR TIME, WHEN WE ONCE AGAIN LIVE UNDER THE CLAIMS OF A DOMINANT GLOBAL "EMPIRE," THIS CHRISTIAN LETTER OF HOPE HOLDS GREAT RELEVANCE.

All of vv. 3–12 make up one long Greek sentence, rich in clauses and praise. To the extent that 1 Peter follows the form of a Pauline letter, this single sentence constitutes the thanksgiving section, similar to 2 Corinthians in using the opening word "blessed" (*eulogētos*) rather than "thanks" (*eucharistō*). Typically, in the thanksgiving section of a letter the author summarizes major themes of the rest of the letter.

"Hope" will be one of the most vibrant themes of this entire letter, perhaps in deliberate contrast to pagan culture that sometimes derided hope and embraced fatalism.[6] Hope gives people a sense of future. The Christians addressed in this letter were living in conditions of social marginalization and ridicule, yet 1 Peter gives them a vision of hope that is not far off or illusory, but rather "living hope." The theme of hope will build throughout the letter, especially in the text assigned for the Sixth Sunday of Easter with its call to "always be ready to give an account for the hope that is in you" (1 Pet. 3:15).

God has "birthed us anew," the letter declares. The verb *gennaō* can mean both "begotten" (the male image) or "giving birth" (the female image); the preposition *ana* adds the sense of "anew." Since baptism is mentioned only once in 1 Peter (3:21), and never in conjunction with "birthing anew," we should be cautious about identifying the new-birth imagery primarily with baptism. While some scholars once viewed 1 Peter as a baptismal homily delivered in a liturgical context, recent scholarship moves beyond such a liturgical interpretation. Roman Catholic scholar Donald Senior argues that "begotten anew" refers to the "entire inaugural experience of the Christian," not just to baptism.[7] The letter is addressed not to baptismal candidates but to the entire community.

New birth delivers us into two parallel gifts—a living hope, and an inheritance.

That the Christian community "inherits" the promises to Israel is a core assumption of 1 Peter, expounded through multiple metaphors and images in this letter (see especially the text for the Fifth Sunday of Easter). "Inheritance" probably still refers to the land of Israel, especially after the traumatic reconquest of Palestine by Rome in 70 C.E. and the forcible exile of many—a memory kept alive by Roman propaganda that would have resonated especially with the exiles of this letter. But for 1 Peter, the Old Testament understanding of inheritance extends beyond the physical land. Indeed, the word "Israel" never appears in this letter, nor does the word "church." "The notion of a holy land is superseded by that of a holy community," argues John Elliott.[8]

First Peter candidly admits that we have "not seen" Jesus. Two references to "not seeing" in v. 8, encompassing both the past ("although you have not seen him") and the present ("although you do not see him now"), sound a parallel refrain. Neither Peter's community nor people today are given physical experiences of "seeing" Jesus in the way the first eyewitnesses did. Yet they "love" Jesus. They rejoice. The rest of the letter will flesh out these declarations in the realm of ethics to show how new birth through Jesus' resurrection holds radical consequences for every aspect of life.

Responding to the Text

Familiar language of "born again" dominates the first chapter of 1 Peter, but with a logic quite different from that of today's fundamentalists. First and foremost, the language of new birth in 1 Peter is always plural. It is "we" who have been birthed anew, not "I." In our individualist culture, preachers need to underscore this communal dimension over and over! Part of the problem is that in English we cannot hear the difference between the plural "you" and the singular "you"—so people tend to assume that in the Bible the "you" is singular. My students from the American South recommend the term "y'all" to make the distinction. Every reference to "you" in 1 Peter should then be read as "y'all"! New birth is not an individual experience, but rather a community experience. Similarly in 1 Pet. 1:23, the declaration is again plural—"y'all have been birthed anew."

The second difference from fundamentalism's use of "born again" language is that new birth happened "through the resurrection of Jesus Christ" (v. 3). It is not a matter of "I was born again on June 10, 1961," nor even "I was born again at my baptism." In 1 Peter, you were born again at the moment of Jesus' resurrection. In the midst of the relentless pressure of fundamentalist individualism, when pressed for the specific details of a born-again experience, we need to learn to say, "I was born again in Jesus' resurrection." It may sound strange, but that is the theology of this wonderful letter.

While we have all been birthed anew, this letter also acknowledges quite honestly that none of has actually "seen" Jesus. Neither the author nor the recipients can claim a personal, one-on-one encounter with the risen Christ. Yet the community (the plural "you"!) is praised for its deep "love" for Jesus and for its rejoicing. The power of this letter comes in its persuasive picture of how together, as a community, we can experience the intensely personal and transformative life of "new birth" to a "living hope"—and how we can love Jesus in the world today.

NEW BIRTH HAPPENED "THROUGH THE RESURRECTION OF JESUS CHRIST" (V. 3). IT IS NOT A MATTER OF "I WAS BORN AGAIN ON JUNE 10, 1961," NOR EVEN "I WAS BORN AGAIN AT MY BAPTISM." IN 1 PETER, YOU WERE BORN AGAIN AT THE MOMENT OF JESUS' RESURRECTION.

ACTS 2:14a, 22-32 (BCP, alt.)

See the comments on the First Reading, above.

THE GOSPEL

JOHN 20:19-31 (RCL, BCP, RC)

Interpreting the Text

Each year the Gospel for this day situates the Christian community in relationship to Thomas, the disciple who finds faith difficult. In vv. 30-31 the narrator speaks directly to us as readers (recall John 19:35, "so that *you also* may believe"), blessing us and inviting us to enter into the Easter story as we journey toward faith.

While Jesus' appearance to the disciples takes place on the same day as the morning's empty tomb appearance, neither Mary's proclamation of "I have seen the Lord" nor the beloved disciple's faith (John 20:8) seems to have had any impact on the disciples. We find them huddled together in a locked room "out of fear of the Judeans." (This translation of *judaioi* reflects the geographical sense of the term elsewhere in John—Jesus "did not wish to go about in Judea because the Judeans were looking for him," John 7:1—and it avoids anti-Judaism by underscoring that Jesus and his Galilean disciples were all foreigners in the Judean city of Jerusalem.)[9]

Jesus appears to the disciples in compassion and love, with the greeting, "Peace to you." In showing his hands and side to the disciples, Jesus identifies himself in terms of his wounded body that shows the visible marks of his torture. Were his scars still tender? Jesus may pass through locked doors, but his risen body still bears the marks of the nails. Like our own scars, these scars inscribe Jesus' bodily history.

Jesus "breathes" on the disciples, an echo of God's breath that brought creation to life in Gen. 1:2; 2:7; and Ps. 104:29-30 ("When you send forth your breath they are created; and you renew the face of the ground"). Jesus' breath at Easter brings forth new creation. Raymond Brown underscores the strong creation grounding of John's Gospel: "The Gospel opened with the theme of creation in the Prologue . . . and the theme of creation returns at the end."[10] Such an emphasis on creation can be an important corrective to docetic or "heavenist" readings of John. Just as God breathed new life into the dry bones in the desert of Ezekiel (Ezekiel 37), so on Easter the risen Jesus now breathes new life into the disciples and into the physical world.

With this breath Jesus bestows the Holy Sprit. Rather than harmonizing John's understanding of the giving of the Spirit with the Pentecost chronology of Acts, we can seek to enter John's own rich symbolic world. Vivid imagery for the promise of the Spirit throughout the Gospel (the water of life, John 7:38-39; the Paraclete, John 14:16) has prepared readers for the full bestowal of the Spirit in John 20:22 on Easter evening.

Thomas is famous as the disciple who missed out on the Easter meeting with the risen Jesus—but we should be cautious about labeling him "doubting Thomas," since the word "doubt" does not occur in this passage. An individual character in John's Gospel, Thomas may also represent an entire community in early Christianity who cherished his unique memory.[11] Thomas's characterization is rich and complex, defying easy categorization. Thomas has appeared twice before in the Johannine narrative, always as a somewhat ambiguous, albeit enthusiastic, figure. We first meet Thomas in the story of the resurrection of Lazarus, when he blurts out, "Let us go too so that we might die with" Jesus (11:16). But it is difficult to know whether Thomas is expressing courageous discipleship unto death or "cynical sarcasm in the face of likely persecution," as suggested by some.[12] At Jesus' farewell discourse, Thomas is the disciple willing to risk admitting, "We don't know" (John 14:5), reflecting an honesty and longing for proof that many Christians can relate to. Twice the Gospel mentions that Thomas is called the "Twin" (Didymus, 11:16; 21:2); perhaps Thomas is a "Twin" to us all.

The preacher will have to decide whether Thomas is being singled out for rebuke in this passage, as Elaine Pagels argues in her provocative study of the experiential dimension of faith, *Beyond Belief: The Secret Gospel of Thomas*.[13] In her view, this Johannine scene was written as a deliberate refutation of the more experiential Thomas-community's theology, represented by the sayings in the noncanonical *Gospel of Thomas*. Other scholars disagree, arguing that Thomas's characterization in John is no more negative than that of Mary Magdalene or Peter, who also do not come to full faith without "seeing" the risen Jesus. In the Gospel of John, the beloved disciple is the only person who believes without seeing.

> IN THE GOSPEL OF JOHN, THE BELOVED DISCIPLE IS THE ONLY PERSON WHO BELIEVES WITHOUT SEEING.

All others, like Thomas, have to be brought from some degree of misunderstanding to full faith.

Eight days later Jesus does show his wounded body to Thomas in love and helps him come to faith. The risen Jesus is the crucified Jesus, who is known by his wounds and his scars. Thomas's confession of faith, "My Lord and my God," is one of the most powerful confessions in the entire Gospel (comparable to Martha's "I believe that you are the Christ, the Son of God," John 11:27).

Responding to the Text

How can the gospel speak to those who "do not see"? How can we, too, come to believe? Lutheran theologian Joseph Sittler's sermon "The View from Mt. Nebo" gives voice to the many Christians who, like Thomas, grapple to believe despite a lack of personal experiences of seeing the risen Lord. Sittler situates himself in the perspective of Moses, who only viewed the Promised Land from afar but never experienced it personally. "Moses on Mount Nebo was in the situation of many of us . . . he could not enter into what he saw." Says Sittler about his own faith as a pastor:

> IN THE SAME WAY THAT JESUS INVITES THOMAS TO TOUCH AND FEEL HIS SCARRED BODY ("REACH OUT YOUR HAND AND PUT IT IN MY SIDE," V. 27), SO THE EASTER TEXTS INVITE US TO TOUCH AND FEEL THE SCARS OF CHRIST'S WHOLE WOUNDED WORLD TODAY.

> It is only honest to say that I have never known fully that kind of life within the full, warm power of experience. I have not seen any burning bushes. . . . John Wesley's "strangely warmed" heart at Aldersgate Street—this is not my street. I have not the possibility to say of the Christian faith what many honest persons have said about it. But I have come to see that to declare as a gift of God that which I do not fully possess is, nevertheless, a duty of obedience. Is the opulence of the grace of God to be measured by my inventory? Is the great catholic faith of nineteen centuries to be reduced to my interior dimensions? . . . No.[14]

In other words, Sittler's situation reiterates the blessing of John 20: "Blessed are those who have not seen and yet believe."

When we are given experiences of actually seeing and feeling the risen Christ in a vivid way in our lives, this text reminds us that that may often be in woundedness and marginalization. Jesus' scars inscribe his own history, much as our own scars tell our life story. I have a scar on my head from a car accident, and another on my leg from a hiking accident. In the same way that Jesus invites Thomas to touch and feel his scarred body ("Reach out your hand and put it in my side," v. 27), so the Easter texts invite us to touch and feel the scars of Christ's whole wounded world today. Thomas's recognition of the body of the beloved Jesus came from touching his scars. The preacher can invite worshipers to touch and feel the scars of torture in our world today, to face the deep wounds of violence. And we can proclaim God's Easter promise of healing and resurrection for our scarred bodies and for all creation.

Notes

1. Daniel Berrigan, *Whereon to Stand: The Acts of the Apostles and Ourselves* (Baltimore: Fortcamp Publishing, 1991), 40.

2. For an excellent short treatment of this question, see Gerard S. Sloyan, *Why Jesus Died* (Minneapolis: Fortress Press, 2004).

3. Joseph Fitzmyer, *The Acts of the Apostles,* Anchor Bible ªNew York: Doubleday, 1998), 309.

4. *Luther's Works,* vol. 35, "preface to the New Testament."

5. Donald Senior, *1 Peter, Jude, 2 Peter,* Sacra Pagina 15 (Collegeville, Minn.: Michael Glazier, 2002).

6. Ibid., 31.

7. Ibid., 48.

8. John Elliott, *1 Peter,* Anchor Bible 36B (New York: Doubleday, 2000), 336.

9. For a discussion of Galilean-Judean tensions and the argument for translating *judaioi* as Judeans, see Richard Horsley, *Galilee: History, Politics, People* (Valley Forge, Pa.: Trinity Press, 1995), 13.

10. Raymond E. Brown, *The Gospel according to John,* Anchor Bible 29A (Garden City, N.Y.: Doubleday, 1970), 1037.

11. See Gregory Riley, *Resurrection Reconsidered: Thomas and John in Controversy* (Minneapolis: Fortress Press, 1994).

12. Wes Howard-Brook, *Becoming Children of God: John's Gospel and Radical Discipleship* (Eugene, Ore.: Wipf & Stock, 2003), 254.

13. Elaine Pagels, *Beyond Belief: The Secret Gospel of Thomas* (New York: Random House, 2003).

14. Joseph A. Sittler, *Grace Notes and Other Fragments* (Philadelphia: Fortress Press, 1981), 50–53.

THIRD SUNDAY
OF EASTER

APRIL 10, 2005

REVISED COMMON	EPISCOPAL (BCP)	ROMAN CATHOLIC
Acts 2:14a, 36-41	Acts 2:14a, 36-47 or Isa. 43:1-12	Acts 2:14, 22-33
Ps. 116:1-4, 12-19	Psalm 116 or 116:10-17	Ps. 16:1-2, 5, 7-8, 9-10, 11
1 Pet. 1:17-23	1 Pet. 1:17-23 or Acts 2:14a, 36-47	1 Pet. 1:17-21
Luke 24:13-35	Luke 24:13-35	Luke 24:13-35

Today's texts proclaim resurrection as homecoming. God gives hope and a home to "all who are far away" (Acts 2:39), to "exiles" who are displaced (1 Pet. 1:17), and to all of us who long to find a home in God. Like the Emmaus travelers, we walk away from Jerusalem, away from the events of resurrection, away from God's call. Stuck in our own fears and what "we had hoped" for (see Luke 24:21), we cannot see the presence of the risen Christ in our midst. But Jesus accompanies us, breaks bread, and brings us near. These texts set our hearts on fire!

FIRST READING
ACTS 2:14a, 36-41 (RCL);
ACTS 2:14a, 36-47 (BCP)

Interpreting the Text

Peter's sermon draws to a close, calling hearers to an urgent response. God has made the crucified one both Lord and Christ! Although Peter's reference to "the one whom you yourselves crucified" can be read as attributing blame to Jews, the point is not to blame. Rather, the point is show dramatic contrast, discontinuity—that God's action has reversed human action by raising Jesus. "Therefore," Peter declares imperatively, "know with certainty" that God has countered the humans' act of crucifixion with an amazing act of enthronement. Peter's opening word, "with certainty" (*asphalōs*, Acts 2:36), is the adverbial form of *asphaleia*, a word from Luke's prologue that lays out the overarching purpose for the Gospel (Luke 1:4). Peter's speech shares the same goal as the Gospel—to persuade us of the "certainty" or "security" of God's work in Jesus.

Peter's message cuts hearers to their heart. "What shall we do?" they ask—the same question three groups of people asked John the Baptist in Luke 3. At the Jordan River, John commanded repentance: "Share your coat and food," "collect no more than what is due," and "rob no one by violence" (Luke 3:10-14). Peter, too, assures his hearers that they can leave the past behind through repentance. Repentance means a radical turning from the old ways to a new life, a new counter-community in the gospel. Be baptized for the forgiveness of your sins, and receive the gift of the Holy Spirit, Peter counsels. "Let yourselves be saved," reflects a better translation for v. 41 than "save yourselves."

Responding to the Text

God's promise is for everyone, for "all who are far away." "Far away" (*makran*) carries a geographical meaning in Acts, signifying distant nations. God will send Paul to the Gentiles who are "far away" (Acts 22:21). But the paradigm for "far away" (*makran*) in Luke-Acts is much more personal and near at hand—it is the prodigal son, whose father ran to greet him when he was yet "far away" (Luke 15:20). Peter's speech suggests that there are yet many more faraway prodigal sons and daughters for whom God is waiting. They, too, will call upon the name of the Lord. God wants to embrace all who are far off to bring them near. As in Eph. 2:17, the allusion is to Isa. 57:19, the proclamation of "peace, peace to the far off and the near," says the Lord, and "I will heal them."

> PETER'S SPEECH SUGGESTS THAT THERE ARE YET MANY MORE FARAWAY PRODIGAL SONS AND DAUGHTERS FOR WHOM GOD IS WAITING. THEY, TOO, WILL CALL UPON THE NAME OF THE LORD. GOD WANTS TO EMBRACE ALL WHO ARE FAR OFF TO BRING THEM NEAR.

ISAIAH 43:1-12 (BCP, alt.)

Interpreting the Text

Middle Eastern and African Christians today caution that Isa. 43:3-4 must not be misused in political debates to advocate advancement for the modern nation of Israel at the expense of other nations. God does not offer to trade Egypt and Ethiopia as a ransom for Israel in any geopolitical sense—and we must critique any such misuse of this theology. So what does the prophet mean in telling Israel that God "will give people in return for you, nations in exchange for your life"?

In the assembly of all nations, the God of Israel is revealed as the first, last, and most powerful of all the gods; a move that brings sixth-century B.C.E. Israel's monotheism a step closer to the radical declaration that God is the only god. Among the nations (including Egypt, Ethiopia, and Seba) God is the one who gathers together all those scattered among the farthest nations (Isa. 43:5-6). God is the one who saves; beside the one God there is no other savior. "You are my witnesses," God declares (Isa. 43:12). The promise of reconciliation, reunion, and salvation under the one God rings sweetly in the ears of the sixth-century B.C.E. Israelite community torn apart by war and exile.

Responding to the Text

In the ears of modern-day communities, the promise of reconciliation and reunion also calls us to give witness to our experiences of redemption, rescue, and salvation. God's redeeming work need not condemn other nations and peoples or mandate their destruction. Instead, we can witness to the power of God's faithfulness and love for *all* nations—"you are precious in my sight, and honored, and I love you" (Isa. 43:4).

> GOD'S REDEEMING WORK NEED NOT CONDEMN OTHER NATIONS AND PEOPLES OR MANDATE THEIR DESTRUCTION. INSTEAD, WE CAN WITNESS TO THE POWER OF GOD'S FAITHFULNESS AND LOVE FOR ALL NATIONS.

ACTS 2:14, 22-32 (RC)

See the comments on the Second Reading for the Second Sunday of Easter.

RESPONSIVE READING
PSALM 116:1-4, 12-19 (RCL); PSALM 116 or 116:10-17 (BCP)

This psalm expresses the singer's love for God; a love that comes from the realization that God listens to cries of distress and anguish (v. 4). Therefore the psalmist asks, "What shall I return to the LORD for all [God's] bounty to me?" Offerings of wine, vows, service, thanksgiving, and praise flow from the singer's lips. It is a prayer of rededication to God in the presence of God's people. The psalmist emphasizes this communal aspect of thanksgiving (116:14, 18, 19), showing a desire to be public with such offerings and praise.

See the comments on the Responsive Reading for the Second Sunday of Easter (RCL).

SECOND READING
1 PETER 1:17-23 (RCL, BCP)
1 PETER 1:17-21 (RC)

Interpreting the Text

"Home" is a strong theme of 1 Peter, addressing "exile." Both the letter's opening address to "the exiles of Diaspora" (1:1) and the closing reference to Rome as "Babylon" (5:13) suggest some form of exile. In today's text, the key word is the Greek word *paroikia*, "exile" (see also the reference to the recipients as *paroikos* in 2:11). *Para* means "alongside" and *oikos* means "home." John Elliott suggests that the recipients were people displaced from their own ancestral home, "by-dwellers." In the ancient world, *paroikos* was a specific legal term for a class of resident aliens who had few rights. Socially vulnerable, they lived among neighbors who were sometimes very hostile. "In addition to natives dispossessed of their lands which were annexed to expanding cities, this group included strangers from abroad."[1] The Greek Old Testament (the Septuagint) uses the term *paroikos* for Abraham and Sarah when they went to Egypt and resided there temporarily because of famine. It uses it also for Moses when he fled to Midian after killing the Egyptian, as manifested in the naming of his son Gershom, "for I have been an alien residing in a foreign land." In the Septuagint *paroikos* is a term used of the foreigners residing in Israel's own midst, who had some rights as legal aliens but could not eat the Passover or participate fully in Israelite life.

First Peter, then, is written to Christian communities in Asia Minor that were not only experiencing a metaphorical or spiritual exile but also whose members likely included a number of literal resident aliens. It is written to give them a sense of *oikos,* or home. The language of "house" and "home" is strongest in chapter 2, but the theme predominates throughout the letter (for example, 4:17). "The symbolization of the community as the *household of God* . . . serves as the root metaphor and organizing ecclesial image in 1 Peter," argues Elliott.[2] First Peter is written to address the tension people experienced by God's people who were baptized into a new royal identity but at the same time marginalized, displaced, and even abused by the society in which they resided. The author gives people a new sense of community identity and "home." The letter crafts a strategy of granting a limited measure of authority to the alien society and government, while rooting the community's primary allegiance or home in God.

Christians have been "ransomed," a word used in the Roman world for the buying of a slave's freedom. This word, too, probably resonated at more than just a metaphorical or theological level to the audience. The threat of slavery haunted people in the ancient world. Even in rural areas of these provinces of Turkey, readers would have known that captives in war were enslaved and deported by their conquerors. This letter is addressed to a number of Christians who are themselves "house slaves" (2:18; on this see the comments on the Second Lesson for the Fourth Sunday of Easter). The blood of the spotless Lamb that ransoms them invokes the exodus story, a reminder of the Passover lamb's blood and this great event of God's liberation from slavery in Egypt.

Being ransomed by God and "begotten anew" brings about ethical consequences for the community. Since we have been renewed and purified, we must "love one another from the heart." The entire letter emphasizes the connection between our new home in Christ and the new life this identity requires.

Responding to the Text

The strong message of home and homecoming in 1 Peter can speak to people's deepest longings today. Marcus Borg identifies the story of exile and homecoming as one of three "macro stories" at the heart of the Bible—in addition to the exodus story of liberation from bondage and the priestly story of sin, guilt, sacrifice, and forgiveness. In Borg's view the church suffers from its excessive focus on the priestly story to the near-exclusion of the other two stories.[3] In our time millions of people experience a sense of homelessness—whether literal homelessness, life as refugees in a foreign country, loss of home or family after divorce or death, or the existential experience of spiritual homelessness. First Peter's extensive use of *oik-* words—*paroikos* as well as *oikos*—invites the preacher to image the gospel as homecoming for exiles.

> FIRST PETER'S EXTENSIVE USE OF OIK- WORDS—
> PAROIKOS AS WELL AS OIKOS—INVITES THE PREACHER
> TO IMAGE THE GOSPEL AS HOMECOMING FOR EXILES.

Annie LaMott tells the story of a little seven-year-old girl who became lost one day and couldn't find her way home. "The little girl ran up and down the streets of the big town where they lived, but she couldn't find a single landmark. She was very frightened. Finally, a policeman stopped to help her. He put her in the passenger seat of his car and they drove around until she finally saw her church. She pointed it out to the policeman, and then she told him firmly, 'You could let me out now. This is my church, and I can always find my way home from here.'"[4]

Today's task is to preach the message of 1 Peter so that every exile can find a sense of home in God—so that each person can say of God, and of their church, "This is my church, and I can always find my way home from here."

The Gospel
LUKE 24:13-35 (RCL, BCP, RC)

Interpreting the Text

The journey to Emmaus offers a moving resurrection story of accompaniment and the breaking of bread. Roman Catholic missiologist Robert Schreiter calls this story a "master narrative" into which Christians can lay their own life story and thereby discover Jesus' presence in their own journeys.[5] Journeys and meals are two favorite Lukan settings. The entire second half of the Gospel centers on Jesus' journey to Jerusalem, punctuated with meals at the homes of Pharisees, friends, outcasts, and others. The Emmaus journey recapitulates core Lukan themes.

Perhaps most important, this story fulfills Luke's purpose of *epignōsis* (recognition), set out at the beginning of this Gospel. In Luke 1:4, Luke tells Theophilus that his goal is "so that you may recognize" (*epignōs,* often translated "know") the certainty about Jesus concerning which you have been catechized. Such "recognition" (*epignōsis*) of Jesus' presence—a deep "Aha" kind of sight—articulates Luke's goal for the post-Easter disciples on the Emmaus road and for each one of us also. *Epignōsis* opens our eyes to recognize Jesus' presence in our midst, walking with us.

The disciples do not immediately recognize the resurrected Jesus—a reminder that resurrection is not something strictly physical, not simply the resuscitation of a corpse. Their journey toward recognition or *epignosis* takes place on the road to Emmaus, a village of uncertain location that had suffered a long history of military violence. Mentioned as a military camp for Judas Maccabeus (1 Macc. 3:40), the village of Emmaus was burned by the Romans in punishment for participating in the revolts of 4 B.C.E. following the death of Herod.[6] The memory of that traumatic destruction still would have been known in the time of Luke—along with memories of crucifixion (two thousand rebels were crucified by the Romans in 4 B.C.E.). Emmaus was a place of trauma and defeat.

Luke names Cleopas but leaves the other disciple unnamed, perhaps as an invitation for all readers to see themselves as the second disciple in the story. The two dejected disciples are walking away from Jerusalem, away from the terrible events of the past week. Indeed, they are walking in the wrong direction, according to the command that Jesus will give in 24:49 to "stay in the city" (Jerusalem). In a wonderful act of ministry and accompaniment, Jesus is willing even to accompany the two disciples as they walk in the wrong direction—going away from the city of Jerusalem.

Along the journey, the disciples tell and retell all that had happened, but without comprehension. The phrase "we had hoped" (v. 21) sums up their situation. Their hope is extinguished.

A stranger who joins them listens and asks questions. But the disciples' eyes are kept from "recognizing" (*epignōnai*, the verbal form of the noun *epignōsis*) that it is Jesus—a link to the same Greek word from Luke's prologue (1:4). The disciples mistake this stranger for a *paroikos* ("exile" or "sojourner"), the same word used by the author of 1 Peter for its original readers. The disciples pour out their hearts about all that has happened, even correctly referring to Jesus as a "prophet mighty in deed and word before God and all the people" (v. 19) and acknowledging that the tomb was empty, "just as the women had said" (v. 24). But this is not a profession of faith. The two disciples are stuck in their inability to put the pieces of the narrative together. Robert Schreiter compares their storytelling to that of trauma survivors, who "can get all the words right, but something still is missing. . . . We struggle to find the one thing that will help us overcome the pain, transform the memory, allow us to get on with our lives."[7]

The stranger provides the transformative key by reframing the disciples' perspective regarding the events in Jerusalem. He places their story about the Lord's death into the larger story of God's action in the world, as recorded in the prophets and the scriptures. It was "necessary" (*dei*, v. 26) for the Christ to suffer, but death was not the end of the story.

The second part of this event, the meal, completes the disciples' breakthrough to "recognition" (*epignōsis*), the purpose laid out in Luke's prologue. It was getting dark, an unsafe time to be on the road. In countries today living under foreign military occupation, curfew often begins at dusk—and perhaps that was so under Roman military occupation of Palestine. The two disciples prevail upon the stranger to stay with them. In Luke's Gospel, breaking of bread is often the setting for divine encounters, whether at the homes of Pharisees, at the feeding of the thousands, or at the Last Supper. As Jesus breaks bread once again, the disciples' eyes that were kept from "recognition" on the road (v. 16) are now opened. This is the final piece needed for the "Aha" moment of recognition, of *epignōsis*—a process that began as Jesus opened the scriptures on the road. It is this act of sharing, of bread breaking, that transformed the disciples' memory and recognition. Now they could look back with burning hearts and "recognize" that it was Jesus who had been walking with them all along.

How do people experience *epignōsis* (recognition), that "Aha" kind of sight that Luke wants for us? How do we see Jesus alive and walking with us in our neighborhood? The artist Fritz Eichenberg, who worked with the Catholic Worker Community, experienced that kind of sight when he depicted "Christ in the Breadline" at a New York City shelter—Jesus standing in line with the other homeless men, huddling to keep warm.[8] Resurrection is not always immediately apparent, as Eichenberg knew. The risen Christ may look just like any other homeless man. The preacher's task is to help open people's eyes to "recognize" Jesus walking with us, even when at first he is hidden from our sight.

We all bring our "we had hoped" to this text: We had hoped it wasn't cancer; we had hoped the relationship would not end in divorce; we had hoped the war could be averted; we had hoped the terrible wound would heal and we could be normal again; we had hoped Jesus was the one to redeem Israel (v. 21).[9] The preacher can gently help people lay their deepest "we had hoped" into this master narrative of Emmaus, and to begin to connect their own personal disappointed hopes into the larger journey of transformed hope. People get "unstuck," Schreiter suggests, by reframing their stories in terms of God's big story for our world. The story of Emmaus can help them begin to see how to tell their story differently.

> THE PREACHER'S TASK IS TO HELP OPEN PEOPLE'S EYES TO "RECOGNIZE" JESUS WALKING WITH US, EVEN WHEN AT FIRST HE IS HIDDEN FROM OUR SIGHT.

The Emmaus story is foundational for the church. From now on, God's people will experience the risen Jesus as the two disciples did that first Easter Eve, in the scriptures and in bread breaking. The presence of Jesus in the shared meal points to the sacred dimension in all our meals. Preachers can evoke recognition or *epignōsis* of the living Christ at the table of our world, sharing bread with us today.

Such recognition sets our hearts on fire, as reflected in the disciples' question, "Did not our hearts burn within us while he talked with us on the road?" The Emmaus story invites us to envision Jesus in every context, accompanying us on the roads of our lives today. In Chicago, where I teach, we can say with the disciples, "Did not our hearts burn within us as Jesus walked with us on 55th Street, as he opened to us the scriptures?"

Walking, bread breaking, scripture sharing—central to the recognition of God's presence in this story—remind us to take time to walk our neighborhood, to be willing to greet the unexpected stranger.

The concept of "accompaniment," modeled by Jesus in Luke 24, has become a central model for cross-cultural ministry, a gift from the Christian community in

Latin America. A document of the Evangelical Lutheran Church in America envisions mission as walking together with global churches in a "journey where the presence of God is revealed to us. . . . We journey side by side, with neither companion ahead or behind, above or below, the other. . . . Accompaniment implies companionship of mutual respect and signals mutuality in our relationships. . . . The accompaniment model holds the potential to create a radical shift in power within today's global relationships."[10]

Notes

1. John H. Elliott, *1 Peter,* Anchor Bible 37B (New York: Doubleday, 2000), 94.

2. Ibid., 113.

3. Marcus Borg, *Meeting Jesus Again for the First Time: The Historical Jesus and the Heart of Contemporary Faith* (New York: HarperCollins, 1994) 126. See also Borg, *The Heart of Christianity* (New York: HarperCollins, 2003), 176.

4. Annie LaMott, *Traveling Mercies* (New York: Doubleday, 2000), 55.

5. Robert J. Schreiter, *The Ministry of Reconciliation: Spirituality and Strategies* (Maryknoll, N.Y.: Orbis, 1998), 40.

6. Flavius Josephus, *Jewish War* 2.55-75 (62 and 71 on Emmaus); *Ant.* 17.271–95.

7. Schreiter, *Reconciliation*, 43.

8. See Fritz Eichenberg, *Works of Mercy*, ed. Daniel Ellsberg (Maryknoll, N.Y.: Orbis, 1992). Eichenberg's woodcut print *Christ in the Breadline* is on the front cover of the book.

9. I am grateful to Dan Erlander for this insight.

10. "Global Mission in the Twenty-first Century" (Chicago: Evangelical Lutheran Church in America Division for Global Mission, 2000), 12.

FOURTH SUNDAY OF EASTER

APRIL 17, 2005

REVISED COMMON	EPISCOPAL (BCP)	ROMAN CATHOLIC
Acts 2:42-47	Acts 6:1-9; 7:2a, 51-60 or Neh. 9:6-15	Acts 2:14a, 36-41
Psalm 23	Psalm 23	Ps. 23:1-3a, 3b-4, 5, 6
1 Pet. 2:19-25	1 Pet. 2:19-25 or Acts 6:1-9; 7:2a, 51-60	1 Pet. 2:20b-25
John 10:1-10	John 10:1-10	John 10:1-10

Today's readings invite us to consider what good shepherding looks like and also how to protect the flock from bad shepherding and violence. The new resurrection community celebrates the "abundant life" of the Good Shepherd through its joyful lifestyle of prayer, testimony, *koinonia*, and abundance. We are Jesus' sheep who know his voice and follow him. Led by our Shepherd, we follow Jesus into a new way of life—a transformed community and a transformed economy, where all can share together in God's abundant pastures.

FIRST READING

ACTS 2:42-47 (RCL)

Interpreting the Text

Peter's Pentecost speech—the text for the past two weeks—leads Christians joyfully to sell their possessions and embark on a new community, as embodied in the Greek word *koinonia* (translated as "sharing" or "fellowship"). Acts 4:32-34 offers a similar description of this early Jerusalem community where believers had all things in "common" (*koina*) and no one said anything was one's own "private" (*idia*) property.

The joy and power of early Christian *koinonia* witness to God's abundance in the face of apparent scarcity. Creation provides enough for everyone if we share. This is manna life, recalling Israel's lessons in the wilderness.[1] "The principle of creative economic cooperation and sharing between neighbors—as a practical technique of survival, not simply as an ethical virtue—was one of the corner-stones of Jesus' teachings about the way that the Kingdom of God might be gained," writes Richard Horsley. For displaced Jewish peasants and urban dwellers in Jerusalem, the *koinonia* described in Acts 2 and Acts 4 constituted a "conscious attempt to create a 'village' in the streets and slums of the city."[2] Similarly, the model of a "village within the city" became the pattern also for Pauline Christian communities in cities of Asia Minor and Greece. Originally a term of economic partnership, *koinonia* came to be used in the New Testament also to describe our deepest spiritual communion in Christ. *Koinonia* is a far-reaching New Testament word that embraces everything from Eucharistic communion (1 Cor. 10:16) to sharing in Christ's sufferings (1 Pet. 4:13) and in one another's suffering (Phil. 2:1; 3:10) to communion in God (2 Cor. 13:13).

In Acts 2 the Christian community carries on the miraculous work of Jesus himself. The community performs "wonders and signs" (v. 43), echoing the wonders and signs that Jesus himself did, as narrated in Peter's speech (Acts 2:22). Publicly in the temple, and also "day by day" in houses, the Christians "broke . . . bread with glad and generous hearts . . . and [had] the goodwill of all the people" (vv. 46-47). Their bread breaking echoes the Gospel feeding stories as well as the Emmaus description in Luke 24:30, 35, where Jesus was made known to the disciples in the breaking of bread. The quotidian quality of their witness shines through in the phrase "day by day," repeated in vv. 46 and 47. The community grows and grows, day by day, steadily, with God adding to their numbers those who are being saved.

Whether these Acts descriptions are Lukan compositions or accurate historical descriptions is impossible to know. Luke certainly views them as normative, foundational visions for all Christian community. Joy and sharing in prayer and bread breaking must extend seamlessly to economic sharing in grass-roots community, embodying an alternative to the exploitive

KOINONIA IN JESUS CLAIMS OUR WHOLE LIFE, BRING-ING US TOGETHER WITH ONE ANOTHER WITH GLAD AND GENEROUS HEARTS.

imperial economy of "haves" versus "have-nots." Such Christian community "turns the imperial world upside down" (cf. Acts 17:6). *Koinonia* in Jesus claims our whole life, bringing us together with one another with glad and generous hearts. It witnesses powerfully to the world, as the Lord adds to the numbers of those being saved.

While some have tried to claim that this was a failed Lukan experiment and that after the famine narrated in Acts 11:28-29 Christians quickly returned to private property, there is no basis for this claim in Luke. Indeed, the entire New Testament lifts up a vision of *koinonia* that is joyful, radical, and life giving—a vision at the heart of the early church.

How can we today, in urban churches, re-create the *koinonia* of a "village in the city" that Acts modeled? What does vibrant Christian community look like today, and how can congregations embody such biblical abundance and sharing? Dietrich Bonhoeffer wrote about Christian community in his *Life Together*. Acts calls us also to joyful economic sharing, along with bread breaking and prayers. People young and old who have lived in intense Christian community testify to what a life-changing experience such *koinonia* can be. Whether volunteering overseas with the Mennonite Central Committee or in a local community such as the Jesuit Volunteer Corps, Lutheran Volunteer Corps with their communal houses, or the Holden Village retreat center and other camps or retreats, community is an experience that forms people in profound and life-changing ways. Living out *koinonia* as a "village in the city" is never easy for us today—nor was it for the first-century Christians. Yet the experience is unforgettable.

In a world of increasing gaps between rich and poor, both globally and locally, the economic aspects of *koinonia* in the church become especially urgent. Ecumenically, the World Council of Churches, Lutheran World Federation, and Roman Catholics recommend *koinonia* as a biblical model for deepening sacramental "communion" in diversity. The Lutheran World Federation at its tenth assembly in Winnipeg in 2002 contrasted the exploitative aspects of economic globalization with the biblical vision for true communion or *koinonia* and called for "an economy that serves life":

> The unequal distribution of wealth and goods leaves more than one billion people under the spell of endemic hunger. Many nations of the South find themselves under the unbearable burden of economic debt. . . . As a Lutheran community we call for the development of an economy that serves life. . . . We also emphasize, with Martin Luther, that economic practices that undermine the well-being of the neighbor (especially the most vulnerable) must be rejected and replaced with alternatives. Luther also reminds pastors that they are obliged to unmask hidden injustices of economic practices that exploit the vulnerable.[3]

ACTS 6:1-9; 7:2a, 51-60 (BCP)

Interpreting the Text

As the book of Acts reveals, *koinonia* was not without problems for the early church. A perception of scarcity threatened to overpower the new multicultural community's economy of abundance, exacerbating tensions along old linguistic/ethnic lines. Both Hellenists and Hebrews were Jewish Christians. Some of the Greek speakers charged that their Greek-speaking widows were being neglected in the *diakonia*—a word variously translated as "daily service" or "distribution."

Stephen was not one of the Twelve, nor was Philip, but Stephen became the first Christian martyr—and Philip the first preacher to Samaria. Both preached eloquently, a reminder that *diakonia* begins at the table but also includes the word.

"Signs and wonders" continued to characterize the community. The Christian community's explosive growth threatened the status quo relationship between Jewish authorities and Roman occupying military powers. Stephen's lengthy inflammatory speech highlighting Israel's chronic disobedience sealed his fate. When he even labeled the Sanhedrin and Jewish high priest "stiff-necked people" (Acts 7:51), the crowds charged him.

Responding to the Text

Stephen's death reflects the double meaning of the word *martyria*. The "witness" to Jesus now becomes the "martyr," stoned in a lynching-like scene in which Saul also takes part. Acts narrates the death of Stephen in close parallelism to the death of Jesus. Both Jesus and Stephen utter a loud cry before their death (Luke 23:46; Acts 7:60). Most important, both Jesus and Stephen pray for forgiveness for their executioners ("Father, forgive them; for they do not know what they are doing," Luke 23:34; "Lord, do not hold this sin against them," Acts 7:60). This Luke/Acts parallelism demonstrates the continuation of Jesus' ministry, including martyrdom, in the lives and deaths of his followers.

ACTS 2:14a, 36-41 (RC)

See the comments on the First Reading for the Third Sunday of Easter, above.

NEHEMIAH 9:6-15 (BCP, alt.)

The larger context of this reading recounts a celebration of the festival of booths shortly after the return of some of the Israelites from exile. During the celebration, Ezra offers his prayer or confession.

This prayer rehearses Israel's whole salvation history. Like a catalog, beginning with creation and the assertion of God's life-giving actions (v. 6), Ezra recounts the times when God noticed Abram's faithfulness (v. 8), saw the ancestors' distress in Egypt, heard their cry at the Red Sea (v. 9), and recognized their hunger and thirst in the desert (v. 15). A pattern emerges from the text describing salvation history as God's continual recognition of and response to Israel's faithfulness, distress, and need. Such intimate connection with the community of faith creates no cause for wonder at the celebratory and doxological introduction to this section: "You are the LORD, you alone. . . . [T]he host of heaven worships you" (v. 6). Such celebratory recognition of God's intonation with the community stands as the preface to a larger textual section enumerating the ways that Israel welcomed God's care and concern with presumptuous disobedience and "stiff necks" (9:16).

Ezra's prayer opens us to the idea that God's awareness and intimacy with us as creatures means that God works to turn our distresses, needs, and faithfulness into the stories of joy that we tell again and again throughout generations.

RESPONSIVE READING
PSALM 23 (RCL, BCP); PSALM 23:1–3a, 3b–4, 5, 6 (RC)

Psalm 23 deepens the refrain of trust from the typical lament psalm, building on the shepherd image. The voice shifts as we enter more deeply into the middle verses of the psalm. Whereas the psalmist begins and ends by speaking *about* God in the third person ("Yahweh" is named in vv. 1 and 6), in the very center of the psalm we address God directly, in the second person ("you," v. 4). This "you" constitutes the crucial theological anchor of the entire psalm, expressing heartfelt trust and gratitude to God that "you are with me." Throughout the psalm, the use of the first person singular ("I," "my," "me") also gives a feeling of personal intimacy, and that makes this a favorite psalm for the church.

SECOND READING
1 PETER 2:19–25 (RCL, BCP); 1 PETER 2:20b–25 (RC)

Interpreting the Text

This reading is one of the most dangerous in the entire lectionary. If you must read it, I urge you not to start the reading with v. 19—or else to preach *against* this reading. A senior colleague of mine tells of his awakening to the danger of this passage while teaching this passage from 1 Peter in a New Testament course years ago. A woman who had been beaten by her husband broke down weeping in his class; soon other victims were sharing their own similar stories of abuse and violence.

First Peter's story of Christ's example in the pattern of Isaiah 53 (vv. 22-24) is powerful, even hymnic. The wonderful reference both to Jesus' shepherding and to our going astray like sheep in v. 25 seems to fit the theme of Good Shepherd Sunday. Jesus' bruises heal us—an early theme of Christian exegetical tradition from Isa. 53:5, quoted widely in early Christian literature. But the problem comes in the way 1 Peter develops Jesus' bruises and beatings, patterned on Isaiah 53, as a model or "example" for other victims to imitate today, "so that you should follow in his steps" (v. 21). When this text is read out of context in parishes today, its bruising weight falls on women and other victims of domestic violence. It becomes a text of terror. Pastorally, it is not a Good Shepherd text!

This admonition to endure beatings may have made sense as a survival strategy, or even as a missionary strategy, when first-century Christians were a powerless minority. The author may have been a victim of political beatings himself. He writes specifically to "house slaves" (*oiketai*, v. 18) as fellow victims, strategizing together about how to survive and live out a Christian witness within a hostile culture. Verse 18 makes clear that this counsel addresses only slaves—not "wives" (wives are addressed in 3:1) and not Christians in general. Moreover, the counsel to endure beatings is addressed only to house slaves living in *non*-Christian households—not to those where the householder is a Christian, the situation of most victims of violence and abuse today. But when these exhortations to follow Christ's example are generalized and read out of context in churches, they no longer function as the counsel of one marginalized victim of oppression to another but rather as the authoritative word of the church commanding victims of violence to endure silently. What was once a subversive voice of hope for the first-century marginalized Christians now becomes the voice of the abuser—a dangerous shift of voice.

> WHEN THIS TEXT IS READ OUT OF CONTEXT IN PARISHES TODAY, ITS BRUISING WEIGHT FALLS ON WOMEN AND OTHER VICTIMS OF DOMESTIC VIOLENCE. IT BECOMES A TEXT OF TERROR. PASTORALLY, IT IS NOT A GOOD SHEPHERD TEXT!

Responding to the Text

I recommend that you either omit vv. 19-21 or 19-20, or at least follow the Roman Catholic lectionary by beginning the pericope with v. 20b ("If you endure when you do right and suffer for it . . ."). If you begin with v. 20b, you retain the ethical exhortation/example focus, but without the specific exhortation to suffer beatings. Better still, in my view, is to begin with v. 22—a move that puts the focus on Jesus and on his suffering as the Lamb of Isaiah 53, culminating in the wonderful christological proclamation of Jesus as the Good Shepherd. While such delay of the start of the reading until v. 22 would downplay the parenetical/ethical use of what may be an early Christ hymn, it probably is more faithful to the original intent of the Christ hymn (like Phil. 2:6-11)—singing praise of Jesus who suffered on the tree for us and was raised to exaltation by God.

The exhortation to imitate Jesus in enduring beatings in vv. 19-21 was probably added by Peter to an earlier hymn.

Few passages in the New Testament preach imitation to such an extent as 1 Peter 3. The New Testament offers other ways to follow Jesus besides imitating him in suffering beatings by violent abusers. One rationale for omitting vv. 19-20a or 19-21 would be that Lutherans have never focused on the imitation of Christ as the central method of doing ethics. Further rationale for omitting vv. 19-20a or 19-21 is that the shapers of the lectionary have already violated the sense unit of the pericope by omitting the introductory verse that identifies the specific audience as "household slaves," v. 18—presumably because they do not want the lectionary to endorse slavery. But the omission of v. 18 has the effect of generalizing to all Christians what was written as specific counsel for a specific group (household slaves). You might also add v. 18 to the pericope, thus restoring the entire sense of the unit and making clear that the audience is household slaves—in which case you would need to preach against slavery.

The important point is that parishes cannot read this counsel originally addressed to household slaves without being attentive to the damage it inflicts on other victims today. Violence against women and children is rampant in our congregations. Preachers face an urgent exegetical responsibility to speak against scriptures that seem to promote such violence. A good shepherd or good pastor today will not exhort the flock to suffer beatings, but will rather teach and preach against violence and will care for victims who are beaten.

The Gospel

JOHN 10:1-10 (RCL, BCP, RC)

Interpreting the Text

For the next four Sundays, the Gospel texts take us into the rich realm of Johannine discourse—into "thick languages, dense discourses, tantalizing relationships between discourse and narratives, and puzzling theology."[4] At first glance, the shepherd text appears straightforward, not puzzling. The beloved shepherd "figure" (*paroimia*, v. 6) from John 10 speaks to people on many levels. "Shepherd" was a political term for rulers in both Israelite and Greco-Roman traditions. Biblical shepherds exhibited positive qualities (both Moses and David were shepherds; see Exod. 3:1; 1 Sam. 17:15), but Israel's prophets also lamented the bad shepherd-politicians who exploited their flock (Ezekiel 34; Jeremiah 23; Zechariah 11). Shepherd imagery would have been familiar also to Gentile hearers from a long tradition of iconography and literature beginning already with Plato's *Republic* 343–345.[5] In John's Gospel, the sheep and shepherd resumes in the final post-resurrection scene, with the risen Jesus' threefold charge to Peter, "Tend my sheep" and "Feed my lambs." The intimacy and comfort of Jesus' shepherd imagery speaks to people today in much the same way that it appealed to hearers in John's community, to both Jews and Gentiles.

Yet, paradoxically, the Good Shepherd discourse of John 10 "exceeds the other discourses in difficulty."[6] Far from idyllic or pastoral, when viewed in its larger narrative context, the chapter is divisive, even alienating. It widens the controversy between Jesus and the Pharisees of chapter 9 ("All who came before me are thieves and bandits," v. 8), and it ends with the Pharisees' attempts to stone Jesus because of his provocative speech claiming equality with God. This is the last conversation that Jesus would have directly with any Pharisees. After this they plot to kill him. The preacher will have to decide whether to introduce the larger polemical context of the discourse or whether to stay focused on the intimate and wonderful imagery of today's pericope itself.

THE PREACHER WILL HAVE TO DECIDE WHETHER TO INTRODUCE THE LARGER POLEMICAL CONTEXT OF THE DISCOURSE OR WHETHER TO STAY FOCUSED ON THE INTIMATE AND WONDERFUL IMAGERY OF TODAY'S PERICOPE ITSELF.

Both this Sunday and next Sunday Jesus makes his great "I am" statements of John's Gospel, introduced with the familiar "Amen, amen I say to you." The provocative "I am" without a predicate in 8:58 likened Jesus directly to God, a claim that still echoes through today's text. Jesus states that he himself is the door or "gate" to the sheepfold (v. 7). He has already said that anyone who does not enter the sheepfold by the gate is a thief and a bandit (v. 1)—a possible veiled reference to the Pharisees. With the claim to be the gate, Jesus lays out an urgent either/or choice between himself as the only legitimate gate and all others. Jesus woos us, as his sheep, to desire to share in life in his sheepfold and to enter only by him. This urgency may reflect the historical situation of John's own community—its effort to persuade crypto-Christians to go public about their faith even at the risk of expulsion from the synagogue. "Whoever enters by me will be saved," Jesus promises. We will "find pasture." The stakes are life and death—and what a life! "The thief comes only to steal, kill, and destroy," Jesus warns. In contrast, Jesus extends what is perhaps the most beloved and life-giving declaration of the entire Gospel: "I came that they might have life and have it abundantly."

The word "abundantly" (*perisson*) links the shepherd discourse to the whole biblical world of abundance, from the story of manna in the wilderness to the abundance of paradise itself. The most direct connection is to the feeding of the five thousand in chapter 6. In that story, the disciples gathered up the fragments that were "left over" or "abounding" (*perisseusanta*), filling more than twelve baskets with the barley fragments that "overflowed" (*eperisseusan*, 6:12-13). The word *perisson* can also be translated as "exceedingly" or "overflowing." "Abundance" expresses the age of salvation dawning in our midst. In Jesus, we participate already in an eschatological paradise symbolized by the loaves and green pastures that satisfy even our deepest hunger. Life abundant means life beyond our imagination, like the fragments that overflowed the baskets. It is eternal life in Jesus' shepherding love.

Responding to the Text

In a world of violence, the Good Shepherd teaches us a model of shepherding leadership through compassion and love, not coercion. For a good shepherd image from popular culture, I recommend the movie *Babe* (1995)—the charming story of a pig who becomes a prize-winning "sheepdog." Babe shepherds the sheep not by biting or intimidating them, but by treating them with kindness. In contrast to the dogs who use domination and ferocity to make the sheep do their will, Babe speaks to the sheep with respect: "If you would be so kind, would the three ladies with collars on please stand outside the pen?" The sheep oblige the little guy. They hear his voice and they follow him. The dogs, who think the world runs only on intimidation and violence, are shocked and finally converted by the model of Babe's gentle shepherding.[7]

The preacher can also draw out the shepherd's expansive invitation to the "abundant" life of the risen Christ, connecting this vision to the early Christian *koinonia* and abundance expressed in the first reading from Acts. In an article entitled "Enough Is Enough," Walter Brueggemann advocates a biblical theology of abundance in contrast to an ideology of scarcity.[8] Brueggemann's thesis is that the entire Bible is all about abundance:

> We live in a world where the gap between scarcity and abundance grows wider every day. . . . But the peculiar thing, at least from a biblical perspective, is that the rich—the ones with the abundance—rely on an ideology of scarcity, while the poor—the ones suffering from scarcity—rely on an ideology of abundance. How can that be? . . .

> When we gather as church each Sunday, we should ponder the stories that declare scarcity to be false: an impromptu hillside meal with as much in leftovers as when it began, a barren desert blossoming with manna, an earth fully equipped to meet everyone's needs. And a question should be burning in our hearts: "What if it is true? What if one of the links between the Creator's generosity and the neighbor's needs is us, this community?" If that is not true, then scarcity rules and we are in sorry shape. But if it is, and if we believe it is, we can begin life anew as stewards of God's abundance.

Notes

1. For a wonderful biblical study on manna and abundance, see Daniel Erlander, *Manna and Mercy: A Brief History of God's Unfolding Promise to Mend the Entire Universe* (The Orders of St. Martin and Theresa, 1992), available from Augsburg Fortress or from the author.

2. Richard Horsley and Neil Asher Silberman, *The Message and the Kingdom: How Jesus and Paul Ignited a Revolution and Transformed the Ancient World* (Minneapolis: Fortress Press, 2002), 103.

3. "Message of the LWF Tenth Assembly in Winnipeg, 21–31 July 2003," Section IX, pp. 14–15 (http://www.lwf-assembly.org/PDFs/LWF_Assembly _Message.pdf). See also the Assembly Study Book chapter, "Transforming Economic Globalization," by Cynthia Moe-Lobeda, Karen Bloomquist, et al. at http://www.lwf-assembly.org/lwfimages/Studybook-Part3-09.pdf.

4. Robert Kysar, *Preaching the Gospel of John* (Minneapolis: Fortress Press, 2002), 2.

5. Adele Reinhartz, *The Word in the World: The Cosmological Tale in the Fourth Gospel* (Atlanta: Scholars Press, 1992), 107–9.

6. Ernst Haenchen, *John,* Hermeneia (Philadelphia: Fortress Press, 1984), 2:50.

7. I am grateful to Ann E. Hafften for her Good Shepherd sermon on "Babe," April 29, 1996, the Evangelical Lutheran Church in America Churchwide Office, Chicago.

8. Walter Brueggemann, "Enough Is Enough," *The Other Side* (November–December 2001) (http://www.theotherside.org/archive/nov-dec01/brueggemann .html).

FIFTH SUNDAY OF EASTER

APRIL 24, 2005

REVISED COMMON	EPISCOPAL (BCP)	ROMAN CATHOLIC
Acts 7:55-60	Acts 17:1-15	Acts 6:1-7
	or Deut. 6:20-25	
Ps. 31:1-5, 15-16	Ps. 66:1-11 or 66:1-8	Ps. 33:1-2, 4-5, 18-19
1 Pet. 2:2-10	1 Pet. 2:1-10	1 Pet. 2:4-9
	or Acts 17:1-15	
John 14:1-14	John 14:1-14	John 14:1-12

Today's texts are about life and death—the death of Stephen, our new life as "living stones," and Jesus as the "way, the truth, and the life." The life that God brings out of death is not an escape from earth. Rather, resurrection life brings us into community to be the "home" or "household" of God here on earth, in the many rooms that God has prepared for us. We are God's living stones, a "house"—*oikos*—the root word for ecology, built together as God's own people in the household of the world. With the celebration of Earth Day on April 22, it is important to emphasize the earth-affirming dimension of resurrection life.

> WITH THE CELEBRATION OF EARTH DAY ON APRIL 22, IT IS IMPORTANT TO EMPHASIZE THE EARTH-AFFIRMING DIMENSION OF RESURRECTION LIFE.

FIRST READING
ACTS 7:55–60 (RCL)

See the comments for the First Reading, Fourth Sunday of Easter, BCP.

ACTS 6:1-7 (RC)

See the comments for the Fourth Sunday of Easter, BCP.

ACTS 17:1-15 (BCP)

We must be careful not to foster anti-Judaism when preaching either this incident or the stoning of Stephen. Acts' claim that Paul evangelized in Jewish synagogues "as was his custom" probably lacks historical veracity. While it makes for action-packed drama, the episode of near lynching by Jews in Thessalonica does not fit with Paul's own self-description of his mission first of all to Gentiles. Nowhere in his letters does Paul himself tell of any "custom" of preaching first in Jewish synagogues before going to Gentiles. Paul's own accounts must be viewed as more reliable historically, since they are so much earlier. The late date of Acts can be seen in the way it repeatedly shifts blame away from the Romans and onto the Jews.

We can still see that the principal conflict behind this episode is not with the Jews but with the Roman Empire. Because Jews would not participate in worship of the emperor or empire, they faced sporadic harassment from the local populace and sometimes from the empire itself. They had to prove their loyalty to the empire. Jewish leaders in Thessalonica had negotiated a careful accommodation with Roman imperial rule that they now perceived Paul and the disciples of Jesus as threatening. They accused Christians of "turning the imperial world (*oikoumene*) upside down" by preaching another king, Jesus, rather than Caesar. These charges were political—they undermined the "dogmas" of the emperor (v. 7).

After a dramatic escape by night, Paul and Silas brought many to faith in Beroea. Greek-speaking women and other people of high standing believed, as well as many Jews.

This text and all its drama show how dangerous it was to preach the anti-empire message of Jesus while living in the heart of that very empire. The story asks the question, Do we yet dare risk our lives to preach such a dangerous gospel?

DEUTERONOMY 6:20-25 (BCP, alt.)

This passage brings the biblical story to life for every generation. Set in the context of Moses giving the Ten Commandments (Deut. 5:1-21) and other ordinances, Deuteronomy invites us to tell and retell the story of "our" exodus to explain the meaning of the law. The author pictures inquisitive children asking the typical child's question, "But why?" The answer is a beautifully simple account of slavery and liberation, of God's faithfulness and the people's response. With the "we" and "us" as the personal pronouns in this text, the story becomes the story of whoever tells it. *We* (as the tellers of the story) were Pharaoh's slaves; *we* are heirs of God's faithfulness and liberation. God's statutes and commandments are part of our story; they keep us alive (Deut. 6:24). By entering into the storytelling of Deuteronomy, we bring the account of God's liberation and love for God's commandments across the generations, into the present moment.

PSALM 31:1-5, 15-16 (RCL)

This psalm is often identified as a lament, but the singer's perspective is one of certainty. God is a refuge, a rock (v. 2), a righteous deliverer (v. 1), a strong fortress, a guide (v. 3), and a faithful God (v. 5). The rock imagery in vv. 2-3 fits especially well with 1 Peter's image of Jesus as a "cornerstone" and a "living stone" into whom we ourselves are being built as stones in the household of God. While the psalmist cries out from places of distress (cf. vv. 1, 4), the tone is not one of hopelessness but one of conviction in God's deliverance. Such surety ties this text to today's Gospel text with Jesus' statement "I am the way, the truth, and the life" (John 14:6).

PSALM 66:1-11 or 66:1-8 (BCP)

Corporate praise, thanksgiving, and witness to God's communal salvation are the central threads running through the first twelve verses of Psalm 66. Yet it is not just Israel or the Hebrew people who are saved when the sea turns to dry land, but the entire earth. The psalmist asserts that this salvation merits worship from all the earth (v. 4), even from the enemies who cringe in God's presence (v. 3). Communal sentiment shifts, however, in the second half of the psalm to an individual testimony of God's works.

PSALM 33:1-2, 4-5, 18-19 (RC)

The psalmist invites us to rejoice and be glad that we belong to God, who is righteous. Verse by verse, Psalm 33 describes who God is in ways that provide confidence, hope, and trust in the Lord whose steadfast love will deliver us from death and keep us alive in famine (v. 19). The message: God is good.

SECOND READING
1 PETER 2:2-10 (RCL);
1 PETER 2:1-10 (BCP);
1 PETER 2:4-9 (RC)

Interpreting the Text

This rich passage strings together an amazing concentration of Old Testament allusions—from the savory taste of God's goodness (Psalm 34) to the rejected cornerstone and stumbling stones of Isaiah, to those who were "not my people" becoming "my people" from the prophet Hosea. Few passages in the entire New Testament employ such rich metaphorical language to express God's grace and our election. The preacher will have to choose among the wealth of possibilities. All focus on our identity as God's people.

Extending the "birthed anew" imagery from 1:23, the passage first invites us to see ourselves as infants who have "just now been birthed" (*artigennēta*). As newborns we long to nurse on spiritual "milk." Milk is not a sign of spiritual immaturity or weakness, as in 1 Cor. 3:1-3 or Heb. 5:12-14, but rather the way to "grow into salvation." The milk is the word of God (translating *logikon* as "of the word").[1] We have tasted and seen that the Lord is good—an allusion to Psalm 34:8.

Verse 4 introduces another wonderful, illogical, geological metaphor—Jesus as a "living stone." "Living" (*zōnta*) is a favorite adjective for this author, signifying resurrection—a "living hope" (1:3), the "living word" (1:23). Jesus is brought from death to life in 1 Peter. Even we ourselves come to life as "living stones."

> FEW PASSAGES IN THE ENTIRE NEW TESTAMENT EMPLOY SUCH RICH METAPHORICAL LANGUAGE TO EXPRESS GOD'S GRACE AND OUR ELECTION. THE PREACHER WILL HAVE TO CHOOSE AMONG THE WEALTH OF POSSIBILITIES. ALL FOCUS ON OUR IDENTITY AS GOD'S PEOPLE.

The phrase "come to him" is a present participle, not an imperative, so we must decide whether to translate this entire sentence as an imperative command or the more literal "coming to him." All depends on the verb *oikodomeisthe* ("you are built up") later in the sentence—whether we or God are the ones doing the building. If indeed the imperative is intended, as both the RSV and NRSV suggest (but not the KJV), the invitation is practically irresistible.[2]

Jesus is now a living stone who invites us to join in being built into his house. A whole wealth of Old Testament "stone" images are at play here, most important the rejected cornerstone of Ps. 118:22, but also the "chosen and precious" cornerstone of Isa. 28:16 and the stumbling stone of Isa. 8:14. These are favorite prooftexts employed by a number of New Testament authors to explain the rejection of Jesus—see Mark 12:10; Acts 4:11; Rom. 9:33. Only 1 Peter, however, takes the image one step further by bringing the stone itself to life, calling Jesus not just the cornerstone but the *living* stone. The text brings us to life as well, as living stones to be joined with Jesus in building up the spiritual house. "Spiritual house" may be an allusion to the temple—because of the reference to "sacrifices"—but more likely is simply the church as a household, as in 4:17. The author is heaping up images in order to give a sense of "home" and identity to beleaguered "exiles" (see the reference to *paroikoi* again in 2:11) who have no other house or *oikos*.

The final powerful set of images in this text underscores our election and chosenness. Weaving together a host of biblical references, including the royal priesthood and holy nation of Exod. 19:6 ("You shall be for me a priestly kingdom and a holy nation"), 1 Peter gives us an identity as royalty—like the old Imperial Margarine commercial where crowns appear magically on the heads of those eating their toast. This whole section is built around contrasts—the contrast between our former darkness and the marvelous light into which we have been called, and the two dramatic contrasts between "once" (*pote*) and "but now" (*nun de*) from Hosea. We who "once" were nobodies are now "God's own people." We who once had not received mercy now have been shown mercy.

Responding to the Text

"Once upon a time"—so begins many a classic story. First Peter crafts a story for downtrodden exiles in Asia Minor. "Once upon a time we were nobodies. But now we have been made somebodies in Christ." In fleshing out the contours of this story, the author taps into the story of Hosea's no-people, the story of Isaiah's stumbling stone, and the story of the lowly cornerstone that was rejected yet was precious to God.

It is Jesus' story, and it is our story too. Once upon a time we were rejected stones on the rock pile—rejected because we were misshapen or we had a crack. Jesus, too, was a rejected stone on the pile. "But now" the very stone that was rejected has become the cornerstone of a whole new house, a whole new community.

Perhaps it is because I was a geology major in college that I love 1 Peter's use of stones to depict new life. We all walk past stone piles every day, but only a few people see the stones as "living." Stones tell a history, each one different. Drawing on Girard Manley Hopkins's poetic assertion that "the world is charged with the grandeur of God," the author of 1 Peter sees even stones as charged with God's grandeur. First Peter weaves geological images into this story of "once upon a time" to build the contrast, "but now." Resurrection makes somebodies out of nobodies by making us into living stones—hewing us, shaping us, building us together into a home, into a community with others. This image gives hope for all of God's chosen and precious stones on earth who have experienced rejection.[3]

> THE "LIVING STONE" IMAGE SPEAKS MOST POWERFULLY TODAY TO MARGINALIZED PEOPLE, TO EXILES, TO THOSE STRUGGLING TO SEE HOPE FOR THEIR HOUSES AND THEIR LAND.

The "living stone" image speaks most powerfully today to marginalized people, to exiles, to those struggling to see hope for their houses and their land. Palestinian Christians call themselves the "living stones" of the Middle East. They remind us that our pilgrimages to the Holy Land must include more than just visiting the ancient (dead) stones of archeological sites. In the shadow of Israeli bulldozers threatening to demolish their houses, Palestinians experience what it is to be the Bible's living stones, longing for a house, a homeland, that no one can destroy.

THE GOSPEL

JOHN 14:1-14 (RCL, BCP);
JOHN 14:1-12 (RC)

For the next two Sundays, the Gospel readings are taken from John 14. "In my father's house are many dwellings," Jesus says, using the Greek word *monē*, which means "resting place" or "way station" (from the Greek verb *menein*, "remain"). Many fundamentalists like to point to Jesus' farewell words in vv. 1-2 as the "first teaching about Rapture in the Bible."[4] They argue that Jesus' statement that he is going to "prepare a place for you" means that he is going *away*, to heaven, to get a place ready for those who will be "raptured" out of their cars or houses for seven years. This theology has gained ascendance in our churches through the tremendous popularity of the *Left Behind* novels. When texts such as this one are assigned in the lectionary, we can use the occasion to counter and correct such "Rapture" theology.[5]

> THIS THEOLOGY HAS GAINED ASCENDANCE IN OUR CHURCHES THROUGH THE TREMENDOUS POPULARITY OF THE *LEFT BEHIND* NOVELS. WHEN TEXTS SUCH AS THIS ONE ARE ASSIGNED IN THE LECTIONARY, WE CAN USE THE OCCASION TO COUNTER SUCH "RAPTURE" THEOLOGY.

We should notice first of all that Jesus' departure is his death. This entire speech is the testament a dying leader leaves on the eve of death. "Death is in the air," Francis Maloney points out about this passage.[6] Jesus is not speaking about ascending up to heaven, but about dying.

Notice too that Jesus does not specify where the "Father's house" is located. Is it in heaven, as Rapture proponents argue? Not necessarily, or at least not exclusively in the Gospel of John, because later in the same chapter, Jesus says that he and the Father will come and make their "dwelling"—using the very same word—in the believing person: "We will come and make our dwelling (*monēn*) with them" (14:23). Here the image surely means God's mystical indwelling in the believer. It is in this sense that the Father also "dwells" in Jesus (v. 10). The Gospel of John is the most mystical of all our Gospels, and it is very hard to pin down locations or chronologies in this Gospel.

Some, such as N. T. Wright, have revived the argument that the "Father's house" refers to the Jewish temple, and that the many rooms may be places in the heavenly temple, or even "safe places where those who have died may lodge and rest, like pilgrims in the temple . . . while awaiting the resurrection which is still to come."[7] But Robert Gundry cautions against viewing Jesus' "many dwellings" or "many mansions" as rooms either up in heaven or in the temple. For Gundry, the crucial clue is that Jesus never promises that he upon his return will take the disciples *away* to the "dwellings" or "mansions" in the Father's house, as one might expect. Rather, what Jesus promised to the disciples is that "Where I am, you will be also." Gundry views the key to chapter 14 as the two parallel occurrences of *monē*—

vv. 2 and 23. These verses provide a "reciprocal relationship: As believers have abid-ing-places in Christ, so Jesus and the Father have an abiding-place in each believer."[8] If Gundry is correct about the reciprocity between the parallel occur-rences of *monē* in vv. 2 and 23, then the point is how "God makes a home with us."

In Gundry's view, the "father's house" (*oikia*) in John's Gospel is not so much heaven as God's household or family on earth. Indeed, the word "house" is prob-ably better translated as "household" both here and in John 4:53 and 8:35. This translation would also fit well with the strong message of *oikos* or household, from First Peter. In a strong and mystical sense, John wants to underscore that we are *already* in some sense living in the mystical "dwelling places" in the Father's house-hold that Jesus says he has prepared for us. The passage is about "not mansions in the sky, but spiritual positions in Christ."[9] Jesus is the vine and we are the branches who "dwell" or "abide" in him, to use the similar mystical imagery and wording that is found in John 15. It is not a matter of being "raptured" away from planet Earth up to the Father's house in heaven. The dwelling Jesus is preparing for us is something quite different.

In the Gospel of John, imagery of ascending and descending has a rich, double meaning that makes a strictly "heavenist" interpretation impossible. Far more important than going up to heaven in John's Gospel is the in-ness and one-ness Jesus wants us to experience already with God—the same in-ness and one-ness that Jesus has with the Father. The Gospel's focus is on the rich relationship of mutual "in-dwelling," the eternal life that is already ours. Never would John's Gospel say that Jesus and God are now up in heaven, waiting until the end times to come back to earth and take us away to heaven in the Rapture for seven years of tribulation on earth, until the so-called Glorious Appearing. God dwells with us now, on earth, in mystical communion through the Spirit or *Paraclete*, in John's Gospel. To split Jesus' second coming into two parts and impose the linear time line of Rapture, followed by tribulation and then an earthly return, imports a chronol-ogy that is totally foreign to this Gospel.

Responding to the Text

In *Homing in the Presence,* poet theologian Gerhard Frost tells this story:

One day as I walked down the airport ramp to board a plane, a family of four was in front of me. The older child appeared to be about four and her every step was a bounce. She radiated expectancy and joy. Her father looked down at her and asked, "Where are we going?" "To Grandma's!" she shouted, punctuating her words with a higher bounce.

She didn't say "to Bismarck" or "Billings," but "to Grandma's." As far as she was concerned, she was going to a person—the place didn't matter. She was an eloquent witness to the fact that we home in those who love us, in peo-ple more than places.[10]

So, too, with the many rooms of John 14, what matters is not where the rooms are geographically, but whose rooms they are. "We are going to God's." Our home is with God, John tells us. Rooms up in heaven, in the temple, or little chambers in limbo are not what this passage is about. Rather, the passage is about the assurance that Jesus is preparing a place for us with God.

"Where are we going when we die?" Frost continues. "Everyone has the right to ask, but perhaps it's the wrong question. Rather, we would wonder, To whom am I going? Again and again during his lifetime on earth, our Lord Christ said, "I go to my Father."

We are going to God's—that is all that matters in John 14.

Notes

1. This is the suggestion of John H. Elliott, *1 Peter,* Anchor Bible 37B (New York: Doubleday, 2000), 400.

2. At issue is the main verb of the sentence, which can be translated either as the exhortation to "*be* built up" (middle imperative) or the indicative statement of fact, "You are being built up" (a passive indicative). The KJV takes the main verb as indicative and translates the participle as "coming": "To whom coming, as unto a living stone, disallowed indeed of men, but chosen of God and precious, Ye also, as lively stones, are built up a spiritual house." Elliott also follows this indicative line in his translation: "Continuing to come to him . . . you yourselves, also, as living stones, are being built up" (406).

3. For more "living stone" imagery for preachers I recommend Barbara Lundblad's *Transforming the Stone: Preaching through Resistance to Change* (Nashville: Abingdon, 2001).

4. Tim LaHaye with Steve Halliday, *The Merciful God of Prophecy: His Loving Plan for You in the End Times* (New York: Warner Books, 2002), 155.

5. See Barbara Rossing, *The Rapture Exposed: The Message of Hope in the Book of Revelation* (Boulder, Colo.: Westview Press, 2004).

6. Francis J. Moloney, *Glory, Not Dishonor: Reading John 13–21* (Minneapolis: Fortress Press, 1998), 33.

7. N. T. Wright, *The Resurrection of the Son of God* (Minneapolis: Fortress Press, 2003), 446.

8. Robert Gundry, "'In My Father's House Are Many *Monai*' (John 14:2)" *Zeitschrift für die Neutestamentliche Wissenschaft* 58 (1969): 68-72.

9. Ibid., 70.

10. See Gerhard E. Frost, *Journey of the Heart: Reflections on Life's Way,* compiled and edited by Naomi Frost (Minneapolis: Augsburg Books, 1995), 112-13; originally published as *Homing in the Presence* (HarperCollins, 1978).

SIXTH SUNDAY OF EASTER

MAY 1, 2005

REVISED COMMON	EPISCOPAL (BCP)	ROMAN CATHOLIC
Acts 17:22-31	Acts 17:22-31	Acts 8:5-8, 14-17
	or Isa. 41:17-20	
Ps. 66:8-20	Psalm 148 or 148:7-14	Ps. 66:1-3, 4-5, 6-7, 16, 20
1 Pet. 3:13-22	1 Pet. 3:8-18	1 Pet. 3:15-18
	or Acts 17:22-31	
John 14:15-21	John 15:1-8	John 14:15-21

Christian faith will clash with the established world powers. Followers of Jesus must expect to face harassment and suffering in the world. Yet we need to be clear about what is meant by "world." According to Acts it is the "imperial world"—the *oikoumenē* or "civilization"—that falls under God's judgment, not the created world. A strong creation focus in the First Reading under-scores the goodness of the created world. Even in the Gospel of John the word *kosmos* carries a dual meaning. God will never give up on the world.

GOD WILL NEVER GIVE UP ON THE WORLD.

FIRST READING

ACTS 17:22-31 (RCL, BCP)

Interpreting the Text

Luke regards Athens as the philosophical and cultural center of the ancient world. For the Christian mission to be fully realized, Paul must go to Athens to debate the philosophers. In his own letters, Paul himself never mentions preaching in Athens, and it is highly unlikely that he delivered any such speech. (His only reference to Athens is in 1 Thess. 3:1.) Luke composed this dramatic speech, like the other speeches in Acts. It does not reflect Paul's own theology. But Luke makes this speech the "second most important Pauline speech in Acts," the high point of Paul's second missionary journey.[1]

Paul's Areopagus speech addresses the complex relationship between three worlds—the world of the gospel, the world of classical philosophy, and the

Roman imperial world (*oikoumenē*). Jerusalem, Athens, and Rome are all present in this speech. Unlike the other speeches in Acts, Paul makes no references to the Hebrew scriptures. He begins by commending the Athenians' religiousness and establishing common ground with them through his repetition of the word "all" and his emphasis on creation. Paul shares with the philosophers an affirmation of God's creation of the "world" (*kosmos*) as good. God made the *kosmos* and "all" that is in it, including humans (v. 24). Our common humanity cuts across "all" nationalities. We are all created from one ancestor, and we are all God's offspring. We all seek after God, who is not far from us. Paul shows a deferential respect for the Athenians' religious spirit even while he views their temples as empty. God who gives life and breath to "all" does not live in shrines made by human hands.

Christianity builds upon classical philosophy but ultimately must contend with it. Resurrection precipitates the clash, as does Paul's call for repentance. Paul's preaching about Jesus' resurrection first caused the Athenians to bring him by force to the Areopagus to defend himself (Acts 17:18). Resurrection now brings Paul's speech to a climactic conclusion in v. 31: God "has given assurance to all by raising him [Jesus] from the dead." Resurrection leads to divided responses among the Athenians in vv. 32-34. Some hearers mock Paul, while others come to faith.

Intertwined with the clash of philosophies is the clash of empires, reflected in Paul's statement that God has appointed a day to "judge the imperial world (*oikoumenē*) in righteousness" (v. 31). To understand the political dimension of the judgment of the "world" in v. 31, we need to distinguish between the Greek words *oikoumenē* and *kosmos*, unfortunately both translated into English as "world." I use the translation of "imperial world" for *oikoumenē* to convey the political connotations that *oikoumenē* has throughout the New Testament. (In Luke 2:1, for example, Emperor Caesar Augustus decreed that the whole *oikoumenē* should be registered for the imperial taxation. See also Acts 19:27; 24:5.)

The events in Thessalonica leading up to Paul's speech set the stage for the anti-imperial reference to *oikoumenē* in v. 31. Only days before his arrival in Athens, Paul had to be smuggled out of Thessalonica in the dead of night. There, synagogue leaders dragged Christians before the Roman authorities, charging them with defying Roman "dogmas" by claiming that there is a king other than Caesar, Jesus (Acts 17:7). Ironically, the leaders in Thessalonica grasp very well the subversive heart of Christianity. They accuse followers of Jesus of "turning the imperial world (*oikoumenē*) upside down."

THE "WORLD" THAT IS OVERTURNED IN 17:6 AND PUT UNDER JUDGMENT IN 17:31 IS NOT THE "CREATED WORLD" OR *KOSMOS* BUT RATHER THE "IMPERIAL WORLD" (*OIKOUMENE*).

The "world" that is overturned in 17:6 and put under judgment in 17:31 is not the "created world" or *kosmos* but rather the "imperial world" (*oikoumenē*). The *kosmos* is good. God made the *kosmos* and everything in it, Paul tells the Athenians. But nowhere in the New Testament does any Christian refer to the *oikoumenē*—the imperial world—as part of God's good creation. Instead, God has fixed a day to "judge the *oikoumenē* in righteousness," Paul tells the Athenians (v. 31)—and that day will mean the judgment of empire.

Responding to the Text

"God made every nation from one ancestor." In our time of fundamentalism, perhaps this is the most important message to preach. We are all God's offspring and relatives of one another. Rather than encouraging a kind of Christian exclusivism, even Christian "jihad," we need to remember this message of oneness and kinship as we preach the radical gospel of resurrection for the world today. The mission of the gospel necessitates discerning which aspects of culture we can build on and affirm, versus other aspects that must be opposed. Recognizing the difference between the *kosmos* as God's good creation, and the *oikoumenē,* or empire, can help in that discernment.

ISAIAH 41:17-20 (BCP, alt.)

Second Isaiah addresses the needs of three constituents and God's response. Verse 17 calls attention to the poor and needy deprived of access to water, the most basic elements needed to sustain life. God will bring water for poor people even to the driest places.

Second, God extends the cup of life to "all" people. God will shake the foundations of the earth so that "all may see and know, all may consider and understand" that God creates life and intends for life to flourish for "all" (Isa. 42:20).

The third constituent in this text is the creation itself, in need of water to renew and sustain itself. God who created the heavens and the earth will not forsake creation (see Genesis 8–9 for the covenant with Noah), nor will God cease creating and shaping life. God will ensure that the world receives water—the most common element in all created things.

Religious leaders attending an International Conference on Faith and Ecology offer us this straightforward understanding:

Land does not belong to us. We belong to the land. Water is not a commodity. Water sustains life. Nobody can claim possession of the air. It is to be shared by everyone. *Land, water, air and people are one. They belong together in one earth community, the community of life.*[2]

ACTS 8:5-8, 14-17 (RC)

The death of Stephen and the terrifying persecution in Jerusalem, spearheaded by Paul, lead to a scattering, or "dispersion," of Jesus' followers throughout Judea and Samaria, just to the north. With Philip's preaching in Samaria, we see the Lukan geography beginning to be fulfilled "in Jerusalem and in all Judea and Samaria and to the end of the earth" (Acts 1:8). Given the well-known tension between Jews and Samaritans—a strong feature of Luke but never mentioned in today's text—it is striking that Samaria is the first area of mission

It is also remarkable that the person to initiate the mission outside Jerusalem is not one of the original twelve apostles but a newcomer, Philip, chosen as a result of the Hebrews-Hellenists controversy. Like Stephen, Philip will play a key role in the story of Acts, bringing about the conversion of Samaria and the conversion of the Ethiopian eunuch on the Gaza road to the south and west.

Philip preaches, heals, and does great "signs" in Samaria, so there is "great joy in the city" (v. 8). He also baptizes the people, but only in the name of Jesus. Not until Peter and John come to lay their hands on them do the Samaritans receive the Holy Spirit. This two-stage sequence of baptism followed by the Holy Spirit at a later time should not be generalized to other settings. Luke nowhere says that one of the twelve apostles' presence is necessary for receiving the Holy Spirit—indeed, Peter's Pentecost sermon suggests that the gift of the Holy Spirit will flow from baptism and forgiveness. A joyous desire to bridge ethnic divisions and extend apostolic fellowship in the Holy Spirit seems to motivate the apostles' visit.

Responsive Reading

PSALM 66:8-20 (RCL);
PSALM 66:1-3, 4-5, 6-7, 16, 20 (RC)

In this psalm, all the earth worships God (v. 4) in a physicality of passion, confidence, and praise. In the opening seven verses, we hear seven calls to action. The great active language invites us to come, see, and hear, and to join in the music of praise. Using exodus imagery, the songs, stories, and communal celebration extend the word of liberation and freedom along with praise for the reign of a faithful and powerful God.

In v. 8 we hear an eighth call to action, the summons to blessing: "Bless our God, O peoples, let the sound of praise be heard, who has kept us among the living and has not let our feet slip." In case we missed it the first time, the closing v. 20 says it even more succinctly: "Blessed be God who has not rejected my prayer nor removed your steadfast love from me."

The Easter psalms may be used as main texts for preaching or can also serve very well for short verses repeated through the sermon, as memory aids, and as a way of punctuating the main points in complementary texts.[3]

PSALM 148 or 148:7–14 (BCP)

Summons to praise God is the essence of this psalm, as the psalmist calls upon the entire created world to join in glorifying God. One by one, the created elements become part of the worshiping congregation. Mountains, fruit trees, stars, weather, and water—the joyous sound builds as all join with humans in praising their Creator. The final stanza gives thanks for God's people, Israel.

SECOND READING

1 PETER 3:13–22 (RCL);
1 PETER 3:8–18 (BCP);
1 PETER 3:15–18 (RC)

Interpreting the Text

First Peter uses the verb "suffer" (*paschō*) more times than any other New Testament book. Christ suffered, and his followers will also suffer. Those who suffer for righteousness are "blessed"—*makarioi*, an echo of the beatitudes of Matthew. We will hear another echo of the beatitudes in next Sunday's "blessing" of those who are "reviled" (1 Pet. 4:14). The particular sufferings that the community endures are "slander" or being "spoken" against (*katalalein,* v. 16)—the intense harassment and discrimination experienced by a suspect minority group—rather than physical persecution. (See the comments for the Seventh Sunday of Easter for more detail.)

> EMPIRE AND ITS LOCAL PROPONENTS INTIMIDATE AND TERRORIZE PEOPLE. THEIR FEAR AND INTIMIDATION SERVE TO PROP UP THE SYSTEM OF VIOLENCE AND INJUSTICE. BUT CHRISTIANS MUST NOT BE INTIMIDATED BY FEAR.

"Do not fear their fear" is Don Senior's translation of 3:14, similar to KJV's "Be not afraid of their terror." Empire and its local proponents intimidate and terrorize people. Their fear and intimidation serve to prop up the system of violence and injustice. But Christians must not be intimidated by fear. The counsel here, as throughout the entire letter is plural—addressed to the entire community. This is counsel that can serve us, too, in a post–September 11 world. When our own government tries to use fear to silence or intimidate us, or when it argues that violence is necessary, we must not fear its fear.

The charge not to capitulate to the fear of empire can be seen also in the author's modification of an Old Testament quote in 1 Pet. 2:17, a verse unfortunately not included in the lectionary. As Gerhard Krodel observes, "The quotation from Prov. 24:21, 'Fear the Lord and fear the King,' is changed to 'fear God, *honor* the emperor.'"[4] First Peter's change of "fear" to "honor" in reference to the emperor in 2:17 is careful and deliberate—in fact, it is key to the whole view of empire. While we must "honor" governors and government, their rule is only temporary, not God-given. We must never "fear their fear." This letter would never say as Paul does that "government is instituted by God" (Rom. 13:1-2).

Using courtroom language, the author counsels hearers to be ready to give their defense or testimony (*apologia*) to their accusers. The content of that testimony is hope—"always be ready to give account for the hope that is in you all." Our world is desperately in need of hope, and 1 Peter can help us find that word of hope.

The author also makes clear that Christians must never respond with violence. Faced with malignity or provocation from the government or from its local representatives, we are to give our account with "gentleness and reverence," not with vengeance. Our nonviolent response will put our opponents to shame (v. 6).

One of the strangest aspects of this passage, and indeed of the New Testament, is the declaration that Christ went to preach to the spirits in prison. This is the origin of the Apostles' Creed statement that he "descended to hell." Artists depict this scene of the "harrowing of hell," as Christ pulling Adam and Eve up from hell, saving those who died before the time of Jesus. But the spirits in prison are more likely the fallen angels of Gen. 6:1-4, and the letter seems to place the event after Jesus' resurrection—after he was "made alive in the spirit." It is also not clear how this event fits with the "preaching even to the dead" in 4:6. The Greek is difficult and has many textual variants.

The only reference to baptism in the entire letter also comes in another extremely difficult sentence, both grammatically and theologically. Baptism transforms us and makes an appeal to God. All this is through the resurrection of Jesus Christ. The reference to Jesus' exaltation at the right hand prepares us for this week's celebration of Christ's ascension—although we should be cautious about imposing a Lukan chronology on 1 Peter.

Responding to the Text

Standing up to empire and to the fear it tries to instill in us is perhaps the most important theme to preach in our congregations. Part of the preacher's task is to help people see the imperial nature of the world today. First Peter can help us in this diagnosis, as can global Christians who point out the similarities between the Roman Empire and the United States. Even though our situation is different from that of the early Christians, we, too, live in the heart of an empire. And we, too, are counseled not to "fear its fear."

We can also take to heart the command to "be prepared to give an account for the hope that is in you" by encouraging people to tell stories of hope to one another. Here are two such stories and testimonies:

In 1993 Gloria Luster started the "Power of Hope Garden" in abandoned empty lots in inner-city Baltimore. Her organic garden helps to feed the city's disadvantaged community, employing the labor of local homeless and low-income residents. By transforming a neighborhood that others viewed as hopeless, Gloria gives testimony to the hope that is in her.[5] "We are not just planting vegetables here, we are planting hope," she says.

> STANDING UP TO EMPIRE AND TO THE FEAR IT TRIES TO INSTILL IN US IS PERHAPS THE MOST IMPORTANT THEME TO PREACH IN OUR CONGREGATIONS.

On the other side of the world, Kenyan theologian Dr. Musimbi Kanyoro knows the seemingly hopeless reality of the AIDS crisis, the debt crisis, corruption, genocide in Rwanda, grinding poverty, and much more. But "Jesus of the gospel is my hope and the ultimate hope for Africa," she says. Christian mission is about sustaining hope in the midst of everything in the world that seeks to negate it:

> It is extremely easy to flirt with hopelessness in Africa, especially today. . . . But even amidst what would seem to be misery, African people have a will to live that can only be described as stubborn hope.
>
> Think of the African woman who gave birth on a tree during the recent floods in Mozambique! Can you imagine a pregnant woman spending five days on a tree, going in labor and giving birth to a baby on a tree? There cannot be a better symbol of hope for Africa than this story that shows that despite our difficulties, life goes on.
>
> To have faith and to hope means to engage hour by hour with life in such a way that our deeds express that which we hope for, while acknowledging the realism of disappointment, frustration, anger, brokenness, and even despair. The challenge is always to dare to hope, and in daring to wrestle with all that seeks to deny us hope. There is no other alternative than to have faith and to hope. Without hope for Africa, there will be a vacuum and that vacuum will be filled by defeat.
>
> This season of Easter teaches us that for Christians and for the church universal, hope is ultimately hope in Christ. . . . Living out this hope beyond the intellectual frame of mind is a challenge we face every day. Mission has to be about sustaining this hope amidst all that seeks to negate it. Mission has to deal with the everyday questions that people ask, including those that push hope to the brink of hopelessness.[6]

Musimbi Kanyoro concludes, "Hope is the greatest gift that the church can give to the world."

The Gospel
JOHN 14:15–21 (RCL, RC);
JOHN 15:1–8 (BCP)

The Gospel lection continues in sequence from last Sunday's reading and prepares us for the ascension, which we will celebrate on Thursday. Today's Gospel offers no narrative or dialogue. The preacher can set the narrative context by reminding people of the disciples' deep grief as Jesus gives his farewell speech to them. In anticipation of his departure, Jesus teaches the disciples about the ways that he will remain with them. He loves them. He will not leave them "orphaned."

The Farewell Discourse circles around familiar themes with an "almost wave-like effect."[7] The waves that bracket today's section are the themes of love and the exhortation to keep Jesus' commandments. In v. 15 Jesus first addresses the love command specifically to the disciples. When the love theme returns again in v. 21, Jesus broadens the audience to us all in love: "*They* [literally, "the one"] who have my commandments and keep them are they who love me . . . and I will love them." Between these two references to love, Jesus introduces two promises, "in-ness" and the *Paraclete*. Jesus will be "in" us and we will be "in" him (v. 20); the Spirit also will be "in" us (v. 17). As with the many rooms in the Father's house earlier in the chapter, the Johannine geography of "in-ness" is highly mystical. Rather than trying to explain, we can invite parishioners into John's metaphorical world and rich imagery. "Imagery invites participation," writes Kysar, in arguing for a poetic, metaphorical style of preaching John.[8]

The Paraclete furnishes one of the most important images for Jesus' ongoing presence with the community. First introduced as the "Spirit of truth," the Paraclete is the Holy Spirit sent in Jesus' name who will act as an advocate on the disciples' behalf. Anticipation of persecution by the Roman authorities may have been an element of the historical context for which the Johannine Farewell Discourse was shaped in the late first century. If so, translation of the word *Paraclete* as "Advocate" underscores this sense of juridical advocacy and encouragement. Besides calling to remembrance all that Jesus taught and witnessed (v. 26), the Paraclete will assist Christians in making their own witness in time of trial.[9] Most of all, the Paraclete makes Jesus present even when he is absent.

The preacher may want to address John's hostility toward the "world" (*kosmos*) in today's reading and again in next week's text from John 17. The view of the *kos-*

mos in this Gospel is more negative than that of Acts. Jesus accuses the "world" (*kosmos*) of being unable to receive or see the Paraclete, in contrast to the disciples (v. 17). Jesus will make even broader antiworld declarations in chapters 15 and 17, when he states that the world "hates" him (15:18) and that he is "not praying for the world" (17:9). Such statements can foster a dangerous disdain for the physical world or a sectarian theology of "Christians against the world." The Gnostics loved the Gospel of John in part because of such dualisms. Yet the great proclamation that "God so loved the world" (John 3:16) stands as a corrective against antiworld dualism in this Gospel. The Johannine view of the world is highly enigmatic, even divisive—yet God does not give up on the world in this Gospel. Jesus continues to send the disciples into the world, even after he explicitly states he is not praying for the world (17:18).

We must seek to understand the function of John's antiworld polarity in this discourse. Jesus is using the contrast between the disciples and the "world" as a way of comforting the disciples. The goal is to assure the grieving disciples that they will continue to "see" him even after his departure, even when the world will not see him (v. 19). For the preacher, the challenge is to preach the intensely personal message of comfort and presence without painting the "world" in starkly negative, sectarian terms.

Responding to the Text

"I view my role as encourager," the head of a major philanthropic foundation told our group of pastors and theologians last year. His reference to the word "encourager" triggered for me the realization that "encourager" is also the word "Paraclete" in the Gospel of John. The Greek noun *paraklete* and the verb *parakaleō* can be variously translated as "exhort," "comfort," "entreat," "advocate," "counsel," or "encourage"—each of which has different connotations. The apostle Paul

> AS PREACHERS, WE FACE THE CHALLENGE OF DISCERNING WHEN OUR CONGREGATIONS NEED A COMFORTER, WHEN THEY NEED AN ADVOCATE, OR WHEN THEY NEED AN EXHORTER—ALL OF WHICH CAN BE CORRECT TRANSLATIONS FOR THE MULTIVALENT *PARAKLETE* AND *PARAKALEO*.

uses the verb *parakaleō* to exhort people and also to comfort. As preachers, we face the challenge of discerning when our congregations need a comforter, when they need an advocate, or when they need an exhorter—all of which can be correct translations for the multivalent *paraklete* and *parakaleō*.

We all struggle with the trauma of Jesus' absence, the trauma of the world's hopelessness, the trauma of grief. Jesus assured the disciples that they would never be orphaned because they would have the Spirit-Paraclete in their midst. Listening to the philanthropist/mentor, I was inspired to adopt a consistent translation for "Paraclete" as "encourager"—and also to try to take on the role of "encourager" as a model for my ministry. We all need encouragers and encouragement. The functions of exhorting, admonishing, advocating, prodding, and counseling people can be subsumed under the overarching banner of "encourager." By living out our own callings as "encouragers," we can witness to the presence of God's spirit as the "Encourager" or Paraclete in our midst.

Notes

1. Joseph A. Fitzmyer, *The Acts of the Apostles,* Anchor Bible 31 (New York: Doubleday, 1998), 601.

2. From a statement by an International Conference on Faith and Ecology, "Land, Water, Air: People Struggling for Life in a Globalizing Economy," Bangalore, India, 10–15 December 2001.

3. I am grateful to Jamie Jazdzyck, my research assistant, for this explication and other psalms and alternate readings for the Sixth and Seventh Sundays of Easter.

4. Gerhard Krodel, *The First Letter of Peter, Hebrews, James, 1 and 2 Peter, Jude, Revelation* (Philadelphia: Fortress Press, 1977), 74. Cited in David Tiede, "An Easter Catechesis: The Lessons of 1 Peter," *Word and World* 4 (1984): 197.

5. Sue Edison-Swift, "A Gardener of Hope: Gloria Luster," *Lutheran Woman Today,* February 1995; http://www.webofcreation.org/education/articles/luster .htm.

6. Musimbi R. A. Kanyoro, "Hope: The Ultimate Alternative for Africa," World Mission Institute, Chicago, April 27–29, 2000, unpublished manuscript, quoted by permission of the author.

7. Richard Cassidy, *John's Gospel in New Perspective* (Maryknoll, N.Y.: Orbis, 1992), 65.

8. Robert Kysar, *Preaching John* (Minneapolis: Fortress Press), 222.

9. Cassidy, *John's Gospel,* 61.

THE ASCENSION
OF OUR LORD

MAY 5, 2005

REVISED COMMON	EPISCOPAL (BCP)	ROMAN CATHOLIC
Acts 1:1-11	Acts 1:1-11	Acts 1:1-11
	or Dan. 7:9-14	
Psalm 47 or Psalm 93	Psalm 47 or 110:1-5	Ps. 47:2-3, 6-7, 8-9
Eph. 1:15-23	Eph. 1:15-23	Eph. 1:17-23
	or Acts 1:1-11	
Luke 24:44-53	Luke 24:49-53	Matt. 28:16-20
	or Mark 16:9-15, 19-20	

FIRST READING
ACTS 1:1-11 (RCL, BCP, RC)

See the comments on the First Reading for the Seventh Sunday of Easter.

RESPONSIVE READING
PSALM 47 or 93 (RCL);
PSALM 47 (BCP);
PSALM 47:2-3, 6-7, 8-9 (RC)

Enthronement psalms sweep us into a great procession, ritualizing God's royal rule over the earth with the enthronement formula, "Yahweh reigns" (93:1) or "God reigns" (47:7, 8). Assigned for Ascension Day, these psalms interpret Jesus' ascension as his enthronement on high, at God's right hand. Enthronement psalms reenact God's victory over enemies and God's installation as ruler. Psalm 93 describes the royal procession and God's victory over floods and storm. Psalm 47 uses imperatives to summon people to praise, describing how God has "gone up" to ascend the throne amid shouts of joy.

PSALM 110:1-5 (BCP, alt.)

A royal psalm, Psalm 110 is cited extensively in the New Testament to support christological claims about Jesus Christ. The newly enthroned king ("my lord") is invited by God ("the Lord") to ascend the throne. This reference to two "lords" was aptly applied to Jesus (Mark 12:36 and parallels; Acts 2:34). The twice-repeated image of God's right hand in Psalm 110:1, 5 also provides the background for the New Testament enthronement imagery of God making Christ "sit at his right hand" (Eph. 1:20; Heb. 1:13). The new king will rule also with priestly investiture, after the order of Melchizedek.

Second Reading
EPHESIANS 1:15-23 (RCL, BCP);
EPHESIANS 1:17-23 (RC)

While Luke and Acts speak of Jesus' ascension into heaven, only Ephesians speaks of his enthronement. This text is assigned for today because it portrays Jesus Christ as seated in the heavenly places at the right hand of God, as Lord of the church, presiding over its cosmic unity. Ephesians is the source of the church's creedal statements that Christ is "seated at the right hand of the Father," a theme articulated also in last week's text from 1 Peter (3:22).

Today's text comes from the opening thanksgiving section of the letter, consisting of two long, participle-rich Greek sentences. Unlike the authentic Pauline letters, Ephesians was probably not written to one specific church (since the reference to the saints of God "in Ephesus," Eph. 1:1, is not found in the best manuscripts). In this letter, we begin to see the concept of the "church" as encompassing multiple congregations united in Christ's oneness. The author (not Paul) prays with unceasing thanks for the whole church, for its faith and love. The prayer is grounded in cosmic praise of God, drawing on imagery of heavenly unity from Colossians.

Psalm 110 shapes Ephesians' description of Christ's journey to enthronement at God's "right hand" (v. 20) and the proclamation that God has "put all things under his feet" (v. 22). A royal coronation psalm, Psalm 110 projects extravagant hopes for the future Messiah. Ephesians and other New Testament texts pick up these same hopes and ascribe them to Jesus Christ, who is seated high above any other authority, surpassing all political rulers and dominions in this age and in every age (v. 21).

No other New Testament letter speaks with such detail about the "heavenly places" (*epouraniois*, Eph. 1:20; 2:6; 3:10; 6:12). Especially striking is the declaration of Eph. 2:6 that *we*, too, have been raised already to "sit" with Christ in the heavenly places.

THE GOSPEL

LUKE 24:44-53 (RCL);
LUKE 24:49-53 (BCP);
MARK 16:9-15, 19-20 (BCP, alt.)

Interpreting the Texts

The Lukan Ascension narrative takes place on the same long Easter day that began at the empty tomb, then saw Jesus walking on the Emmaus road, and finally appearing to the disciples in Jerusalem. Like the Emmaus conversation earlier in the day, Jesus' concern is to teach about fulfillment of scripture. He opens the disciples' minds to

> THE PREACHER MAY WANT TO EMPHASIZE THE BLESS-ING THAT WAS JESUS' FINAL GIFT TO THE DISCIPLES.

understand the law, the Prophets, and the Psalms—naming all three parts of the Bible—so that they might understand that his death and resurrection were all in accordance with God's word.

Jerusalem is the center from which Jesus' mission will go forth, the place where the disciples will receive "power from on high." In contrast to the post-Easter geography of Mark and Matthew, the disciples are not instructed to go to Galilee in Luke. They are to wait in Jerusalem for the Holy Spirit.

Jesus' last act on earth is to bless the disciples, a farewell gesture reminiscent of biblical prophets and priests (Num. 6:22-27; Sir. 50:20-21; Luke 2:34). As he is blessing them, Jesus is taken up from their sight. The preacher may want to emphasize the blessing that was Jesus' final gift to the disciples. After Jesus departs, his followers return to Jerusalem with great joy, where they too are continually "blessing" God (the same Greek word).

MATTHEW 28:16-20 (RC)

This Matthean story is not an ascension but a resurrection appearance and commissioning. The disciples go back to Galilee, just as the angel sent Mary Magdalene and the other Mary to instruct them. The disciples are back where the Gospel began, where Jesus has "gone ahead" to meet them (Matt. 28:7). Jesus

> MATTHEW NOTES THAT THE DISCIPLES WORSHIPED HIM, "BUT SOME DOUBTED" (28:17).

meets them on the mountain, recalling all the other mountaintops of this Gospel. In one of the most wonderfully candid admissions of an otherwise exalted

Gospel, Matthew notes that the disciples worshiped him, "but some doubted" (28:17); literally, "but *they* doubted." This is a good reminder that doubt is part of faith. The church—indeed each one of us—is always a mix of wheat and tares, sheep and goats, until the end of the age.

Jesus claims "all authority" for himself—a reminder that the empire's authority is only temporary. He tells the eleven to "disciple" all nations, baptizing them and then teaching them to observe all that he has commanded. Catechesis follows baptism. There is no Pentecost in Matthew—only the inclusion of the Spirit in the baptismal formula, "baptizing them in the name of the Father, and of the Son and the Holy Spirit."

Finally, Jesus promises the disciples that he will be "with" them always, an echo of the promise in the name Emmanuel given to him at the beginning of the Gospel. The name Emmanuel means "God with us," Matthew explained in 1:23. Thus, the two promises that Jesus will always be "with" us bracket this Gospel in a wonderful way. In Matthew's Gospel, Jesus is never taken up to heaven. He never departs on a cloud. Presumably, this Gospel wants us to know that Jesus is still "with us," in our midst, as "Emmanuel"—wherever two or three are gathered in his name (Matt 18:20).

IN MATTHEW'S GOSPEL, JESUS IS NEVER TAKEN UP TO HEAVEN. HE NEVER DEPARTS ON A CLOUD. PRESUMABLY, THIS GOSPEL WANTS US TO KNOW THAT JESUS IS STILL "WITH US," IN OUR MIDST, AS "EMMANUEL"—WHEREVER TWO OR THREE ARE GATHERED IN HIS NAME (MATT 18:20).

Responding to the Texts

The preacher faces several challenges in these ascension texts: first, how to present Jesus' departure from the earth not as an occasion for sorrow but celebration; and second, how to translate the kingship and hierarchical language of the enthronement texts (Psalms 47; 93; 110; Ephesians 1) into imagery that speaks to a world no longer governed by kings and monarchs. Contemporary hymn writer Brian Wren explains why he does not use imagery of divine kingship in his lyrics: "Those who use such language doom themselves to thinking of God as influential only in their personal lives or in the life of the church. Though still colorful, this language doesn't resonate except at a very privatized level."[1]

The Mattean emphasis on commissioning is perhaps the most important corrective to enthronement. If Jesus' ascension is to have meaning today, it must not be as a way of inscribing churchly hierarchy (the danger of Ephesians) but rather as a way of expressing Jesus' presence still among us in the world, inhabiting every time and place. Biblical descriptions of Jesus' enthronement in political terms can counteract tendencies to privatize faith today, but this political dimension, too, needs to be expressed in language and analogies that speak to our own *polis* or contemporary context.

In preaching the ascension we do well to follow Luke and Acts in turning our gaze earthward. Brazilian theologian Vitor Westhelle argues that this is the meaning of the statement of the angels in Acts 1:11—that just as we experienced Jesus first on earth, and then departing to heaven, so will we experience him coming again from earth.[2] Earth is the place to look for Jesus' presence. The disciples' response to ascension can be ours as well, to return with great joy, "blessing God," and to set out in mission and ministry in the world.

Notes

1. Interview in *The Christian Century*, May 3, 2000, 506.
2. Vitor Westhelle, unpublished Ascension sermon, Chicago, May 16, 1999.

SEVENTH SUNDAY OF EASTER

MAY 8, 2005

REVISED COMMON	EPISCOPAL (BCP)	ROMAN CATHOLIC
Acts 1:6-14	Acts 1:(1-7) 8-14 or Ezek. 39: 21-29	Acts 1:12-14
Ps. 68:1-10, 32-35	Ps. 68:1-20 or Psalm 47	Ps. 27:1, 4, 7-8
1 Pet. 4:12-14; 5:6-11	1 Pet. 4:12-19 or Acts 1:(1-7) 8-14	1 Pet. 4:13-16
John 17:1-11	John 17:1-11	John 17:1-11a

The mystical "glory" experienced by Jesus and his followers encompasses suffering. Today's texts are about glory and glorification—but not the glorious restoration of the kingdom that the disciples hope for. The arc of Jesus' glory begins with crucifixion and continues through the community's "fiery ordeal" of suffering in 1 Peter. Because of our oneness and *koinonia* in Christ, we can know that when anyone suffers, all of our brothers and sisters in all the world share together in that same suffering. Jesus' spirit of glory "rests" upon us when we suffer, accompanying us as a wonderful companion. Indeed, these final Easter readings take us more and more deeply into companionship with Jesus, with the Spirit, with God, and with one another.

FIRST READING
ACTS 1:6-14 (RCL);
ACTS 1:(1-7), 8-14 (BCP);
ACTS 1:12-14 (RC)

Interpreting the Texts

Jesus has appeared to his followers many times during the forty days following his resurrection, speaking about the kingdom of God (Acts 1:3). Now, as he prepares to depart once more, Jesus instructs them and promises that they will be baptized with the Holy Spirit.

Only Luke among the Gospels distinguishes Jesus' ascension from his resurrection as a separate event. And only Acts puts a forty-day separation between the two events. The church's liturgical year comes from the calendar of Acts. Luke narrates the ascension twice, both at the end of the Gospel and again at the beginning of Acts, with a chronological conflict between the two accounts. In Luke 24:51, Jesus ascends late on Easter day itself (some manuscripts do not include the words "was carried up into heaven"), whereas in Acts 1 his ascension is delayed until "after forty days" (reminiscent of Jesus' forty-day stay in the wilderness, Luke 4:2).

The story of the ascension forms a bridge from Luke into Acts, from the time of Jesus into the time of the church. Acts uses the ascension story not only to narrate Jesus' departure but also to discourage expectations and speculations about the timetable of Jesus' return in glory. In response to questions of the chronology, such as the question posed by the disciples, Jesus replies with words still relevant today: "It is not for you to know the times or the seasons." The words for "times" (*chronoi*) and "seasons" (*kairoi*) do not seem to be distinguishable. The point is that the disciples must not to try to calculate the date of his return and his kingdom (see also Matt. 24:36 and Mark 13:32, "But about that day and hour no one knows"). Only God knows the times, and they are set by God's own authority. We are not to speculate.

> ACTS USES THE ASCENSION STORY NOT ONLY TO NARRATE JESUS' DEPARTURE BUT ALSO TO DISCOURAGE EXPECTATIONS AND SPECULATIONS ABOUT THE TIMETABLE OF JESUS' RETURN IN GLORY.

Acts uses the ascension story also to mark the end of Jesus' resurrection appearances on earth. No more can anyone claim to "see" the risen Jesus in the same way that Mary Magdalene and the other disciples saw him. The forty days of Easter appearances are over. In this sense, the ascension exerts a degree of control against any enthusiasts who would still claim to "see" appearances of Christ. The importance of marking an end to Jesus' appearances can be seen also in 1 Cor. 15:5-8, Paul's list of eyewitnesses who saw the risen Jesus—a list that does not include Mary Magdalene or the other women. The ascension narratives mark a watershed: Henceforth, no one can claim to be an eyewitness, for Jesus is to be known only through the power of the Holy Spirit, in the scriptures, and in the church.

The ascension is not about Jesus' absence but about his presence in the world in a new way. The promised Holy Spirit will come upon the community to take Jesus' place on earth. During the ten days between Ascension and Pentecost we await with joy the promised "power" (*dynamis*) of the Holy Spirit, just as the Spirit came upon the early church. Meanwhile, Jesus calls us to direct our gaze not toward heaven but toward the world, where our

> THE ASCENSION NARRATIVES MARK A WATERSHED: HENCEFORTH, NO ONE CAN CLAIM TO BE AN EYEWITNESS, FOR JESUS IS TO BE KNOWN ONLY THROUGH THE POWER OF THE HOLY SPIRIT, IN THE SCRIPTURES, AND IN THE CHURCH.

mission is now to be his witnesses "in Jerusalem, in all Judea and Samaria, and to the ends of the earth" (Acts 1:8).

The first followers of Jesus awaited the Spirit by gathering together in their upper room on the Mount of Olives. Acts is careful to note that their group includes Jesus' mother and other women. Together they devote themselves to prayer "with one accord."

Responding to the Texts

A mosaic at the Church of the Ascension at Augusta Victoria Hospital on the Mount of Olives in Jerusalem, one of the possible sites of Jesus' ascension, portrays the ascending Jesus flanked by the two angels who tell the nostalgic disciples to stop gazing up into heaven. These two are depicted as ordinary-looking men, gazing lovingly down at us rather than up at the ascending Jesus. They point us in the most important direction of this text—not heavenward but earthward: "Why are you standing looking up toward heaven?" The present-day presence of the Lutheran World Federation hospital at this particular holy site, attending to Palestinian refugees and others, is an apt successor to Ascension on the Mount of Olives.

This earthward attention to mission in the world becomes especially important in light of the recent popularity of the *Left Behind* novels and "prophecy" speculation about when Jesus will return to split the Mount of Olives in two. In today's text, the Mount of Olives is not the place where Jesus' followers await his return, preparing for a final battle. Rather, the Mount of Olives is the place where the disciples devote themselves together to prayer, preparing to be sent out in mission in the world.

EZEKIEL 39:21-29 (BCP, alt.)

These verses conclude Ezekiel's oracles against the nations (Ezekiel 25–36, 38–39), culminating the oracle against the mythic nations of Gog and Magog. The prophet describes the history of Israel's oppression, God's restoration, and God's commitment to again redeem and pour out the Spirit upon the nation.

The verses reflect a faithful model of relationship that moves well past what Bonhoeffer termed "cheap grace." Israel "treated God treacherously," and God turned away for a time and gave Israel into the hands of other nations. Only when God has done the work of forgiveness can reconciliation begin. Verses 21-24 suggest that through God's hiddenness both Israel and other nations would see God's judgment. God here is able to show to Israel and all nations that the people's response has an effect on God, that their relationship is one of authentic, vulnerable love.

Yet, the turning away is not to be understood only as judgment. God returns with a bounty of goodness. The actions of God's people do not change the everlasting love and faithfulness of God. God will "restore the fortunes of Jacob and have mercy on the whole house of Israel," and "will leave none of them behind" (Ezek. 39:25ff.). Forgiveness leads to reconciliation that transforms relationship and brings about trust and liberation.

RESPONSIVE READING
PSALM 68:1–10, 32–35 (RCL); PSALM 68:1–20 (BCP)

Psalm 68 offers a mosaic of analogies and images, many of which are alluded to in the New Testament (although not in today's readings). While soaring images describe God's ride though the heavens (vv. 4, 33), the heart of the psalm comes back to earth to praise God for protecting the marginalized. God is "father of orphans and protect of widows" who "gives the desolate a home" (vv. 5-6). The stop at Mount Sinai, the march through the wilderness, the finding of a home—these glorious events are all rehearsed by the psalmist, who then circles back again to God's goodness in providing for the needy (v. 10). The rider in the heavens recalls holy war imagery, ending in the declaration that the awesome God gives power to the people.

PSALM 27:1, 4, 7–8 (RC)

Psalm 27 offers an intimate look at the uncertainties we face. It balances fear and hope, faithfulness and anxiety. The psalmist opens with a proclamation of hope and conviction, "The LORD is my light and my salvation; whom shall I fear?" The final verses, 13 and 14, provide a similarly confident bookend, "I believe that I shall see the LORD in the land of the living."

At the same time, the psalmist cries anxiously to God, "Do not hide your face from me. Do not turn your servant away in anger . . . do not cast me off, do not forsake me" (Ps. 27:9). Psalm 27 presents an honest faith; one that hopes for God's faithfulness and fears what life might be like if God turned away from the covenanted people.

PSALM 47 (BCP, alt.)

See the comments on the BCP Responsive Reading for Ascension Day, May 5, 2005.

SECOND READING

1 PETER 4:12-14; 5:6-11 (RCL);
1 PETER 4:12-19 (BCP);
1 PETER 4:13-16 (RC)

The themes of suffering and marginalization intensify in chapters 4–5 of 1 Peter. Jesus lived a cruciform life, and so do we. We should not be surprised at suffering. The "fiery ordeal" experienced by the Christians in this letter was not formal state persecution but rather the hostility and ostracism that a low-status minority group suffered from the dominant majority groups in their towns. We know from Governor Pliny's letters to Emperor Trajan, for example, that Christians who refused to eat meat or participate in civic festivals were denounced as unpatriotic and dangerous. The verb "denounce" (*oneidizein*) in v. 14 is the very same word used for the mocking of Jesus on the cross (Matt. 27:44; Mark 15:32). It is also the same word used in the beatitude, "Blessed are you when they mock you" (Matt. 5:11; Luke 6:11). The experience of verbal abuse and public shaming was not limited to Christians. Any community that stuck out for its "superstitions" was a target in the Roman world. Jews often suffered similar harassment from their neighbors because of their separate customs and their refusal to participate in emperor worship.[1]

This letter coaches Christians on how to survive marginalization and public hostility, using a number of strategies: First, we do not suffer alone. Throughout the entire epistle, every single reference to "you" is plural. Suffering can be borne in community with others. Those who suffer "share" deeply with one another and with Christ, as seen in the abundance of *koinonia*-related root words: "you share (*koinoneite*, v. 13) in Christ's sufferings;" the author "shares" (*koinonos*, 5:1) in the glory that is to be revealed. Even the oft-quoted exhortation, "Cast all your anxieties on God, for God cares for you (5:7, quoting Ps. 55:22), a verse that sounds so personal, is actually plural. Together, as a community, we cast our cares on God.

> SUFFERING SETS US IN SOLIDARITY WITH ONE ANOTHER IN A PROFOUND WAY—CEMENTING OUR GLOBAL COMMUNITY IN CHRIST THROUGHOUT THE ENTIRE WORLD.

Because we share together in Christ's sufferings, we can even rejoice (v. 13). We are to "rejoice and be glad" to suffer in the "name of Christ" (v. 14). The name "Christian" in v. 16 is one of the earliest uses of this label.

Using a wonderful image of companionship, the author declares that those who suffer have the Spirit of glory "resting" (*anapausetai*, v. 14) on them. This image expands on Isaiah's description of the servant, "The spirit of God shall rest upon him" (Isa. 11:2). Think of a bird or companion sitting on your shoulder, whispering encouragement and counsel in your ear as you are mocked or shamed. That is the image of the Spirit's presence resting on us.

Suffering is only for a "short time" (5:10). The end is near (v. 7). Indeed, the end will bring a great reversal. We are to "let ourselves be humbled now" (5:6), and even rejoice, knowing that we will be exalted. The judgment that is being experienced first by the "household of God" (another reference to the church as a "house," v. 17) will soon come upon the oppressors.

Suffering sets us in solidarity with one another in a profound way—cementing our global community in Christ throughout the entire world. One of the letter's most expansive insights comes in 5:9, "For you know that your brothers and sisters in all the world are undergoing the same kinds of suffering." The community that shares in suffering is not just local community but worldwide family of sisters and brothers in solidarity.

Grace flows through this entire letter, undergirding exhortation with encouragement, culminating in the description of God as "God of all grace" (5:10). When we have suffered a little while, the "God of all grace" will restore, support, strengthen, and establish us.

Responding to the Text

This text can connect us to Christians who suffer marginalization or harassment today—to Central Americans, to Asian Christians living as tiny minorities in Muslim countries, to Palestinian Christians living under Israeli occupation. We share with our sisters and brothers around the world whose daily experiences of "exile" or harassment echo the *paroikos* (exile) situation of 1 Peter.

Our experiences of "exile" may not be the same. When I have led Bible studies on 1 Peter, I have heard people's painful stories of "exile" and estrangement in their own communities: the stigma of mental illness or disability, the exile of sexual abuse, divorce, prison, joblessness, or other forms of marginalization; the exile of separation from family members who disown us. For some, our exile may be the experience of living within a powerful "Christian" empire

> FIRST PETER HELPS US LEARN HOW TO LIVE IN AN IMPERIAL WORLD WHILE NOT CAVING IN TO IT—HOW TO HONOR THE GOVERNMENT WHILE FEARING ONLY GOD (2:17), HOW TO TESTIFY TO THE HOPE THAT IS IN US.

whose leaders invoke Christianity to justify policies that we cannot support. Whatever our exile, this letter urges us to testify to hope even if we are reviled or mocked. First Peter helps us learn how to live in an imperial world while not caving in to it—how to honor the government while fearing only God (2:17), how to testify to the hope that is in us. This letter brings us back to some of the most basic questions that face Christians. Indeed, the words leap off the page into our own time: How do we live out our faith as an alternative "household" within the most powerful empire on earth?

The Gospel

JOHN 17:1–11 (RCL, BCP, RC)

Interpreting the Text

Each year the Gospel for the Seventh Sunday of Easter, between Ascension and Pentecost, is taken from Jesus' great prayer in John 17, the conclusion of his Farewell Discourse. Throughout the Gospel, Jesus has been speaking in a more intensifying tone of his "hour." Already in 12:23 Jesus had told Philip that the "hour" had come for him to be "glorified," a statement echoed at the beginning of the entire Farewell Discourse in 13:1. Now, as he begins his great prayer to God, Jesus again announces that "the hour has come."

This prayer, like Jesus' other prayers (John 11:41-42 and 12:27-28), is meant to be overheard by us. It is a prayer for all of us. Jesus invites us into a "heavenly family conversation" between himself and God.[2] The conversation witnesses to Jesus' return to God (his "glorification") and to his deep love for his followers. Everything he has he now gives to us, as he is returning back to God.

"Eternal life" (*zoē aiōnion*) is what Jesus gives to us in v. 2. My students are always amazed to learn that in John's Gospel eternal life does not mean living forever, nor life after death, nor even resurrection. For John "eternal life is to know you, the only true God, and Jesus Christ whom you have sent" (v. 3). This statement articulates an amazing "present eschatology" or "realized eschatology," in contrast to the future eschatology of the other Gospels and Paul. John is the "maverick Gospel," with an eschatology and theological definitions quite different from the Synoptic Gospels or Paul.[3]

God's glory bathes this prayer. Jesus addresses three imperatives directly to God, twice requesting God to "glorify" him—"Glorify your son," v. 1; and "Glorify me in your presence," v. 5. The shadow of death falls over every mention of "glory" and "hour" in the Gospel of John. Glorification and Jesus' hour mean the whole sequence of Jesus' passion, death, and resurrection. Jesus has already linked glorification to death with the parable of the seed that must fall to the ground and die (12:23-24). Even though death is not mentioned in this section of John 17, the smell of death is in the air.

With the third imperative, Jesus' prayer shifts from petitioning God about his own glorification to petitioning on behalf of his disciples. Jesus requests God to "keep" or "protect" (*tērou*) the disciples in God's name, so that they may be one (v. 11). "Keep" is a favorite Johannine word, used already in v. 6 to describe how the disciples have "kept" Jesus' word. Jesus says in v. 12 that he "kept" the disciples in God's name while he was with them. Now as he departs, he asks God to keep them in that name, the name that he made known to them (v. 6).

The request of John 17:11 (and 17:21) "so that they may be one," is not Jesus' ecumenical program exhorting denominational unity. Jesus' words are more mystical than programmatic. They foreshadow his crucifixion. We should read this verse first of all as a continuation of the prayer, a window into the very heart of God. The word "one" (*hen*, a neuter form) grounds the disciples' oneness in Jesus' prior mystical oneness and in-ness with God, preparing them for the division and hostility they will face after his death. Horizontal unity among Jesus' followers is thus a (vertical) gift from God, not the result of their own action.

How powerful it is to know that Jesus has prayed to God on our behalf! There is no one for whom Jesus did not pray on his last night. Like the prayer of a parent overheard by the child for whom one intercedes, what this prayer reveals is Jesus' deep love for the disciples and his deep trust in God as he prepares for his death.

Responding to the Text

The great prayer of John 17 evokes longing in us to be fully "one" with Jesus, in the mystical communion of prayer, so that his prayer of love for us becomes not a farewell but rather a homecoming. How do we learn to pray with such oneness in the heart of God? Prayer could be a wonderful sermon theme, since this is the longest prayer of Jesus in the New Testament.

Eternal life and John's amazing "realized" eschatology would be another provocative sermon topic. Most people have no idea that they are already living in eternal life, but that seems to be the Johannine view! Robert Kysar's chapter "Eternity Is Now" traces the theme of eternal life through the Gospel and offers meaty preaching insights.[4]

A third theme for preaching is Jesus' vision "that they may all be one." For those who want to preach on Jesus' prayer for unity in John 17 as a model for Christian unity today, several cautions by Johannine scholar Raymond Brown are appropriate: First, given the overall sectarian orientation of John's Gospel, "the Johannine outlook is not overly ecumenical." And second, "unity should allow for diversity, for the Father and the Son remain distinct persons despite their unity."[5]

Recent scholarship has highlighted the many ways John's theology diverges from the Petrine orthodoxy of the Synoptics, not just on eschatology but on other issues. This Gospel reflects the diversity of earliest Christianity is all its richness for today. Considerable diversity among the four canonical Gospels and Paul's letters show how differently each of the early communities envisioned Jesus and the meaning of his life and death for us. Just as we would not try to harmonize John with the other Gospels, so we should not appeal to this Gospel to try to craft some hegemonic uniformity for the church today. Indeed, John's Gospel represents a minority position on many issues in the early church, with its focus on the beloved disciple, and other quirks—yet what a wonderful minority position!

So if we are to preach John 17 to explore ecumenical unity, we need to lift up models for unity that can also embrace diversity—not sameness—and that can cherish a multiplicity of minority voices. Kysar suggests that John's Gospel invites inclusiveness in a "round table," nonhierarchical church. David Rhoads uses the diversity of the New Testament canon itself to model unity in diversity, noting that the canon places Christian authors with divergent perspectives alongside one another without trying to harmonize them.[6] I use the geological image of a "braided stream," a type of river in which multiple strands of water come together and divide again, criss-crossing in a beautiful braided pattern that sparkles and shifts across the broad streambed. If the church is like a river, we can seek models of ecumenical unity that aim not to merge everyone into one monolithic main channel, but rather affirm the multiplicity of individual strands as they braid and criss-cross and sparkle across the broad spectrum of God's river of unity.[7]

Notes

1. So John H. Elliott, *1 Peter,* Anchor Bible 37B (New York: Doubleday, 200), 78, citing Josephus, *Against Apion* 2.148.

2. Raymond Brown, *The Gospel according to John,* 2 vols., Anchor Bible Commentary 29 (New York: Doubleday 1970), 2:747.

3. *John the Maverick Gospel* is the title of a book by Robert Kysar (Louisville: Westminster John Knox, rev. ed., 1993).

4. Ibid., chap. 4, pp. 97ff.

5. Brown, *John,* 2:775.

6. David Rhoads, *The Challenge of Diversity* (Minneapolis: Fortress Press, 1996).

7. See Barbara Rossing, "(Re)Claiming *Oikoumene?* Empire, Ecumenism and the Discipleship of Equals," in *Walk in the Ways of Wisdom: Essays in Honor of Elisabeth Schüssler Fiorenza,* ed. Shelly Matthews, Cynthia Briggs Kittredge, and Melanie Johnson-DeBaufre (Harrisburg Pa.: Trinity Press International, 2003), 86–87.

THE SEASON
OF PENTECOST

JOHN J. PILCH

For the early Christians, Pentecost (the Greek term for "fifty") actually incorporated the entire period of fifty days from Easter. Only at a later time was the term applied specifically to the fiftieth day, which then became a feast in its own right. This is important, because the fifty days from Easter continued the celebration of Christ's resurrection, called the "most joyful season" by Tertullian and "one great Sunday" by Athanasius. During these days, there was no kneeling for prayer but only standing—in anticipation of the general resurrection. Nor was there any fasting—a foretaste of the messianic banquet to come.

In the fourth century, the fiftieth day was commemorated as the seal of the fifty-day period, blending the themes of Christ's ascension and the Spirit's descent. In the fifth century, however, these two feasts became distinct, with Ascension observed forty days after Easter and Pentecost on the fiftieth day. The vigil of Pentecost became a baptismal occasion in the English church, the white robes of the baptized giving rise to the term "Whitsunday."

But the origins of Pentecost derive from the Old Testament, where it was originally observed as an agricultural festival at the end of the grain harvest that began at Passover. Later Pentecost was used to commemorate the giving of the Law on Sinai and the formation of a mixed group of Egyptian refugees into the people of God. The church retained the latter in order to celebrate not only the events in Acts 2 but also the church's own character as people of the new covenant. "For the law of the Spirit of life in Christ Jesus has set you free from the law of sin and of death" (Rom. 8:2). As the death and resurrection of Jesus dramatized the fact of eternal redemption, Pentecost dramatized the reality of the Christian's possession by the Spirit, making redemption an effective reality in the Christian's life in time.

During this Pentecost season, which comprises virtually one-half of the church year, we will be studying and preaching on many texts that focus on the Christian's life in time. But, lest we forget, it all begins with the Spirit's descent on that awesome day: "And that day about three thousand persons were added. They devoted themselves to the apostles' teaching and fellowship, to the breaking of bread and the prayers" (Acts 2:41-42). Can we do any less? Moreover, as Mark Bangert points out (see "Resources," below), "Presumably through such powerful witness, the Spirit led still others to join the apostles as they took the good news to all nations. Gradually the thousands baptized at Pentecost were joined by thousands more, so that the new royal residence of God, described in 1 Peter, might be manifest to the far corners of the earth."

In these very complicated and difficult times, perhaps we should be praying for and expecting a new Pentecost, a special measure of the Spirit specifically for these times. God bless your sermon preparation during this season, and may your preaching be filled with the Spirit's power and peace.

Resources

Bangert, Mark P. "Holy Communion: Taste and See." In *Inside Out: Worship in an Age of Mission*, ed. Thomas H. Schattauer (Minneapolis: Fortress Press, 1999).

Dix, Dom Gregory. *The Shape of the Liturgy* (New York: Seabury Press, 1982).

Wainwright, Geoffrey. "Pentecost." In *Dictionary of the Ecumenical Movement*, ed. Nicholas Lossky et al. (Geneva: WCC Publications; Grand Rapids, Mich.: Eerdmans, 1991).

THE DAY OF PENTECOST

REVISED COMMON	EPISCOPAL (BCP)	ROMAN CATHOLIC
Acts 2:1-21	Acts 2:1-11	Acts 2:1-11
or Num. 11:24-30	or Ezek. 11:17-20	
Ps. 104:24-34, 35b	Ps. 104:25-37	Ps. 104:1, 24, 29-30, 31, 34
	or 104:25-32	
	or Ps. 33:12-15, 18-22	
1 Cor. 12:3b-13	1 Cor. 12:4-13	1 Cor. 12:3b-7, 12-13
or Acts 2:1-21	or Acts 2:1-11	
John 20:19-23	John 20:19-23	John 20:19-23
or John 7:37-39	or John 14:8-17	

FIRST READING

ACTS 2:1-11 (BCP, RC);
ACTS 2:1-21 (RCL)

Interpreting the Texts

Altered states of consciousness experiences (ASCs) are the routine channel through which God communicates with human beings (see 1 Sam. 3:1).
Reports of such experiences abound in the Bible from beginning (Gen. 2:21) to
end (the entire book of Revelation). Scholars identify two kinds of ASC experiences in the Bible: those by individuals (e.g., Isaiah 6) and those by groups, such
as recounted in these verses from Acts of the Apostles.

ASCs are essentially neurophysiological events that human beings have learned
to interpret. Typically, the experience has three stages. In stage one, the person
entering into an altered level of awareness sees certain colors (but mainly white)
and then sees various geometric patterns. This is an indication and manifestation
of neurological changes taking place in the brain. In stage two, the visionary
strives to make sense of the patterns and other elements she or he is seeing. Stage
three, the deepest stage in which the association areas of the brain are disengaged
or deactivated, brings assorted and often confusing imagery. Afterward, the visionary will seek to make sense of the experience mainly by arranging it in linear

fashion (this is not how the experience occurs) and then interpreting what was seen with the aid of the culture's latent discourse.

The tongues (of fire) that the gathering sees indicate stage one of their trance experience (Acts 1:1-11). These are geometric shapes. The meaning or interpretation given to the shapes (by the group or by Luke) is "tongues." The human behavior that occurs in this trance experience is quite likely glossolalia, speaking in tongues. Anthropologists have documented such experience across cultures. Glossolalia is patterned, noncommunicative speech that occurs in an ASC. Luke, however, reports the event as xenoglossy, speaking in *foreign* languages. Such trance behavior is unknown in the literature of anthropology or cognitive neuroscience. Either Luke has misunderstood the event or intentionally reinterpreted it perhaps to suggest that God now removes the divine punishment inflicted at Babel (Gen. 11:1-9). The fact that the sound comes from the sky indicates God is the cause of what is happening. As often occurs in such cases, judgment among viewers is divided. Some want to know what it means, while others deny its authenticity (vv. 12-13).

The meaning of ASC experiences is not self-evident, because the experience is usually not linear, as in waking consciousness. They require interpretation. Peter interpreted the event for the crowd who witnessed it (Acts 1:14-21). He insisted that the group was not drunk but rather inspired by God to prophesy. By definition, prophecy is the act of expressing God's will for the here and now. God's will is simply that "everyone who calls on the name of the Lord shall be saved" (v. 21).

NUMBERS 11:24-30 (RCL, alt.)

The issue in this lection is institutional control of prophetic ecstatic trance. Prophets routinely receive God's communication in an altered state of consciousness. Seventy men subordinate to Moses received a portion of Moses' spirit, but two men outside the camp received the spirit independently. These would be "unofficial" or nonprofessional prophets. Joshua represents those who would restrict prophecy and subordinate it to institutional control. Moses takes the opposite viewpoint, believing that the community will benefit no matter who receives the spirit.

EZEKIEL 11:17-20 (BCP, alt.)

In vv. 14-20, God inspires the prophet to warn those who did not go into exile in 598 B.C.E. against smug complacency. These people who had remained in Jerusalem claimed that the exiles lost their claim to the land because of infidelity to God. Through Ezekiel, God expressed divine preference for the exiles, promising to give them a heart that will be undivided in its loyalty to God (NRSV: "one" or "new" heart) and the Spirit as well.

Perhaps many believers have not had the experiences of our ancestors in faith such as described in these readings. It would be helpful to learn about them. More than 90 percent of societies analyzed and studied by anthropologists using the Human Relations Area Files at Yale University readily and routinely experience altered states of consciousness. Research by contemporary neuroscientists leads some of these scientists to conclude that God has "hard-wired" human beings to experience the deity. The human body was created to serve this purpose. Preachers who become familiar with this pan-human experience can not only help believers regain an appreciation for these experiences of their ancestors but also help them to discover how to develop the openness and capacity for such experiences in their own lives.

> RESEARCH BY CONTEMPORARY NEUROSCIENTISTS LEADS SOME OF THESE SCIENTISTS TO CONCLUDE THAT GOD HAS "HARD WIRED" HUMAN BEINGS TO EXPERIENCE THE DEITY. THE HUMAN BODY WAS CREATED TO SERVE THIS PURPOSE.

RESPONSIVE READING

PSALM 104:24-34, 35b (RCL);
PSALM 104:25-37 or PSALM 104:25-32 (BCP);
PSALM 104:1, 24, 29-30, 31, 34 (RC)

This psalm, and especially these verses, praise God the Creator, master of life and death. God sends forth the divine breath (Spirit) and renews life in all of its cycles.

SECOND READING

1 CORINTHIANS 12:3b-13
or ACTS 2:1-21 (RCL);
1 CORINTHIANS 12:4-13
or ACTS 2:1-11 (BCP);
1 CORINTHIANS 12:3b-7, 12-13 (RC)

Interpreting the Text

Torn by divisions and strife, the Corinthian community posed a strong pastoral challenge to Paul. In the lections for today, Paul presents two arguments against such behavior. One argument deduces proper conduct for the Corinthians from the conduct of the Spirit, the Lord, and God in the realm of the divine life. Though this listing reflects their hierarchical relationship, these beings live in peace and not in competitive rivalry. The gifts of the Spirit therefore should not cause divisions in the community. The second argument is based on the necessity of human body parts to work harmoniously in order not to damage the body.

Responding to the Text

Sadly, divisions and rivalry exist in modern Western culture just as they did in the agonistic culture of our ancestors. Would Paul's reflections be helpful or just humorous to modern Western culture, driven as it is by competition and the desire to excel?

THE GOSPEL

JOHN 20:19-23 (RCL, BCP, RC)

Interpreting the Text

This is one of the reports of a group's experience of the risen Jesus in an altered state of consciousness or awareness. (Other scriptures report individual experiences of the risen Jesus as, e.g., Paul in Acts 9:3-7 or Stephen in Acts 7:55-56.) In those Jesus groups that succeeded the Jesus movement, such experiences were the necessary foundation for apostolic authority that would be recognized as normative, legitimate, and legal. Today's Gospel basically reports two things: how group leaders were authenticated and whence these leaders drew their power.

The risen Jesus personally commissioned and legitimated leaders. In this case, the leaders are sealed by the gift of the Holy Spirit (v. 22) and commissioned to preach repentance and forgiveness of sins (v. 23). Sin in John's Gospel is the failure to believe in Jesus as the One the Father sent. The best interpretation of this passage, then, is that Jesus commissions these leaders to bring new members into the community. It differs from the commission of Matt. 18:19, which describes how the community should deal with the sinfulness of its present members.

The second important point is that Jesus empowers these leaders by the gift of a very powerful spirit, the Holy Spirit (v. 22). This gift guarantees the efficacy of the leaders' activities.

Responding to the Text

A Baptist psychiatrist attending a workshop on the appearances of the risen Jesus contained in Scripture responded skeptically, saying that he treated people who heard voices and saw things that weren't there. Many contemporary believers would agree with the psychiatrist. On the other hand, some biblical scholars would identify these reports as literary forms, that is, stylized and stereo-typical ways of reporting some conviction. According to them, these leaders strongly believed Jesus would agree that this new behavior is God's will.

In contrast, the pioneering anthropologist Erika Bourguignon, who studied ASC experiences in a sample of 488 world societies at varying levels of techno-logical complexity, discovered that 90 percent of these societies considered such experiences as normal and routine. She suggested that societies that deny or refuse to have such experiences ought to explain why they are not having them. In the Johannine community of believers, no one doubted these reports as liter-ally true, as authentic group experiences of the risen Jesus descended from the sky again to visit the Johannine "children of God" (John 1:12).

The problem that eventually emerged was the subsequent Gnostic emphasis on *personal*, *individual* experiences of Jesus with messages that ran counter to group experiences. The Gnostics sought to legitimate their authority as leaders with these visions. This prompted the non-Gnostic leaders to establish a norm or canon of Scripture for Jesus groups and to deny any messages from individual experiences that deviated from the New Testament canon. They didn't deny the experiences but only that the message had any public import for the community. How are church leaders legitimated in your tradition? Is there a need to improve on this and, if so, how?

> IN THE JOHANNINE COMMUNITY OF BELIEVERS, NO ONE DOUBTED THESE REPORTS AS LITERALLY TRUE, AS AUTHENTIC GROUP EXPERIENCES OF THE RISEN JESUS DESCENDED FROM THE SKY AGAIN TO VISIT THE JOHANNINE "CHILDREN OF GOD" (JOHN 1:12).

JOHN 7:37-39 (RCL, alt.)

Interpreting the Text

The setting of these verses is the Israelite liturgical ritual at the Feast of Tabernacles. In origin it was basically an agricultural feast, specifically a harvest festival. Thus, it was celebrated in autumn for a seven-day period, coming to a conclusion on the eighth day. Eventually, the celebration of the feast was moved to the Jerusalem temple, and thus it became a pilgrimage festival. On the seventh day of the feast, the priests took water from Siloam, circled the altar seven times, and poured the water on the ground. This was a ritual thanksgiving for God's gift of rain. In this setting, Jesus identified himself as the source of living water.

The verses are difficult and challenging to interpret. It is always difficult to identify John's scriptural allusions when a direct reference cannot be found. Per-haps in this case, texts that speak of water coming from the temple mount are the best candidates (e.g., Ezek. 47:1-11; Zech. 14:8). Yet these texts were often asso-ciated with other texts, such as Isa. 43:20; 44:3; et al., that describe the rock in the desert from which water sprang. Some of these texts served as synagogue readings during the month in which this feast was observed. At the temple festival itself, Psalm 114 was recited by pilgrims. Verse 8 describes God as turning "the rock into a pool of water, the flint into a spring of water." The NRSV interprets v. 38 as referring to the believer ("Out of the believer's heart shall flow rivers of living water"). This has support in antiquity, including textual evidence in a second-century papyrus. However, it seems preferable to render the verse literally—"From within him shall flow rivers of living water"—thus allowing the immediate context (vv. 37-38) to point to Jesus as the source of these waters.

Responding to the Text

Preachers are wise not to delve into excessive exegetical detail in their reflections. It is, after all, not a lecture but a sermon or homily they are expected to deliver. On the other hand, translations are inevitably interpretations. In this instance, the preacher has a precious teachable moment to remind the listeners that the Gospels are not transcripts of factual events. They are not instant replay. All, whether preachers or listeners, are called to learn the truth about Jesus as best as one can.

JOHN 14:8-17 (BCP, alt.)

Interpreting the Text

This lection begins with the third of a series of questions that highlight the disciples' misunderstanding of Jesus' words prior to his glorification (see John 13:37; 14:5, 8, 22). Philip's request for a vision of the father follows upon Jesus' statement to Philip that to know Jesus is to know and see the Father. Jesus is "the way, and the truth, and the life" or, in other words, the authentic vision of existence. Philip's request indicates that he has obviously misunderstood Jesus. What does Philip seek? It is quite plausible that he desires an experience of the Father in an ASC. This was common and routine in that culture, as it is in a majority of contemporary mainly non-Western cultures in the world today, as anthropologists tell us. Just two chapters earlier in John's Gospel, Philip was present when Jesus in an ASC heard a response from God to his prayer (John 12:27-30). As Philip's question is reported by John in the evangelist's historical context, it represents the Gnostics' claim to special knowledge derived from special revelation experiences.

THE EMBEDDED RELATIONSHIP BETWEEN JESUS AND THE FATHER REPLICATES (AND THUS LEGITIMATES) THE EMBEDDED RELATIONSHIP BETWEEN MEMBERS OF THE JOHANNINE COMMUNITY AND THE RISEN JESUS PRESENT IN THEIR MIDST.

John's Jesus points in another direction. The embedded relationship between Jesus and the Father replicates (and thus legitimates) the embedded relationship between members of the Johannine community and the risen Jesus present in their midst. They require no special disclosure of the Father in an ASC, because the risen Jesus mirrors the Father to them. If this proves difficult, they ought to focus on the works of Jesus (see John 2–12), which are the works of the Father.

The Greek word for "works" (*erga*) is the same word used by the Septuagint to describe the works of God. God's two great works are creation and redemption; in other words, God bestows life and restores meaning to life. The works of Jesus reported by John can be similarly categorized. Jesus gives life (John 4:46-54; 6:1-15; 11:1-44) and restores meaning to life (John 2:1-11; 5:1-15; 6:16-21; 9:1-41).

Responding to the Text

Contemporary followers of Jesus would surely profit from reflecting on their actions and exploring whether they are life giving or death dealing, or whether they restore meaning to life or suck meaning out of life.

HOLY TRINITY SUNDAY / FIRST SUNDAY AFTER PENTECOST

MAY 22, 2005

REVISED COMMON	EPISCOPAL (BCP)	ROMAN CATHOLIC
Gen. 1:1—2:4a	Gen. 1:1—2:3	Exod. 34:4b-6, 8-9
Psalm 8	Psalm 150	Dan. 3:52, 53, 54, 55
	or Canticle 2 or 13	
2 Cor. 13:11-13	2 Cor. 13:(5-10), 11-13	2 Cor. 13:11-13
Matt. 28:16-20	Matt. 28:16-20	John 3:16-18

FIRST READING

GENESIS 1:1—2:4a (RCL); GENESIS 1:1—2:3 (BCP)

Interpreting the Text

This report of the creation of the world is ascribed to the Priestly tradition (following Wellhausen's documentary hypothesis). God created the world in six days and rested on the seventh, thus hallowing the observance of the Sabbath (Exod. 31:17). Though this story is not as colorful as the Yahwist's report that immediately follows it, it is nevertheless carefully and artistically structured. The days are arranged in this manner:

Formless void and darkness (vv. 1-2)

Day 1. Light (evening and morning, vv. 3-5)

Day 4. Lights in the sky (vv. 14-19)

Day 2. Separation of waters (upper and lower, vv. 6-8)

Day 5. Separation of birds and sea creatures from the water (vv. 20-23)

Day 3. Separation of earth and seas; plants (vv. 14-19)

Day 6. Separation of animals and humans (vv. 24-31)

Day 7. God rests (2:1-3)

Seven is a significant number in biblical literature. In this report, the seventh item is the climax of the story: God rested. The story is entirely about God and God's spirit (NRSV: "a wind from God," v. 1), which put order into the original chaos (NRSV: "formless void"). Wind, breath, and spirit all correctly translate the Hebrew *ruah*, which expressed the power of God. God's power can give life or destroy it. This is what creation effected. As ten utterances of God ("God said," vv. 3, 6, 9, 11, 14, 20, 22, 24, 26, 29) turned chaos into an orderly universe in this story (Gen. 1), so centuries later in the Israelite tradition another ten "words" from God (see Exod. 20:1) sought to insure order and civility in chaotic human life.

EXODUS 34:4b-6, 8-9 (RC)

Exodus 32–34 is an editorial insert between two detailed descriptions of the tabernacle (Exodus 25–31, 35–39). The insert reports the Israelites' worship of the golden calf, their severe punishment, Moses' breaking of the tablets, and the rewriting of the tablets. The insert gathers very diverse traditions relative to God's self-disclosure at Sinai/Horeb. However, scholars are still unable to untangle all these laws and trace them to their precise origins.

Today's verses focus attention on God's name in Hebrew: Yahweh (NRSV, NAB: "LORD"). Since its meaning is disputed, the preacher ought to explain the interpretation selected as a personal choice. Philologically, the name derives from the verb "to be," very likely in the causative form (*hiphil*). One very popular interpretation is "I am who causes things to be," in other words, "I am God the creator."

In this passage, God offers an interpretation of the divine nature: "merciful and gracious, slow to anger and rich in kindness and fidelity." The Hebrew for "merciful and gracious" is melodious to speak: *rahum we hannun*. The latter word is used exclusively as an attribute of God. It reminds a reader of the most important of the ninety-nine Divine Names in Islam: "Al-Rahman al Rahim," "The Compassionate, the Merciful." (For all ninety-nine names, see http://www.baitalkitab .com /baitalkitab/index.htm).

The Hebrew word translated "merciful" derives from the word for womb. Though some scholars have said that mercy might have been perceived as a feminine value, there is an explanation for this phrase as God's self-description that is culturally more suitable. The Middle Eastern cultural belief is that children born from the same mother (same womb) are the most closely bonded of all kin and should exhibit special concern (mercy) for one another. (See Deut. 13:6 and contrast with Gen. 20:12.) The author of this passage presents God as claiming an incredibly intimate relationship of kinship between self and God's people.

The second phrase, "kindness and fidelity," has been traditionally translated "steadfast love (Hebrew: *hesed*) and fidelity or loyalty (*emet*)." The phrase was used chiefly though not exclusively to describe God in the Hebrew Bible. To describe a human being with this phrase is to identify that one as a loyal, devout person. The predecessors of the Pharisees at the time of the Maccabean revolt around 167 B.C.E. were called *hasidim*, devout ones. Nicodemus, to whom the verses of today's Gospel reading were addressed by Jesus (John 3:16-18), is a spiritual descendant of this group.

This is a truly remarkable insight about God's character. Although all theology is based on analogy (that is, everything human beings know and say about God is rooted in human experience), these qualities contrast with what we know about Mediterranean personalities. They were quick to anger (Gen. 4:1-7), unforgiving (Matt. 18:23-35) and severe (Luke 9:51-56). They restricted love and fidelity to real and surrogate kin (Lev. 19:17-18).

> BOTH THE READING FROM GENESIS AND THE SELECTION FROM EXODUS GIVE US INSIGHT INTO THE NATURE OF GOD. GENESIS HIGHLIGHTS GOD'S POWER, WHILE EXODUS DISPLAYS A SOFTER, GENTLER DIMENSION OF GOD.

What a shock! No wonder the sacred author presents Moses as having a keen sense of humor. His response to the meaning of God's self-disclosure might be paraphrased in this way: "Boy, do we need a God like you! We stiff-necked people are going to need your pardon many times over. If you can live with that, please take us as your people!"

Responding to the Text

Both the reading from Genesis and the selection from Exodus give us insight into the nature of God. Genesis highlights God's power, while Exodus displays a softer, gentler dimension of God. Both views are correct, and many other perspectives are possible. The successful preacher will be the one who helps the congregation to deepen their appreciation of the richness of the divine personality.

RESPONSIVE READING

PSALM 8 (RCL)

A fitting response to the reading from Genesis 1, this psalm praises God for creation and recognizes God as "sovereign," all the more after the disappearance of the Davidic dynasty in the Babylonian and Persian periods.

PSALM 150 (BCP)

Just as each of the previous four books of the Psalter ended with a solemn doxology (Pss. 41:13; 71:18-19; 89:52; 106:48), so this psalm concludes the entire book of Psalms with a Hallelujah. Some scholars note that the ten Hallelujah's in this psalm honor the ten words of God in creation as well as in the Decalogue.

CANTICLE 2 or 13 (BCP, alt.)

These chapters from an incomparable paean to human love are principally the words of the young lady expressing her love and yearning for her lover. Perhaps the many references to the beauties of the natural world inspired the selection of these sentiments as the appropriate response to Genesis 1.

DANIEL 3:52, 53, 54, 55 (RC)

Drawn from the hymn sung by Shadrach, Meshach, and Abednego in the furnace, today's verses exhort all creatures on earth to praise God throughout the universe.

SECOND READING
2 CORINTHIANS 13:11-13 (RCL, RC);
2 CORINTHIANS 13:(5-10), 11-13 (BCP)

Interpreting the Text

The Episcopal lectionary suggests including vv. 5-10, in which Paul asks his addressees to examine themselves to determine whether they are living "in the faith." If we interpret faith in its Mediterranean cultural sense of loyalty, he is clearly asking them to forgo divided loyalties and join in harmonious unity in Christ Jesus. In this way, they will continue on the path to becoming perfect (v. 9).

Verses 11-13 then conclude that segment of 2 Corinthians in which Paul has been harsh to the addressees. This harshness helps to understand the imperatives: rejoice, mend your ways, encourage one another, agree with one another, live in peace (NAB); or put things in order, listen to my appeal, agree with one another, live in peace (NRSV). Despite antipathy toward his opponents in this community and the harsh words addressed to them, Paul desperately wants the divisions to end and harmonious fellowship to return. This indeed is his concluding prayer.

Paul sometimes recommends that believers greet one another with a holy kiss (1 Cor. 16:20; 2 Cor. 13:13; 1 Thess. 5:26). Justin Martyr (around 100–165 C.E.) reveals that this is part of the liturgy in his day: "Having ended the prayers, we salute one another with a kiss" (*Apol.* 1.65.2). Perhaps Paul's recommendation derives from his liturgical setting. Surely Westerners understand that in the ancient world and in other parts of the world even today, the "kiss" is shared by two people (including two men) who embrace. Then usually the younger or the one of lower status will kiss the one of higher status on each cheek.

It is not clear what might make the kiss "holy." Perhaps Jesus' comment to Judas: "Is it with a kiss, Judas, that you betray the Son of man?" (Luke 22:48) offers some insight. In the honor-driven culture of the ancient Mediterranean world, betrayal or breach of loyalty is shocking enough. Expressing this disloyalty in non-verbal language (a kiss) whose primary purpose is to express respect and loyalty only compounds the perversion. Thus, perhaps the kiss during the liturgy is holy because by means of it believers express respect and loyalty to each other.

THERE ARE TIMES WHEN ALL BELIEVERS NEED TO BE CALLED TO TASK. THIS IS SURELY ONE OF THE LEAST APPEALING CHALLENGES TO ANY PREACHER,

Responding to the Text

There are times when all believers need to be called to task. This is surely one of the least appealing challenges to any preacher, but as Paul urged Timothy: "Proclaim the message; be persistent whether the time is favorable or unfavorable" (2 Tim. 4:2). For this the preacher must answer.

THE GOSPEL

MATTHEW 28:16-20 (RCL, BCP)

Interpreting the Text

The Gospel of Matthew concludes with an edict (vv. 18-20), just as does the last book of the Hebrew Bible, 2 Chronicles (2 Chron. 36:23). A key verse has traditionally been mistranslated: "Go therefore and make disciples of all nations . . ." (v. 19). The accusative case in this verse ("disciples of all nations") is grammatically identified as an accusative of extent in space. It answers the question "Where?" A more appropriate and grammatically correct translation of Jesus' edict or command would be "to make disciples among all the nations."

During his lifetime, Jesus sent his disciples to preach to "the lost sheep of the house of Israel" (Matt. 10:6). Geographically, these lost sheep were living in Judea,

Galilee, and Perea. Jesus himself believed his mission was only to fellow ethnics ("Israel" is Matthew's customary name for the ethnic group into which Jesus was born). Thus the risen Jesus simply directs his disciples now to go beyond the region of the original mission to the Israelite émigrés living beyond Palestine. The edict is, "Go therefore and make disciples of the lost sheep of the house of Israel living among all the nations." Matthew's purpose behind this account is to explain how his Israelite community of followers of Jesus (presumably living in Syria, see Matt. 4:24) came to be disciples of Jesus. These are the many who "will come from east and west and will eat with Abraham and Isaac and Jacob in the kingdom of heaven" (Matt. 8:11). These Israelite émigrés will return to the theocracy soon to be established in Palestine. Jesus and Matthew's community remained completely within the house of Israel and never went beyond it.

JOHN 3:16-18 (RC)

Interpreting the Text

The evangelist uses the word "world" in both a positive and a negative sense. From the positive perspective, Jesus is glad he came into the world (John 6:32; 11:27). He proclaims himself to be the light of this world (8:12; 9:5; 12:46). Even today's passage reflects a positive view of the world (see also 1:29; 4:42; 6:33, 51; 10:36; 12:47; 17:21). But much more often the word "world" appears in John's Gospel in a negative sense. The world refused to receive Jesus (1:9-10). The world opposes Jesus (16:20; 17:14, 16; 18:36) and his Spirit (14:17; 16:8-11). Actually, the world absolutely hates Jesus and his followers (7:7; 15:18-19; 16:20).

Perhaps a key passage for understanding John's usage is the scene in which Jesus is interrogated by the high priest. Jesus replied, "I have spoken openly to the world; I have always taught in synagogues and in the temple, where all Jews come together. I have said nothing secretly" (John 12:20). If "world" is synonymous with the synagogue, temple, and gatherings of members of the house of Israel, then the negative view is intelligible. At the earliest stage of John's community, its members viewed fellow ethnics as worthy of recruitment to become followers of Jesus. At a later stage (perhaps the late 80s), as Judean audiences began to dismiss the message and even ejected some messianists from synagogues, a negative view of the world emerged and developed.

> A HISTORICALLY SENSITIVE APPRECIATION OF OUR ANCESTORS IN FAITH HELPS TO UNDERSTAND THE CHALLENGING JOURNEY THEY MADE FROM BEING FOCUSED EXCLUSIVELY ON THE IN-GROUP, FELLOW-ETHNICS, TO A MORE INCLUSIVE PERSPECTIVE OF WHO MIGHT BE A FOLLOWER OF JESUS.

Today's verses reflect the positive view. God so loved the people of divine election that God sent the Son to them. Those who would be loyal to him (believe) would gain life eternal and be saved. Those who refused to be loyal to him would reap condemnation, though this was not part of God's plan.

The ambiguous use of language tips us off that John's community is really an antisociety. This means that it is a group that intentionally establishes itself as a conscious alternative to the larger society. Social scientists who study such societies note that they deliberately use language ambiguously for two purposes. On the one hand, outsiders are confused (as was Nicodemus by Jesus' use of the Greek word that could mean "from above" and "again"). On the other hand, the antisociety knows full well what they intend by these words, which then serve to bond them together more tightly.

Responding to the Text

A historically sensitive appreciation of our ancestors in faith helps to understand the challenging journey they made from being focused exclusively on the in-group, fellow-ethnics, to a more inclusive perspective of who might be a follower of Jesus. It is a lesson that perhaps each generation of believers needs to explore and learn.

SECOND SUNDAY AFTER PENTECOST / BODY AND BLOOD OF CHRIST (CORPUS CHRISTI)

MAY 29, 2005

PROPER 4

REVISED COMMON	EPISCOPAL (BCP)	ROMAN CATHOLIC
Gen. 6:9-22; 7:24; 8:14-19 or Deut. 11:18-21, 26-28	Deut. 11:18-21, 26-28	Deut. 8:2-3 14b-16a
Psalm 46 or Ps. 31:1-5, 19-24	Psalm 31 or 31:1-5, 19-24	Ps. 147:12-13, 14-15, 19-20
Rom. 1:16-17; 3:22b-28, (29-31)	Rom. 3:21-25a, 28	1 Cor. 10:16-17
Matt. 7:21-29	Matt. 7:21-27	John 6:51-58

FIRST READING
GENESIS 6:9-22; 7:24; 8:14-19 (RCL)

Interpreting the Text

For today's reading about the Flood story and Noah's role in it, the architects of the lectionary have selected verses only from the P (Priestly) document. According to P, the waters above and below the earth, which God confined there at the very beginning, burst forth upon the earth (Gen. 7:11) and flooded it. P doesn't mention the rain that J (Yahwist) does. Further, P says that Noah brought two pairs of every animal on the ark, while J anachronistically mentions seven pairs of clean and two pairs of unclean animals. And P doesn't mention Noah's sacrifice (8:20-22).

Responding to the Text

The covenant that God establishes with Noah (Gen. 6:18) is the first of four covenants in the P tradition. The full explanation is given in Gen. 9:1-17. God will never again destroy the earth, but the human partners to the covenant must develop and maintain a respect for life. A meaningful link between this reading and the Gospel (Matt. 7:21-29) is the required human response to God's expectations whether in covenant or as mediated in Jesus' Sermon on the Mount.

DEUTERONOMY 11:18-21, 26-28 (RCP, BCP)

Interpreting the Text

The words or commandments of God must be remembered. More than that, they must be internalized, integrated into the very fiber of one's being. Verses 18-21 describe some devices to facilitate remembering: the phylactery worn on the forehead, the mezuzah on the doorpost, and so on. All of these strategies were intended to help Israelites remember the commandments. But that alone is insufficient. They must be obeyed, that is, they must be lived out in reality (vv. 26-28).

Mediterranean culture approves of saying one thing but doing another. The son who had no intention of working in his father's vineyard told his father what

THE WORDS OR COMMANDMENTS OF GOD MUST BE REMEMBERED. MORE THAN THAT, THEY MUST BE INTERNALIZED, INTEGRATED INTO THE VERY FIBER OF ONE'S BEING.

he wanted to hear: "I go, sir" (Matt. 21:30). He honored his father and did not shame him with public disrespect ("I will not!"). As always in his teaching, Jesus' question was not about the honorable thing but about "doing the will of the Father" (Matt. 21:31). In today's verses, Moses poses the same challenge to the Israelites: don't just memorize God's words, obey them!

DEUTERONOMY 8:2-3, 14b-16a (RC)

In vv. 2-3, the author draws lessons from the past for the Israelites, who seemed to have short memories. God's purpose during the forty years after the exodus from Egypt was to test the Israelites' loyalty. Loyalty (called "faith" in the Bible) is a key Middle Eastern value, and whatever is true of human beings must be even truer of God. If humans expect and cherish loyalty, all the more does God do the same. According to the NAB, God sent afflictions as a test to "find out whether or not it was your intention to keep his commandments (NRSV: "to know what was in your hearts"). Verses 14-16 list the various tests, but both segments remind the Israelites of God's providential gift of manna, something unfamiliar but nourishing, in order that they might understand that "not by bread alone does man live, but by every word that comes forth from the mouth of the LORD."

Responding to the Text

The BCP readings appear to intend the same as the RCL readings: God expects a prompt and appropriate response to divine directives. The RC readings from Deuteronomy 8 and John 6 focus instead on manna and the bread of life. In each case, the preacher faces the challenge of making ancient texts come alive and translating concepts from an alien culture (Middle Eastern) to the Western culture of contemporary worshipers.

Responsive Reading
PSALM 46 (RCL);
PSALM 31:1–5, 19–24 (BCP; RCL, alt.)

Psalm 46, the first of the Zion songs in the Psalter, is associated with King Hezekiah and Sennacherib's invasion (701 B.C.E.). While most of Judah was burned, Jerusalem was spared (see 2 Kings 18:13-16). In the face of near certain extinction, God comes to the rescue. Zion survives. (Verse 1 of Psalm 46 inspired Luther's hymn "A Mighty Fortress.")

The author of Psalm 31 must have suffered a hideous disease (v. 11). The first five verses, however, express confidence in the righteousness of God who will deliver him. Of this the psalmist is certain. God is his fortress, and the psalmist trusts God completely. Verses 19-24 thank God for rescue, if for no other reason than to find shelter and readmission to the temple (v. 20).

PSALM 147:12–13, 14–15, 19–20 (RC)

These verses are drawn from the three quasi-independent hymns that constitute this psalm: vv. 1-6; 7-11; and 12-20. The latter hymn focuses on God as Lord of Zion through the creative word. Mention of Zion and repetition of various synonyms for word: command, statutes, and ordinances demonstrate how these verses serve as a suitable bridge between the first reading and the Gospel.

Second Reading
ROMANS 1:16–17; 3:22b–28, (29–31) (RCL)
ROMANS 3:21–25a, 28 (BCP)

Interpreting the Text

Paul himself never uses the word "Romans." He writes "to all God's beloved in Rome." (Rom. 1:1). Throughout his letter he speaks only of "Judeans and Greeks" (see Rom. 1:16; 2:9-10; 3:9; 10:12; see also 1 Cor. 1:24 and passim; Gal. 3:28; Col. 3:11). The best translation of "Judeans and Greeks" for Paul would be "uncivilized and civilized Israelites." It seems that for non-native Romans, to be "Roman" was to be "Greek" or "civilized." In sum, "Judean" and "Greek" indicated a status, while the words "Israelites" and "Gentiles" indicated genealogical and geographical origin. Israelite groups and their "Judaisms" (an appropriate plural for the first century C.E.) held in common a "genealogical story of mythical origin" rooted in Abraham. Paul's assumptions that his audiences knew Israel's story and Israel's scripture and that his essential task was to proclaim how the God of Israel was revealed in the resurrection of Jesus (thus appointing Jesus Israel's Messiah with a forthcoming Israelite theocracy) makes it quite clear that Paul's message was meant only for Israelites.

At Rom. 3:21, having presented "bad news" or the hopelessness of human existence apart from Jesus Messiah, Paul introduces good news. God presents a much simpler way of setting people in right relationship to the deity, namely, through unswerving loyalty to (faith in) Messiah Jesus (v. 22) in whom the divine quality of uprightness is revealed. All who have faith actually appropriate this uprightness to themselves according to the divine plan.

What else is Paul trying to communicate in these verses? The broader context makes his central point clear (I already mentioned it above): God brings sinners back to right relationship with the deity through unswerving loyalty (faith) in Messiah Jesus. How? The key word here is "blood," the blood of Jesus. In Israelite tradition, "the life of a living body is in its blood" and "it is the blood, as the seat of life, that makes atonement" (Lev. 17:11). This central element of life belongs to the deity alone. When offered in sacrifice to God, it can produce one of two effects: life-maintenance or life-restoration. Just as feuding between human beings requires some reconciliation to keep life-threat (vengeance) at bay and to re-establish life-supporting relations, so Jesus' blood works this effect (called "expiation" in v. 25) with God. Jesus' blood now has a life-effect in terms of life-restoration. Redemption (v. 25) is the restoration of the honor of God's people (considered by Paul to be "all" who sinned but who now have faith in Jesus Messiah).

1 CORINTHIANS 10:16-17 (RC)

These few verses are drawn from a segment of this letter (1 Cor. 10:14—11:1) that offers detailed application of the narration of Israel's story that immediately preceded it (1 Cor. 10:1-13). That part of Israel's story spoke of showing respect for or service of images (usually translated as "worship of idols"; see 1 Cor. 10:14). In Paul's application to the Corinthian context, the service of images is like the behavior of the Israelites in the wilderness, with its desire for evil, service of images proper (this includes eating, drinking, merrymaking, or sexual promiscuity), putting Christ's loyalty to the test, and constant complaining about what

God has decided and provided. To make his point, Paul first refers to the significance of the Corinthians' ritual sharing of the blood and body of Christ, underscoring the fact that the one bread stands for one body without division (today's vv. 16-17). Then Paul cites a truism of Mediterranean sacrificial practice: those who eat of what is sacrificed are partners in the altar, i.e., in the sacrifice linking worshipers with the deity and to one another. Such is the case with the God of Israel and the Israelites who sacrifice. Such is not the case with non-Israelites, since the entities to which they offer sacrifice are not deities but demons. A word to the wise is sufficient!

Responding to the Text

By situating these readings within their appropriate Middle Eastern setting, a preacher will gain and be able to share fresh insight with the congregation. It is stunning but sobering to recognize that Paul's preaching, so redolent of the Israelite story and tradition, would make sense only to those familiar with it. That would mean non-Israelites were not part of his intended audience. Paul's charge was to preach to Israelite minorities living among predominantly non-Israelite populations.

> BY SITUATING THESE READINGS WITHIN THEIR APPROPRIATE MIDDLE EASTERN SETTING, A PREACHER WILL GAIN AND BE ABLE TO SHARE FRESH INSIGHT WITH THE CONGREGATION.

THE GOSPEL
MATTHEW 7:21-29 (RCL);
MATTHEW 7:21-27 (BCP)

Interpreting the Text

These concluding verses to Jesus' Sermon on the Mount pose a sobering warning to listeners to consider how they will respond to the sermon. Perhaps their attention wandered as Jesus spoke. Jesus tells the fate that will befall those who act upon his words and those who are unmoved by them. To call someone "Lord" in Middle Eastern cultures is to recognize this individual as a personal patron. A patron is a person with surplus who is culturally obliged to give it away. Patrons freely choose clients and treat them "as if" they were family members. Patrons thus show favoritism. A fortunate client who is selected by a powerful patron freely accepts the obligation of doing what the patron expects and of singing the patron's praises far and wide for all benefits received.

Matthew's Jesus warns those who have listened to his sermon that it is not enough to *acknowledge* him as patron or broker with God, the ultimate patron. As the culture dictates, a client must fulfill the patron's wishes and behave in a way that pleases and honors the patron. In the Sermon, Jesus the broker has specified what God the patron expects of clients. Now he urges appropriate behavior and warns of fatal consequences for not behaving appropriately. Jesus then contrasts the consequences of a resolute, positive response with the consequences of an inauthentic response. The choice is up to the listeners.

To appreciate what seems to be a self-evident statement about consequences, one needs to understand the Middle Eastern preference for appearances over reality, for the ideal over the real. For a Middle Easterner, to feign compliance is as good as complying. At least it doesn't shame the one expecting a positive result. Jesus says the challenge is more serious than that, and an authentic response to the sermon, to God's expectations, is paramount.

FOR A MIDDLE EASTERNER, TO FEIGN COMPLIANCE IS AS GOOD AS COMPLYING. AT LEAST IT DOESN'T SHAME THE ONE EXPECTING A POSITIVE RESULT. JESUS SAYS THE CHALLENGE IS MORE SERIOUS THAN THAT, AND AN AUTHENTIC RESPONSE TO THE SERMON, TO GOD'S EXPECTATIONS, IS PARAMOUNT.

JOHN 6:51-58 (RC)

In today's reading, Jesus' comments led his contemporaries to *a violent dispute among themselves*: "How can he give us his flesh to eat?" (v. 52). No one interpreted this statement literally. The violent dispute erupts because Jesus once again resorts to the "anti-language" that is so thoroughly characteristic of the entire Gospel of John. John's Jesus and the entire Johannine community use familiar words like "manna," "bread come down from heaven," and "I am" but create new and jarring meanings. What was Jesus *really* saying?

One clue is found in v. 59: "Jesus said these things while he was teaching in the synagogue at Capernaum" (v. 59). It may be best to interpret today's passage as part of a "midrashic homily" Jesus preached in the synagogue. The Hebrew word "midrash" means interpretation or explanation. Homilies by definition must always (1) explain biblical texts and (2) apply them to life. A homily never was and should not now be a sermon, or a speech, or a lecture, even if entertaining. To identify the biblical text that Jesus was explaining is not easy.

We know that in the first century C.E. the Torah was read in the synagogue. It was divided into 150 sections that were read sequentially over a three-year period. A second reading, called the *Haphtarah*, was drawn from the prophets. Some scholars hypothesize that a third reading came from the 150 canonical psalms.

No one has yet discovered this "lectionary," but Aileen Guilding has attempted to reconstruct it. Many scholars disagree with her reconstruction, but most if not all agree with her basic idea. If the lectionary could be reconstructed, we might have some idea of the text upon which Jesus was commenting in the synagogue at that Passover season. This search would be a purely, creative-imaginative exercise were it not for yet another ancient body of Israelite literature known as the Targumim (singular: Targum), which are paraphrases of the Hebrew scriptures in the Aramaic language.

After the Babylonian exile, Israel gradually forgot its Hebrew language and adopted the language the Babylonians spoke, Aramaic or Chaldean. Eventually, they could no longer understand the Hebrew scriptures that were read to them. In the synagogues, therefore, one person would read from the Hebrew text while another person would translate instantaneously into Aramaic. The translations gradually became paraphrases, and sometimes they became much longer and detailed than the Hebrew text. By the sixth and seventh centuries C.E., two collections of such Targumim existed: the Babylonian and the Palestinian. The former in general is more literal, the latter more paraphrastic.

Bruce Malina of Creighton University, Omaha, Nebraska, hypothesized that the sermon in John's text reflects a Palestinian Targum to Josh. 5:5—6:1, the Haphtarah or second synagogue reading, which appears to have been linked with Num. 21:6-9 as the Torah, the first reading. They deal with the Exodus and the manna tradition. John (or Jesus) used this manna tradition to explain how Jesus personally surpassed the deficiencies of manna. In other words, instead of following the Israelite tradition of explaining the Bible by the Bible, John (or Jesus) explained the Bible (the manna tradition) in the light of Jesus. This could and did provoke violent dispute. Not all would have agreed that Jesus is the fulfillment of and substitute for the Torah, the living Word of God.

Responding to the Text

Many modern believers might insist that God would not have made the Scripture so challenging to understand and interpret. Surely God intended it to be readily intelligible to all. Nevertheless, these small excursions into Mediterranean culture and the nature of the Israelite scriptural tradition indicate how much more contemporary believers need to learn. What does the Mediterranean idea of patronage mean to your understanding of God? What does the Eucharist and its relationship to manna mean to you?

THIRD SUNDAY AFTER PENTECOST

JUNE 5, 2005
TENTH SUNDAY IN ORDINARY TIME / PROPER 5

REVISED COMMON	EPISCOPAL (BCP)	ROMAN CATHOLIC
Gen. 12:1-9	Hos. 5:15—6:6	Hos. 6:3-6
or Hos. 5:15—6:6		
Ps. 33:1-12	Psalm 50 or 50:7-15	Ps. 50:1, 8, 12-13, 14-15
or Ps. 50:7-15		
Rom. 4:13-25	Rom. 4:13-18	Rom. 4:18-25
Matt. 9:9-13, 18-26	Matt. 9:9-13	Matt. 9:9-13

FIRST READING

GENESIS 12:1-9 (RCL)

Interpreting the Text

These verses are selected from the collection of stories of diverse origin in Gen. 11:27—15:18, which recount the story of Abraham and Sarah. The collection reflects J, E, and P traditions, but scholars prefer the view that this is a fluid tradition that was frequently revised over time. In Genesis 12, J is reflected in vv. 1-4a, 6-9, while P is reflected in vv. 4b-5. The formal arrangement of the entire collection seems to reflect a rabbinical pattern reporting ten trials and seven blessings. Verses 1-4 present Abraham's first trial: God commands that he leave his country (Haran) and kin (father Terah and his household). P has added an interesting cultural note in v. 5: Abraham took

> THE LINK WITH THE GOSPEL IS QUITE LIKELY MATTHEW'S IMMEDIATE AND UNQUESTIONING RESPONSE TO JESUS' INVITATION TO "FOLLOW ME."

along his brother's son, Lot. Since the customary marriage partner in the patriarchal period was father's brother's daughter, or patrilateral parallel cousin (see Genesis 24), Abraham would have readily available to him an ideal marriage partner for his sons (or daughters). Verses 2-4 summarize the seven blessings, two of which are explained in v. 7: enduring offspring and possession of the land of Canaan.

Verse 7 also reports the first recorded encounter between God and a patriarch in an altered states of consciousness (ASC) experience (see Gen. 17:1; 18:1; 26:2, 24; 35:9; 48:3). This is God's customary medium of communication with human beings whom, as cognitive neuroscience informs us, God seems to have hardwired for the experience.

In general, this story tells how God gives Abraham a command (v. 1) that he obeys immediately and unquestioningly (v. 4). It is God's summons of Abraham to a divinely determined destiny. The link with the Gospel is quite likely Matthew's immediate and unquestioning response to Jesus' invitation to "follow me." It is worth reflecting on how spontaneously modern believers respond to divine invitation.

HOSEA 5:15—6:6 (BCP; RCL, alt.);
HOSEA 6:3-6 (RC)

Interpreting the Text

In today's Gospel (Matt. 9:9-13), Matthew's Jesus cites Hosea according to the Septuagint. This is very likely the intended link between these readings. Speaking to his eighth-century B.C.E. audience, the prophet Hosea presents Yahweh's scorn for Israel when it attends to purely external worship rituals without actually obeying Yahweh's commands. Israel's piety is evanescent, like the dew that evaporates with the rising of the sun. Though it seeks to repent, Israel's repentance is not deep-rooted or lasting. While vv. 1-3 sound like repentance, they are clearly insincere and inauthentic. Verse 3 in particular appears to refer to fertility rituals (spring rains) rather than divine solicitude. God's response is a promise of judgment. God's judgment which "goes forth like the light" is reliable and unshakable. It stands in contrast to Israel's inconstancy, which is like "the dew that goes away early."

Responding to the Text

Israel responds to God in authentic Middle Eastern cultural fashion: it says what it knows God wants to hear. Yet prophets like Hosea and Jesus summon to honesty and authenticity. That is what is most effective in God's sight.

RESPONSIVE READING
PSALM 33:1-12 (RCL);
PSALM 50:7-15 (RCL, alt.);
PSALM 50 or 50:7-15 (BCP);
PSALM 50:1, 8, 12-13, 14-15 (RC)

A psalm of praise, Psalm 33 celebrates the creative power of the word (v. 4)—an idea that was common in the sacred writings of Egypt and Babylon as it was in ancient Israel. Indeed, "word" and "work" stand in parallelism in v. 4: the divine word is personal, effective, and dependable to come to the rescue of Israel as it has need of it.

Most likely originating before the exile in a period of well-being, the verses of Psalm 50 selected for this responsive reading are not really critical of sacrifice. God actually has no need of any of them. What God desires above all is quite in line with Mediterranean cultural values. God desires praise, that is, honor. In other words, God wants recognition of and respect for divine status. This kind of human behavior will obtain from

> WHAT GOD DESIRES ABOVE ALL IS QUITE IN LINE WITH MEDITER-
> RANEAN CULTURAL VALUES. GOD DESIRES PRAISE, THAT IS, HONOR.

God rescue from distress, which in its turn should prompt the recipient to further glorify or honor God.

SECOND READING

ROMANS 4:13–25 (RCL);
ROMANS 4:13–18 (BCP);
ROMANS 4:18–25 (RC)

Interpreting the Text

In Romans 4, Paul uses Abraham to illustrate his point that uprightness with God derives from faith, that is, in Middle Eastern cultural terms, loyalty. Abraham was considered upright because of his loyalty (vv. 1–8) rather than because of his circumcision (vv. 9–12). Righteousness came to Abraham in virtue of a promise (vv. 13–17); hence he is a model of loyalty or faith for those who have accepted Jesus as Messiah.

A popular first-century Israelite belief claimed that Abraham (around 1800 B.C.E.) knew and obeyed the Torah even though he lived long before God revealed it to Moses (around 1250 B.C.E.). Paul challenges this belief. Approximately twenty-nine years after God declared Abraham to be upright (see Genesis 15), Abraham was circumcised (see Genesis 17). Paul repeats throughout this passage that Abraham trusted in God. Trust is the Middle Eastern cultural value interpreted as "hope" in theological jargon. Paul also repeats that Abraham remained loyal to God. Loyalty is the Middle Eastern cultural value interpreted as "faith" in theological jargon. Because of these values, God judged Abraham to be righteous ("Therefore his faith [loyalty] was reckoned to him as righteousness," v. 22).

Responding to the Text

In today's verses, Paul makes an immediate application "to us." This is something every modern believer and many preachers often do. Paul does this by means of midrashic interpretation. The word *midrash* in postbiblical Hebrew means to explain or interpret scripture based, of course, on study (see Sir. 51:23, where "the house of instruction" reflects the Hebrew phrase *beth hammidrash*). One purpose of midrash is to modernize or actualize (to use a modern term) the Old Testament by applying it to a new situation. To do this, Paul emphasizes that Abraham had faith (was loyal), while he completely ignores elements of Abraham's skepticism, like laughing when he heard that at ninety-nine years of age he would produce a son with his ninety-year-old wife (Gen. 17:17).

Paul is more interested in playing with the word "dead." Abraham's body and Sarah's womb were "dead," but God brought life from these dead elements. Thus Abraham's faith in God (loyalty to God) foreshadowed the kind of faith Paul's contemporaries had that God raised Jesus from the dead. Similarly, the consequences for the believer then are new life gained through the death and resurrection of Jesus.

> TRUST IS THE MIDDLE EASTERN CULTURAL VALUE INTERPRETED AS "HOPE" IN THEOLOGICAL JARGON. PAUL ALSO REPEATS THAT ABRAHAM REMAINED LOYAL TO GOD. LOYALTY IS THE MIDDLE EASTERN CULTURAL VALUE INTERPRETED AS "FAITH" IN THEOLOGICAL JARGON.

In today's Gospel (Matt. 9:9-13), Jesus quotes a proverb, joins a quote from Hos. 6:6 to it, and tells his critics to "go and learn what this [these words from Hosea] means" (v. 13). Contemporary believers face the same challenge. Separated by time but especially by culture from biblical events and scenes, contemporary preachers and believers are obliged to bridge these and other gaps in order to arrive at a (Mediterranean) culturally plausible interpretation of text segments. They cannot be selective or uncritical, as Paul was in interpretation.[1] Only then can the preacher or teacher begin to explore cross-cultural applications to modern situations.

THE GOSPEL

MATTHEW 9:9-13 (BCP, RC);
MATTHEW 9:9-13, 18-26 (RCL)

Interpreting the Text

The call of Matthew is situated in a cluster of ten stories about Jesus' mighty deeds (*dynameis*) that the evangelist has gathered in chapters 8 and 9. Though it is not one of these ten stories, healing is one of its motifs. The scene is set in Capernaum, Jesus' own town (v. 1). Capernaum was located on the northwest corner of the Sea of Galilee along the major road of international trade between Damascus and Egypt. Domestic trade among the towns and villages on the shores of the Sea of Galilee also had to pass through Capernaum. This was a

JOHN J. PILCH

perfect location for collecting tolls (a more accurate translation than "taxes") that were levied on all goods in transit. Matthew was a toll collector who worked in the Capernaum customhouse. He also brokered fishing rights on behalf of the government to those who would fish in the Sea of Galilee.

In Jesus' time, a toll collector was a native who contracted with Rome to collect the allotted tolls but paid them personally to Rome in advance. It was the toll collector's hope to collect enough taxes to make a profit, but the gamble rarely paid off. The rich and the educated, a minuscule minority in Jesus' day, routinely criticized toll collectors. The poor rarely had anything on which duties could be levied and would likely sympathize with rather than criticize toll collectors who like themselves were trying to eke out a subsistence.

Jesus, the village artisan (did he pay tolls for transporting his handiwork?), invited Matthew the toll collector to his home, which was very likely located in Peter's father's complex at Capernaum. It is significant that Jesus' disciples and "many" other toll collectors and sinners came to eat dinner there. Apparently Jesus had the ability to marshal sufficient resources to feed a group of this size. In a culture where 95 percent of the population existed at subsistence level, the ability to host such a meal suggests that Jesus was well connected with a network capable of providing provisions.

In a culture where minding other people's business is a major concern, the Pharisees hurl a public challenge against Jesus' honor by asking the quite likely embarrassed disciples, "Why does your teacher eat with tax collectors and sinners?" Jesus, ever the master of riposte in these verbal games of push and shove, responds personally by citing a proverb. Many cultures, including some segments of American culture, are particularly adept at spontaneous, creative, and colorful responses. Jesus' proverb was: "Those who are well have no need of a physician, but those who are sick."

Prior to the relatively recent discovery of the microscope and germs or viruses, sickness was generally viewed as a loss of meaning in human life. Technically, this is called an illness rather than a disease. Healing occurred when meaning was restored even if a cure did not occur. Jesus draws an analogy between his association with tax collectors and sinners and the association of healers with sick people. Historians of medicine tell us that in antiquity healers preferred to discuss illness rather than to treat sick people. If the sick person died, the healer might be put to death as well. It was safer to muse and philosophize. Jesus' activity contrasts with this cultural view because he touched the untouchables and associated with the outcasts in a way that good healers should have done but didn't.

Moreover, sickness in ancient Israel nearly always entailed separation from the community until health returned. This was part of the understanding of purity and wholeness. In a group-oriented culture, separation from the community is a fate worse than death. Jesus' healing ministry in general always included a restoration of the person to community, whether it was persons with repulsive scaly skin conditions (called "leprosy") or toll collectors who in general were a remarkably fair and honest group of people routinely stereotyped, condemned, and shunned by their peers.

The RCL adds verses that recount two healing events, the restoration to wholeness of a woman with a serious menstrual irregularity and the restoration to life of a recently deceased girl (Matt. 9:18-26). Contemporary medical specialists suggest that the woman suffered from a psychological conversion disorder, a condition rooted in the woman's mind. Her faith (= loyalty) worked effectively to remedy the situation. As for the recently deceased girl, it is important to recognize that death was defined differently in antiquity. It was a yearlong process. Given the apparently rapid onset and progress of the girl's condition (at least in Mark 5:21-24, 35-43), contemporary medical specialists hypothesize that she may have been suffering from a severe febrile illness with central nervous system effects. Examples would include bacterial meningitis or cerebral malaria, possibly common in first-century Palestine. Even more plausible is the suggestion that the girl was suffering from a conversion disorder or somatization illness associated with menarche. A comatose condition would emerge from "hysterical" over-breathing. Modern speculation aside, what the Gospels report is that Jesus effectively helped in both instances. The results were impressive. There is no reason to doubt that Jesus gave or restored to life the young girl. He also restored meaning to life of the woman with the menstrual irregularity, reflecting God's activity of giving life (creation) and restoring meaning to life (redemption) in the Israelite story.

> WHAT ROLE DOES GOD PLAY IN HUMAN LIFE, ESPECIALLY IN THE CONTEMPORARY WESTERN UNDERSTANDING OF LIFE AND THE MEANING OF LIFE? OR OF SICKNESS AND HEALING?

Responding to the Text

What role does God play in human life, especially in the contemporary Western understanding of life and the meaning of life? Or of sickness and healing? Is the Western understanding in conflict with traditional biblical views? Or does it help us understand traditional biblical views? Curious believers want to know!

Note

1. Such an evaluation of Paul is obviously anachronistic. Even in modern times, midrash remains a key element of the Jewish interpretation of the Bible. It is part of the method by which Jewish interpreters make ancient texts relevant to modern life. In contrast, most Christian interpretation is committed to historical-

critical methods. These differ from midrash. While it is also possible to make ancient texts relevant to modern life with historical-critical methods, the process is much more complex. For the view of the Roman Catholic Church, see the Pontifical Biblical Commission document, *The Interpretation of the Bible in the Church*, 1994, on the web at http://myweb.lmu.edu/fjust/Docs/PBC_Interp.htm.

FOURTH SUNDAY AFTER PENTECOST

JUNE 12, 2005
ELEVENTH SUNDAY IN ORDINARY TIME / PROPER 6

REVISED COMMON	EPISCOPAL (BCP)	ROMAN CATHOLIC
Gen. 18:1-15 (21:1-7)	Exod. 19:2-8a	Exod. 19:2-6a
or Exod. 19:2-8a		
Ps. 116:1-2, 12-19	Psalm 100	Ps. 100:1-2, 3, 5
or Psalm 100		
Rom. 5:1-8	Rom. 5:6-11	Rom. 5:6-11
Matt. 9:35—10:8 (9-23)	Matt. 9:35—10:8 (9-15)	Matt. 9:36—10:8

FIRST READING

GENESIS 18:1-15, (21:1-7) (RCL)

This story is an excellent illustration of the Middle Eastern practice of hospitality (which likely is the intended link with the Gospel), a process for allowing outsiders to enter a family circle by transforming them from strangers to guests. First they are tested, but in this story, Abraham does not consider a test necessary. The washing of the feet transforms the strangers to guests. Definite rules bind guests and hosts. The guest should not insult the host or usurp his role (hospitality is predominantly extended by the men), or refuse what is offered (the three guests here apparently ate everything Abraham offered). The host should not insult his guests but must protect them and their honor and show concern for their needs and wishes. In other words, the host must earn the good the guests should show.

> THIS STORY IS AN EXCELLENT ILLUSTRATION OF THE MIDDLE EASTERN PRACTICE OF HOSPITALITY (WHICH LIKELY IS THE INTENDED LINK WITH THE GOSPEL), A PROCESS FOR ALLOWING OUTSIDERS TO ENTER A FAMILY CIRCLE BY TRANSFORMING THEM FROM STRANGERS TO GUESTS.

While a guest will rarely if ever reciprocate hospitality, there is something of a quid pro quo in the process. In return for safe passage through hostile territory guaranteed by a host, guests often repay the kindness with some favor or blessing. There are no "free gifts" in the Middle East—not even in the Bible! In this story, one of the guests announced a blessing from God, a son—the best imaginable Middle Eastern gift of all.

Sarah, who by the rules of the culture remains in female space inside the tent yet overhears the promise, insults the guests by laughing skeptically. This is a breach of hospitality, but it reflects more on Abraham than on her. Perhaps for this reason, the guests overlook it and simply reaffirm the promise, in the name of God of course, who is a central figure in the entire story. In the end, the guests leave as friends of Abraham (see James 2:23; in the Muslim tradition, Abraham is known as the friend of God, *el Khalil*).

Responding to the Text

Hospitality toward strangers as demonstrated by Abraham (and later Lot; Genesis 19) can rightfully be expected by evangelizers (Matt. 10:11-14). Those who do not extend it when needed will have to answer for it (see Matt. 25:31-46).

EXODUS 19:2-8a (BCP; RCL, alt.); EXODUS 19:2-6a (RC)

Interpreting the Text

God speaks to Moses in an altered states of consciousness experience (ASC). The place is the mountain of God traditionally identified as Sinai (or Horeb; see Exod. 3:1). God's message is simple: reflect on your experience of the things I have done on your behalf relative to the Egyptians. Consider how I have cared for you. Now therefore the choice is yours: I want you as my treasured possession, more precious to me than all other peoples. If this is acceptable to you, then you must obey my voice and keep the covenant, the sworn agreement between me and you, my people. If you choose to live in this fashion, you shall be a holy people, that is, one set apart from every other people on the earth. The people agreed. One plausible link of this reading to today's Gospel (Matt. 9:36—10:8) is Jesus' sending his disciples only to "the lost sheep of the house of Israel," that is, to God's holy people, and definitely prohibiting them from going to the pagans or the Samaritans.

> HOW DOES ONE EXPLAIN GOD'S OBVIOUS FAVORITISM TOWARD ONE GROUP AND APPARENT DISAVOWAL OF OTHER GROUPS? DID GOD EVER CHANGE THE DIVINE ELECTION AND INTENTION?

Responding to the Text

How does one explain God's obvious favoritism toward one group and apparent disavowal of other groups? Did God ever change the divine election and intention? This is a difficult problem, but it is timely even in our own day, particularly in the context of Christian Zionism. A God-fearing preacher will not shrink from it.

PSALM 116:1-2, 12-19 (RCL);
PSALM 100 (BCP; RCL, alt.);
PSALM 100:1-2, 3, 5 (RC)

Quite likely the entire Psalm 116 was composed at a time of serious illness and perhaps even a sentence of execution ("you have loosed my bonds," v. 16), but the psalmist has experienced rescue. In today's select verses, we hear the psalmist's unshaken confidence ("I will call on him as long as I live") and his gratitude (offer sacrifice in the temple; and call upon the name of the Lord, vv. 17-18).

Psalm 100 is a hymn of praise, and it echoes well the sentiments of the reading from Exodus: "We are his people; the sheep of his pasture (Ps. 100:3)." Scholars point out that in v. 1, the Hebrew literally reports the singular, and the word is more appropriately translated literally as "land" ("lands," RSV; NAB) rather than "earth" (NRSV). The plural "lands" and the word "earth" inappropriately and anachronistically read universal recognition and worship of Yahweh into an Old Testament passage. Though this might embarrass sophisticated contemporary believers, the word "land" does indeed reflect our inward-looking, ethnocentric, exclusivist ancestors in faith. They are concerned only with their fellows. Matthew's Jesus shared the same restrictive view.

ROMANS 5:1-8 (RCL);
ROMANS 5:6-11 (BCP, RC)

Interpreting the Text

In Romans 5, Paul turns to a new emphasis. While he previously spoke of the complete hopelessness of human existence without Jesus Messiah (Rom. 1:18—3:20), and then reflected on salvation through faith in Jesus Messiah (Rom. 3:21—4:25), Paul now reflects on the life of a person who has accepted Jesus as Messiah. Justification and righteousness recede from major consideration, while God's love comes to the fore. In today's verses, Paul considers what is it like to be right with God.

> THE TWO MAIN CONSEQUENCES OF BEING IN RIGHT RELATIONSHIP WITH GOD ARE PEACE (V. 1) AND HOPE (V. 2).

The two main consequences of being in right relationship with God are peace (v. 1) and hope (v. 2). The peace of which Paul speaks is the calm and relief that human beings experience after wrestling with and resolving great doubts or problems. In the anti-introspective culture of the Middle East (see 1 Sam. 16:6), doubts and other such problems tend to be externalized, that is somatized. Some call this a psychosomatic problem, but the more appropriate contemporary term is a conversion disorder. When the problems are resolved, the solution does indeed bring peace and restore wholesomeness and physical health.

Hope or trust can be understood as confidence to such a high degree that one puts everything into the hands of the trusted person. Here the object of such hope or trust is the confidence of sharing in God's honor. Paul boasts about this hope. In Middle Eastern terms, boasting is the way in which one acknowledges one's personal lord and master, in this case, God. Sin is an act that shames another person. If through sin a person has shamed God and thereby become a shameful person, what a remarkable reversal of life-situation it is to share now in the immeasurable honor and glory of God. This is truly an amazing gift from God. Indeed, Paul goes on to explain this in vv. 5-8. That Jesus, who didn't deserve to die this kind of death, agreed to die for sinners is an incredible thought. In a cultural world that operates predominantly by informal exchanges known as dyadic contract (I do you a favor, you owe me; you repay the favor, I owe you, etc.), that Jesus would do us a favor that is truly impossible for us to repay is absolutely astonishing. Yet that is indeed how God proves divine love for us. God's ways are not the ways of human beings.

Responding to the Text

Appreciating or, even better, adopting a Middle Eastern way of thinking requires a truly exhausting effort. Peace and hope seem to be universal human aspirations. They very well may be, yet they are understood differently in different cultural settings. More, they are achieved by different cultural strategies. Understanding the Middle Eastern perspective will prevent both preachers and listeners from psychologizing the Bible, or interpreting the Bible from a psychological perspective. Specialists in cross-cultural psychology note that so long as Western models and concepts dominate psychology, it will remain irrelevant and useless in understanding the rest of the world.

THE GOSPEL
MATTHEW 9:35—10:8 (9-23) (RCL);
MATTHEW 9:35—10:8 (9-15) (BCP);
MATTHEW 9:36—10:8 (RC)

Interpreting the Text

A social-scientific perspective on Jesus' selection of Twelve whom he gathered around himself identifies the group as a special kind of *coalition* called a *faction*. In general, a coalition is a group that gathers for a specific purpose over a limited time with no intention of being permanent. That reveals one dimension of the Twelve. The group was not intended to be a permanent institution. A key characteristic of a coalition is its many-sided network of relations directed toward the achievement of limited goals. We don't know Jesus' explicit goals, but the Twelve surely did. This is what they had in common. Moreover, joining a coalition does not mean one has to quit other more basic groups such as one's family. The fishing conglomerate that was comprised of the families of Jonah (including his sons Simon and Andrew) and Zebedee (and his sons John and James) along with their hired hands is a coalition.

A faction is a special type of coalition characterized by the charisma of a central person who gathers followers and maintains firm loyalty of his core group. Jesus initiated his faction by calling Simon, Andrew, James, and John (Matt. 4:18-22). In today's reading, he rounds out the core group by selecting and naming a total of Twelve. In a faction, individual members have strong relationships with the central figure but less loyalty to and concern for one another. When the mother of John and James boldly requested Jesus to grant her sons special status in the faction (Matt. 20:20-28), the other ten were understandably angry! It is likely that they wished they had thought of this and done it first. While shameful in a limited good society, such a request is quite intelligible in a faction. Some members of a faction often divide their loyalties with other factions and leaders. Judas, who was selected by Jesus as part of the core group, may in reality have only given him limited loyalty, even though Judas held the common purse.

Matthew's Jesus specifies the limited goals of his faction; "Go nowhere among the Gentiles, and enter no town of the Samaritans, but go rather to the lost sheep of the house of Israel" (v. 5). They proclaim the same message that Jesus did at the outset of his career, a proclamation taken over from John the Baptist: "The kingdom of heaven has come near" (v. 7; Matt. 4:17; compare Matt. 3:2). In addition, Jesus raises the status of these followers by empowering them to heal and cast out demons.

SINCE ONLY GOD HAS POWER TO HEAL (EXOD. 15:26) AND EXORCISE, HUMAN BEINGS WHO SHARE IN THIS POWER MUST RECOGNIZE THAT THIS POWER IS NOT A PERSONAL POSSESSION.

Effectively Jesus makes the Twelve brokers of God's power over spirits and disease just as he is. Since only God has power to heal (Exod. 15:26) and exorcise, human beings who share in this power must recognize that this power is not a personal possession.

This is the context for understanding the concluding verse of today's reading (RCL, BCP, RC): "You received without payment; give without payment" (v. 8). In truth, there never was and still is no "free gift" in the Middle Eastern world. Every gift has strings attached. Gift giving is done with a view of expected repayment! (A Middle Eastern proverb observes, "Don't thank me; you *will* repay me!")

In the verses that immediately follow (9-15 BCP, 9-23 RCL), Jesus advises his apostles to take no gold, silver, copper, etc. They are to travel light and rely on hospitality, that is, kindness extended to *strangers* (the kindness that one extends to relatives is called steadfast loving kindness, not hospitality). If the apostles received hospitality, they should evangelize; if not, they should move on. The charge to the disciples that they "give without payment" is a prohibition to expect or demand anything over and above normal Mediterranean hospitality.

Verses 16-23 surely describe the life experiences of Jesus' groups after Jesus died. There is no evidence that fellow Israelites treated Jesus and his followers in the way described here. The family situations described in vv. 21-22 and Jesus' advice to "endure" to the end is probably difficult for Westerners to appreciate. In the Middle East of antiquity and the present, family is the paramount social institution. Every member must be loyal and totally attached to her or his family of origin. Transferring this loyalty and complete attachment to some surrogate family, like a Jesus group, would turn a family against its own members. Not only that, all the friends of the family of origin would turn against such renegade members. Jesus requires the equivalent of social suicide, promising that the surrogate family will replace it (see vv. 37-39; Matt. 12:46-50).

WHAT DOES IT MEAN TO BE HANDPICKED BY JESUS AS A FOLLOWER? HOW SHOULD EVANGELISTS MINISTER?

Responding to the Text

There is much to ponder in this reading. What does it mean to be handpicked by Jesus as a follower? How should evangelists minister? How does Middle Eastern hospitality differ from the Western understanding? Is the Middle Eastern concept of family at all practicable in Western culture? Because the Bible doesn't offer all the direct answers for living, the preacher and listeners have their work cut out for them even with very familiar readings.

FIFTH SUNDAY AFTER PENTECOST

REVISED COMMON	EPISCOPAL (BCP)	ROMAN CATHOLIC
Gen. 21:8-21	Jer. 20:7-13	Jer. 20:10-13
or Jer. 20:7-13		
Ps. 86:1-10, 16-17	Ps. 69:1-18	Ps. 69:8-10, 14, 17, 33-35
or Ps. 69:7-10 (11-15)	or 69:7-10, 16-18	
16-18		
Rom. 6:1b-11	Rom. 5:15b-19	Rom. 5:12-15
Matt. 10:24-39	Matt.10:(16-23) 24-33	Matt. 10:26-33

FIRST READING

GENESIS 21:8-21 (RCL)

Interpreting the Text

This story of Hagar and Ishmael combines P (vv. 1b-5), J (v. 7), and E (vv. 6, 8-21) elements in its narrative. Since sons are "social security" for parents in antiquity, Sarah is concerned that Isaac should be the sole heir in order to take proper care of her when the time comes. It's a matter of life for her. Abraham is, of course, pained by Sarah's request, but God assures him this is the divine intention. God instructs Abraham to obey Sarah, a cultural situation that would indeed require a direct command from God (Prov. 31:3, 10-31). God promises to make Ishmael's descendants into a "great nation" (LXX, see Gen. 25:12-18; Muslims trace their ancestry to Abraham through Ishmael, who is always mentioned first in the Koran). Then God comes to the rescue of Ishmael in the desert. In fact, God has rescued everyone in the story: the concerns of Sarah and Hagar about their respective families are effectively addressed, and Ishmael will thrive in the desert.

> SURELY THE INDISCRIMINATE PROVIDENCE OF GOD IS EVIDENT IN THIS STORY AS IN THE GOSPEL ABOUT THE GOD WHO REVEALS SECRETS.

Surely the indiscriminate providence of God is evident in this story as in the Gospel about the God who reveals secrets. Preachers and listeners have a golden opportunity with this reading to reflect upon the place of Ishmael's descendants in the plan of God even to this day. In the Koran, *Surah* 14:35ff. presents some interesting parallels to the reading from Genesis and the Gospel.

JEREMIAH 20:7-13 (BCP; RCL, alt.); JEREMIAH 20:10-13 (RC)

Interpreting the Text

Scholars identify today's reading as part of a series scattered through Jeremiah 11–20 that has been called "The Confessions of Jeremiah" or "The Intimate Papers of Jeremiah." They stem from the last period of his life, from the fall of Jerusalem (597 B.C.E.) to his death in Egypt not long after 587 B.C.E. God inspired Jeremiah to steadfastly preach that capture by the Babylonians and exile in Babylon was the divine will. The people should not resist it. This would certainly be treason. Who could believe it? Because of this message, Jeremiah had to suffer endless harassment and punishment. Understandably, his experience left him feeling quite isolated and abandoned. Still he remained firmly convinced that this was God's inspired message for him to preach.

THE VERSES WE READ TODAY REFLECT JEREMIAH'S UNSWERVING CONFIDENCE DURING WHAT MUST HAVE BEEN HIS MOST INTENSE PERSONAL CRISIS. FORMER FRIENDS NOW HAVE BECOME HIS MEANEST DETRACTORS, BUT JEREMIAH'S CONFIDENCE IS SOLIDLY ROOTED IN GOD'S PROMISE TO HIM (1:8, 19).

The verses we read today reflect Jeremiah's unswerving confidence during what must have been his most intense personal crisis. Former friends now have become his meanest detractors, but Jeremiah's confidence is solidly rooted in God's promise to him (1:8, 19). In all of his difficulties, Jeremiah remained unswervingly loyal. The word "needy" (NAB: "poor") in v. 13 is not an economic description. It rather designates those who have temporarily lost ascribed status, reputation, and honor and who place all their hope in God to restore it. Jeremiah is supremely confident that God will vindicate him.

Responding to the Text

In today's Gospel, Matthew's Jesus encourages confidence similar to that of Jeremiah: "Have no fear of them" (v. 26); "do not fear those who. . ." (v. 28); and "do not be afraid" (v. 31). Perhaps few preachers or listeners have ever found themselves in a position like Jeremiah's or the ones Jesus describes. If, however, such an occasion arose, whence would one draw confidence that one's position is truly God's will?

RESPONSIVE READING

PSALM 86:1–10, 16–17 (RCL);
PSALM 69:7–10 (11–15) 16–18 (RCL, alt.);
PSALM 69:1–18 or 69:7–10, 16–18 (BCP);
PSALM 69:8–10, 14, 17, 33–35 (RC)

Psalm 86 is a postexilic personal lament in which the author has woven a tissue of texts memorized from other parts of the Bible into a "new" psalm. In times of stress, it is comforting to recall such memorized passages and reassure oneself that the Lord is indeed "good and forgiving." Verse 16 helps understand the psalmist's confidence: "Give strength to your servant; save the child of your serving girl." Servant and child are synonyms in this verse. A servant born in the house of his master was deemed more faithful and dependable (see Exod. 21:1ff.). His petitions stood a better chance of being heard expeditiously by the master. This psalm is a prayer well calculated to move God to pity, mercy, and forgiveness.

Psalm 69 manifests many traces of Jeremiah's influence upon Israel's piety after his death. This, of course, is postexilic Israel. The verses read today do indeed reflect elements of Jeremiah's prayer of confidence in the First Reading. It is especially the lowly ones, those who seek God, the poor, God's very own who are in bonds, who have every reason to be confident of God's help. The verses build a suitable bridge to the Gospel exhortation, "Do not be afraid."

SECOND READING

ROMANS 5:12–15 (RC);
ROMANS 5:15b–19 (BCP)

Interpreting the Text

In this text segment, a familiar Pauline thought pattern emerges. Sin reigned from Adam until Jesus Messiah (then); Jesus' obedience ended that reign and inaugurated a new period of grace (now). Sin and death are personifications. Sin is an active force within and among all human beings. It has been present since the very beginnings of the human race. In Israelite tradition, sin expresses itself chiefly through the "flesh." Flesh is not synonymous with body but rather describes a person viewed from the perspective of unredeemed weakness. Death is also a personified, cosmic force. It works two effects: death obviously destroys the human body, but it also causes definitive separation from God. For Paul, sin is the twin of death.

Paul's main interests are Adam and Jesus, whom he views as contrasts. Each one worked a change in the world. Adam unleashed an active hostile force (sin) that had the power to cause definitive alienation from God (death), the source of all life. The force (sin) was accepted and ratified by all individuals who personally committed misdeeds (v. 12). In contrast, Jesus' redemptive death unleashed uprightness and life for all who accept (believe in or are loyal to) him. The tragedy of Adam's failure is offset by the magnificent fullness of Jesus' redemption.

The far-reaching consequences of Adam's disobedience are reported according to a rabbinic division of time into three periods. The first extended from Adam to Moses, during which time there was no law to disobey (v. 14). Yet Adam's transgression was so powerful that the death it caused (separation from God) dominated. During this period, all humanity lived in sin and subjection to death. The second period extended from Moses to the Messiah, during which the law occasioned many failures. The third period from the Messiah onward brought the gracious gift of Jesus the Messiah that resulted in acquittal or justification and, above all, life for all. Humanity in the image of the new Adam enjoys God's righteousness and "reigns in life."

> SIN REIGNED FROM ADAM UNTIL JESUS MESSIAH (THEN); JESUS' OBEDIENCE ENDED THAT REIGN AND INAUGURATED A NEW PERIOD OF GRACE (NOW).

Responding to the Text

It is important to note while Paul is talking about the reality that modern Christians term "original sin," that Paul never used that phrase. It originated with Augustine. The reality of the first creatures' sin and its universal damaging impact on all creation are a constant throughout history. However, with regard to the various aspects of this notion, there were significant differences in the tradition throughout history. It could be worthwhile to point that out.

ROMANS 6:1b-11 (RCL)

Interpreting the Text

In Romans 5–8 Paul highlights God's love and exhorts the believers living in Rome to "consider yourselves dead to sin and alive to God in Christ Jesus" (6:11). According to Paul, sin in the singular is not some sort of human failing. Rather, sin is more correctly understood as a force or a power that drives a person toward an almost unavoidable proneness to failure or to committing an evil deed. Mediterranean culture views human beings as subject to nature rather than as controlling it. In the Mediterranean understanding, nature includes an invisible world of powers and forces that mischievously, capriciously, or sometimes even with deliberate calculation interfere in human life and cause human beings to behave in ways that displease God. This world of power and forces is the context in which Paul understands sin.

According to Paul, the good news is that Jesus' death and resurrection have destroyed the effectiveness of this force or power called sin. Furthermore, baptism snatches believers from the power of this force and incorporates them into new life with God. This is something very real and very welcome to the Mediterranean way of thinking. While some people in this world use amulets, gestures, or incantations to ward off evil, believers through baptism are intimately united with the very One who has defeated the source of all evil. But people still fail and still commit sins. It is to this situation that Paul speaks when he exhorts his letter recipients thus: thanks to baptism our old self was crucified (v. 6) and we are now "alive to God in Christ Jesus" (v. 11). Therefore, we should live accordingly.

Responding to the Text

Understanding sin as a force or power is a useful balance to the understanding of individual, personal transgressions. The broader understanding helps to put the narrower one into a good perspective. Perhaps one might reflect upon strategies for constraining or weakening the force as a way of reducing individual, personal failures.

THE GOSPEL
MATTHEW 10:24-39 (RCL);
MATTHEW 10:(16-23), 24-33 (BCP);
MATTHEW 10:26-33 (RC)

Interpreting the Text

Privacy did not exist in ancient village life. Just as in the contemporary Middle East, minding everybody else's business is a major occupation. Crowds tracked Jesus down even when he sought out deserted places (Matt. 14:13). Village children were trained to spy out the secrets of other families while keeping the secrets of their own families intact. In this society, if people do not know what others are up to, they suspect that they must be up to no good. Surely they are plotting something damaging to everyone in the village. Jesus forbade his disciples from keeping the children away from him (Matt. 19:13-15) because he wanted everyone to know that he wasn't trying to hide anything.

Life in such a world is oppressive. For this reason, people in this culture resort to secrecy and deception in order to gain some breathing room. During the Festival of Booths, Jesus' disciples urge him to go to Jerusalem and seek honor from the crowds. Jesus replies, "I am not going to the festival" (John 7:8). Yet after his brothers left, he also went but *in secret* (John 7:10). Jesus' secretive behavior explains why the Jerusalem crowd was divided in their opinion about his reputation. Some said, "He is a good man," while others said, "No, he *is deceiving* the crowd" (John 7:12). Given the prevalence of secrecy and deception in this society, how could one ever believe another person?

People resorted to various strategies to persuade others that they were indeed telling the truth. One strategy was to call God as witness to the truth of one's statement. Ruth seeks to assure her mother-in-law, Naomi, that she truly intends to remain with her rather than return to her family by saying, "May the LORD do thus and so to me, and more as well, if even death parts me from you" (Ruth 1:17).

The fact that one of the commandments prohibits summoning God to witness a lie ("You shall not make wrongful use of the name of the LORD your God . . ."; Exod. 20:7) suggests that even oaths did not guarantee that truth was being told. Jesus' oft-repeated phrase in John's Gospel, "Amen, amen I say to you" (more appropriately translated "Truly, truly I say to you") is echoed in the contemporary Middle East by the oft repeated "Believe me!" The plea has a ring of exasperation in it.

Today's Gospel is good news indeed: God the patron will uncover everything that is covered and will reveal all secrets (Matt. 10:26). To enjoy these benefits, one had best acknowledge publicly that Jesus is God's favored broker (Matt. 10:32). Earlier in this Gospel (Matt. 6:1-18), Jesus criticized the Pharisees who drew attention to their fasting, almsgiving, and praying in order to be seen by others and thereby to win honor from the crowds. While the Pharisees behaved in culturally acceptable fashion, Jesus urges his disciples to do these same good deeds "in secret" (Matt. 6:1-18). Jesus' advice redefines honor, his culture's core value. The Pharisaic ostentatious practices of almsgiving, prayer, and fasting are normal and expected. They make a claim to honor and respect. In contrast, Jesus says that the honor bestowed by God is far superior to that which humans give. Do good deeds to gain honor from God rather than from human beings!

> TODAY'S GOSPEL IS GOOD NEWS INDEED: GOD THE PATRON WILL UNCOVER EVERYTHING THAT IS COVERED AND WILL REVEAL ALL SECRETS (MATT. 10:26).

Verses 34-39 (RCL) describe anticipated trouble from adversaries, in particular one's family of origin. Since this was the core social institution in this society, it demanded absolute loyalty. Associating with certain categories of undesirable people (a consequence of Jesus' call for inclusive table fellowship) would bring dire consequences in its wake as described here. Membership in Jesus groups would tear a family apart even beyond the family of origin to the in-laws. The Jesus group was to be a surrogate family to replace one's blood family.

Responding to the Text

On the one hand, the American press believes that citizens have "the right to know" many things. They are suspicious of secrecy, especially in government, and seek to reveal these secrets. On the other hand, Americans are concerned about all the personal information about them that has been gathered and stored by various organizations including the government. They want some personal information to remain forever secret. How will American believers react to God's revelation of all secrets?

> HOW WILL AMERICAN BELIEVERS REACT TO GOD'S REVELATION OF ALL SECRETS?

SIXTH SUNDAY AFTER PENTECOST

JUNE 26, 2005
THIRTEENTH SUNDAY IN ORDINARY TIME / PROPER 8

REVISED COMMON	EPISCOPAL (BCP)	ROMAN CATHOLIC
Gen. 22:1-14	Isa. 2:10-17	2 Kings 4:8-11, 14-16a
or Jer. 28:5-9		
Psalm 13	Ps. 89:1-18	Ps. 89:2-3, 16-17, 18-19
or Ps. 89:1-4, 15-18	or 89:1-4, 15-18	
Rom. 6:12-23	Rom. 6:3-11	Rom. 6:3-4, 8-11
Matt. 10:40-42	Matt. 10:34-42	Matt. 10:37-42

FIRST READING

GENESIS 22:1-14 (RCL)

Interpreting the Text

In the Mediterranean world of antiquity, when a boy reached the age of puberty, he was forcefully and unceremoniously pushed out of the women's world in which he was raised with minimal male presence or influence. Bar mitzvah dates only to the Talmud (sixth century C.E.). The boy would now have to take his proper, hierarchically determined place in the male world. This shocking experience caused him to run back to the women, who continued to expel him from their company. Having had little contact with men to this point, the boy experienced a gender-identity crisis. What did it mean to be a man? How should a man behave?

In Mediterranean culture, males distinguish themselves by two skills: an ability to bear physical pain without flinching or crying (recall the Faithful-Servant Songs in Isaiah), and a mastery of language (think of Jesus' use of parables). When adolescent boys enter the men's world, fathers initiate their sons into bearing pain without complaint. Later the grown sons initiate their children into bearing pain in the same way. Proverbs (13:24; 19:18; 22:15; 23:13-14; 29:15, 17) and Ben Sira (30:1-13) contain more than one exhortation to fathers to physically punish their son if they hope that he will grow up to be an honorable adult.

These notions help a Western reader understand the story of a surprisingly docile Isaac in the face of a terrifying ordeal about to be dealt to him by his father.

One contemporary author of Mediterranean ancestry expresses this cultural ideal thus: "In a fight, I would never give up or say 'enough,' even though the other were killing me. I would try to go to my death, smiling. That is what we mean by being 'macho'" (Oscar Lewis, *Children of Sanchez*). Isaac may not have been smiling as he faced death, but an American believer wonders why he didn't overpower his father or simply run away.

Child sacrifice in the Bible is reported in 2 Kings 3:27; Jer. 7:31; and Ezek. 16:20, but it is forbidden in Exod. 13:15; Deut. 12:29-31; and 1 Kings 16:34. It is possible that the Isaac story represents an earlier stage of tradition that legitimated the substitution of an animal for child sacrifice. Some scholars think that the present version of the story suggests (in v. 5) that Abraham recognized that this was only a test of his loyalty to God. He tells the servant: "I and the boy will return. . . ." It is more probable that Abraham resorted to deceit with his servant to hide God's command and his determination to obey it. Even though frightened and likely confused, Abraham and the boy remained faithfully obedient. God was satisfied with Abraham's willingness. Isaac did not actually have to be sacrificed after all.

> IT IS LEGITIMATE TO ASK HOW FAR OBEDIENCE SHOULD GO. IS IT EVER AN EXCUSE TO SAY, "WE WERE JUST FOLLOWING ORDERS," EVEN IF ONE THINKS THE ORDERS CAME FROM GOD?

Responding to the Text

Social scientists caution about using the word "abuse." Abuse in one culture is often a virtue in another. One needs to be careful of cultural imperialism. The key ideas in this passage are Abraham's obedience to God and Isaac's obedience to Abraham. Yet it is legitimate to ask how far obedience should go. Is it ever an excuse to say, "We were just following orders," even if one thinks the orders came from God?

JEREMIAH 28:5-9 (RCL, alt.)

Interpreting the Text

In Jeremiah 27–28, two prophets, Jeremiah and Hananiah, have a face-off. True to form, Jeremiah preaches bad news that is equivalent to treason. His message is that God intends that Judah will be defeated by Babylon and be taken into exile. They should not resist it. Hananiah preaches the opposite. The problem is complex. To begin with, the Hebrew language did not have a word for "false prophet." In the Hebrew Bible, both Jeremiah and his opponent, Hananiah, are called "prophet," that is, a spokesperson for God's will in the here and now. Faced with conflicting messages presumably from God given by two prophets, how is a listener to decide on authenticity?

Jeremiah's argument is that, among predecessor prophets, messages from God were generally bad news: "war, famine, and pestilence against many countries and great kingdoms" (v. 8). As for peace? Only when the prophet's message is confirmed or verified can one be certain that the LORD truly sent that prophet. This, of course, simply reiterates the Deuteronomic opinion. God tells Moses that if the event announced in the name of God by the prophet "does not take place or prove true," it's not God's message (Deut. 18:20-22). The prophet who presumes to speak in God's name something that God has not communicated shall die (Deut. 18:20). If *listeners* would die before the event took place, they would never know for certain whether it was an authentic word from God or not. In the face-off between Jeremiah and Hananiah, the latter prophet died in the same year after Jeremiah exposed him as a fraud (Jer. 28:17).

Responding to the Text

Determining who speaks authentically for God or in the name of God is notoriously difficult. It is no easier in the contemporary world than it was in the past or has ever been. One constant in God's messages (whether those of Jeremiah or of Jesus in today's Gospel) is that they are almost always not what one expected, nor even what one would want to hear. Have modern believers contributed any new insights to the task of evaluating those who claim to speak for God?

HAVE MODERN BELIEVERS CONTRIBUTED ANY NEW INSIGHTS TO THE TASK OF EVALUATING THOSE WHO CLAIM TO SPEAK FOR GOD?

ISAIAH 2:10-17 (BCP)

In these verses the prophet announces that God will remove the two major obstacles to the divine plan as announced in vv. 2-4: human pride and haughtiness. Judah thought of itself in much too elevated a manner. Yahweh the LORD of hosts will rise up and put these people into their proper places. Notice the tenfold occurrence of "against" (vv. 12-16). God is opposed to all attempts at autonomy and self-sufficiency that remove life from divine dominion.

IGNORING GOD OR INTERPRETING APPARENT HUMAN SUCCESS AS UNCONNECTED TO DIVINE ASSISTANCE IS DISASTROUS.

With God everything is possible. Ignoring God or interpreting apparent human success as unconnected to divine assistance is disastrous. To the wise, a prophetic word is sufficient.

Interpreting the Text

"Whoever welcomes a prophet in the name of a prophet will receive a prophet's reward" (Matt. 10:41a). Was Jesus thinking of this report in Kings? The barren woman of Shunem insists that Elisha become a regular guest. In reciprocity, Elisha, "the holy man of God," intercedes with the deity to make her conceive and give birth within the year. The woman is designated as "a wealthy woman," but she does not seem to be independently wealthy. The fact that her husband has servants (v. 22) suggests this. Still the woman, who recognized Elisha as "a holy man of God," pressed him to be a guest at their home. She prepared special lodging for him.

A "holy man of God" is a type of person found in every culture. Such a person is presumed to have facile and direct access to the deity. Thus is a holy man capable of brokering favors from the deity to those who seek them. Holy persons (men and women) make contact with the realm of God in altered states of consciousness (ASCs). Sometimes they even journey to that realm (see, e.g., Rev. 4:1-2) to learn God's will. The narrator also attributes to Elisha great tenderness in responding to human need. Elisha's promise, "This time next year you will be fondling a baby son," contains an unusual expression (fondling or embracing) that is used to describe emotional reunions (Gen. 29:13; 33:4; 48:10) or sexual caressing (Eccl. 3:5). A woman could hardly hope for a better reward.

> WHO WOULDN'T ASPIRE TO BECOME A HOLY PERSON SUCH AS DESCRIBED BY CULTURAL ANTHROPOLOGISTS? WHO WOULDN'T WANT TO GAIN INTIMATE FAMILIARITY WITH GOD AND BEINGS IN GOD'S REALM?

Responding to the Text

Christians in general believe in a universal call to holiness from God. Everyone is invited; all are welcome. However, who wouldn't aspire to become a holy person such as described by cultural anthropologists? Who wouldn't want to gain intimate familiarity with God and beings in God's realm? A response to that call could possibly produce that special result, God willing.

RESPONSIVE READING
PSALM 13 (RCL)

This lament by an individual Israelite is brief and to the point. The petitioner laments "How long?" and in v. 5 proclaims his indebtedness for having been heard by God.

PSALM 89:1-4, 15-18 (RCL, alt.);
PSALM 89:1-18 or 89:1-4, 15-18 (BCP);
PSALM 89:2-3, 16-17, 18-19 (RC)

The phrase "steadfast love" in v. 2 (NRSV) refers to God's promises to David for an everlasting dynasty (v. 4). God would remain faithful to David, sustain good order in the world, and fulfill the covenant struck with Moses. When tragedy threatens that dynasty and creation itself seems about to collapse (vv. 5-14), the people lament and urge God to rescue them. This psalm is primarily a liturgical lament for a military defeat, but the lament could apply to any defeat. Moreover, the hope for rescue mirrored in these verses is rooted in God's fidelity to divine promises.

SECOND READING

ROMANS 6:12-23 (RCL);
ROMANS 6:3-11 (BCP);
ROMANS 6:3-4, 8-11 (RC)

Interpreting the Text

For a reflection on Rom. 6:1b-11, see the commentary on the RCL Second Reading assigned for the Fifth Sunday after Pentecost, above. It is relevant to the BCP and RC selections for this Sunday.

I turn now to Rom. 6:12-23. The imperatives in this section mark it as a fervent exhortation that flows naturally from the first eleven verses. Thinking that his premise is clear and convincing, Paul feels free to command his readers. His directive is: don't allow that alienating force (sin) to govern your manner of life (v. 12). Do not yield to the powerful desires, cravings, and intentions of your natural self. These pit you against God. Give yourselves over once and for always (literally) to slave service of God (v. 22) so that God might use you as an instrument of goodness.

> DO NOT YIELD TO THE POWERFUL DESIRES, CRAVINGS, AND INTENTIONS OF YOUR NATURAL SELF. THESE PIT YOU AGAINST GOD. GIVE YOURSELVES OVER ONCE AND FOR ALWAYS (LITERALLY) TO SLAVE SERVICE OF GOD (V. 22) SO THAT GOD MIGHT USE YOU AS AN INSTRUMENT OF GOODNESS.

What kind of freedom is a freedom for rendering "slave service"? This is something very different from the Western notion of freedom. Westerners understand themselves as free from external obstacles or restraints so that they may freely choose a personally determined goal. Such an idea is impossible for Paul to conceive. A person in his culture simply cannot live in total independence, subject to no one. To be free from the power of sin means to accept another master, namely, God (v. 22). This is why the baptized person (now a slave of God in Christ) cannot continue to be a slave of the power of sin.

Responding to the Text

To fashion a response to this reading will require an adjustment of one's understanding of freedom. Is it worth it?

THE GOSPEL
MATTHEW 10:40-42 (RCL);
MATTHEW 10:34-42 (BCP);
MATTHEW 10:37-42 (RC)

Interpreting the Text

These verses from Matthew report the serious family consequences of the choice to join a Jesus group (vv. 37-39) and the assistance one might expect as compensation for loss of family ties experienced (vv. 40-42). Family is the central social institution in the ancient and contemporary Mediterranean world, just as economics is in our world. Jesus' requirement that his followers should love him more than they love mother, father, son, or daughter is shocking not only to his first-century listeners (v. 37) but also to contemporary Western believers.

The ancient Middle Eastern family was very large and quite extended. The basic family consisted of a father (and mother) and the sons, single and married, with their entire families living in one place. Daughters lived there only until marriage, when they moved to their husband's patriarchal household. The ideal marriage partner was a patrilateral parallel cousin (father's brother's daughter), a practice that bound this close-knit family even closer! The resultant mentality of such a practice is "our family" against "everyone else."

> FAMILY IS THE CENTRAL SOCIAL INSTITUTION IN THE ANCIENT AND CONTEMPORARY MEDITERRANEAN WORLD, JUST AS ECONOMICS IS IN OUR WORLD. JESUS' REQUIREMENT THAT HIS FOLLOWERS SHOULD LOVE HIM MORE THAN THEY LOVE MOTHER, FATHER, SON, OR DAUGHTER IS SHOCKING NOT ONLY TO HIS FIRST-CENTURY LISTENERS (V. 37) BUT ALSO TO CONTEMPORARY WESTERN BELIEVERS.

It is unthinkable to marry anyone other than a relative. The "prodigal son" (Luke 15:11-32) who severed ties with his family committed the equivalent of social suicide. Outside the family, no one can be trusted, no one will help you, as that renegade son quickly learned when his funds ran out. A person who leaves the family not only gives up the basic claim to honor and status but also loses all of the family's economic, religious, educational, and social connections as well. Perhaps most disastrous of all consequences is loss of a connection to the land. These are all serious and life-threatening losses. They are what Jesus had in mind when he spoke of "taking up one's cross" and "losing one's life for my sake" (vv. 38-39).

Did he offer anything in exchange? Yes. He established his own company of followers as a "replacement" family, a new gathering of people linked not by blood-ties but by bonds of commitment to Jesus. This is what Matthew portrays throughout his Gospel. Specifically, Jesus reminds his Mediterranean listeners of another basic social institution in their culture intended to make up for the separation from one's family, namely, hospitality. By definition, hospitality in the Middle East is extended almost exclusively by men and almost exclusively to total strangers. (The care one extends to relatives is called "steadfast loving-kindness.")

Hospitality provides safe passage for a large family, like that of Abraham (see Gen. 12:16), or smaller groups, like Lot's visitors (Genesis 19), through hostile territory, that is, regions where they had no kinfolk. Jesus exhorts new communities of followers to practice hospitality toward each other in order to make up for the loss of family advantage (vv. 40-43). Whereas in Middle Eastern culture the reward for hospitality was largely the honor that accrued to one who extended it, Jesus connects the practice of hospitality among nonrelated believers to a reward that God will personally give. These concluding verses also return attention to missionaries (just as at the beginning of Matthew 10). The prophet, holy person, and others are considered to be sent by Jesus on a mission. Whoever receives them receives Jesus as well and honors the Father who sent Jesus.

Responding to the Text

To appreciate the shock of this reading, one needs to appreciate the notion of collectivistic personality that characterizes the Middle East. In that culture, persons are embedded in groups, mainly family, and derive their identity and support from those groups. Middle Eastern culture is highly integrating. In contrast, Western culture holds a set of isolating values rooted in individualism and individualistic personalities. Making this Middle Eastern text relevant to non–Middle Eastern cultural contexts will challenge preachers and their listeners.

SEVENTH SUNDAY AFTER PENTECOST

JULY 3, 2005
FOURTEENTH SUNDAY IN ORDINARY TIME / PROPER 9

REVISED COMMON	EPISCOPAL (BCP)	ROMAN CATHOLIC
Gen. 24:34-38, 42-49, 58-67 or Zech. 9:9-12	Zech. 9:9-12	Zech. 9:9-10
Ps. 45:10-17 or Song of Sol. 2:8-13 or Ps. 145:8-14	Psalm 145 or 145:8-14	Ps. 145:1-2, 8-9, 10-11, 13-14
Rom. 7:15-25a	Rom. 7:21—8:6	Rom. 8:9, 11-13
Matt. 11:16-19, 25-30	Matt. 11:25-30	Matt. 11:25-30

FIRST READING
GENESIS 24:34-38, 42-49, 58-67 (RCL)

Interpreting the Text

The architects of the lectionary have unwittingly and regrettably omitted key verse(s) for understanding this recomposed reading. All Middle Easterners know that the best way to receive a favor is to get yourself invited to a meal, then refuse to eat until the host grants the favor. Abraham's servant succeeds in obtaining hospitality from Lot but, when the meal is served, he says, "I will not eat until I have told my errand" (v. 33, omitted in today's reading). Lot is helpless and must listen. The servant recounts Abraham's charge to find a wife for his son, the servant's bargain with God, his meeting with Rebekah, his recognition that she is the ideal partner for Isaac, and that all of this is "of God." Then he waits for the decision so that he will know what to do next (v. 49). Laban and Bethuel also recognize that the entire happening is of God, and they agree. Then the servant and his entourage eat (v. 54, omitted in today's reading). Verses 33 and 54 are crucial markers in the entire pericope, because it is the servant's manipulation of the process of hospitality that helps him to attain the favor he needs.

Moreover, the narrator of this story three times assures the reader that Rebekah is truly the appropriate and ideal marriage partner for Isaac (vv. 15, 24, 47). In each passage, she is clearly identified as a patrilateral parallel cousin. Endogamous marriages were the pattern in the patriarchal period.

Responding to the Text

One can only marvel at how adeptly God works within the structure of a specific culture to realize the divine intention. How does God work within Western culture?

ZECHARIAH 9:9-12 (BCP; RCL, alt.); ZECHARIAH 9:9-10 (RC)

Interpreting the Text

It is practically impossible to determine the specific historical context for Zechariah 9–14, though it is certainly later than first Zechariah (about 520–518 B.C.E.). This is a period of instability in the Judean community. People cannot help themselves. God must personally rescue them. In this context, God appears as a Divine Warrior. (The preferable translation is not, "he will cut off" [LXX], but rather, "I, Yahweh, shall banish" [MT]). Judah is the bow and Ephraim the arrow (9:13-14) with which God will vanquish neighboring Phoenicia, Syria, and Philistia. God will also destroy the instruments of war (chariots, war-horses, battle bow, etc.). The king whom Yahweh will establish will be peaceable. Riding a donkey signals the peaceful intent of the rider (see Gen. 49:11; 1 Kings 1:33). The horse was an animal symbolizing pomp and used during invasion and war (see Exod. 14:9; Zech. 1:7-11).

The word "meek" appears to link this First Reading with the Gospel (Matt. 11:25-30). God the victorious Warrior King does not "lord it over others," neither does he boast. Quite in line with Mediterranean culture, the humble person (v. 9) takes one step behind his rightful place so that others can elevate him to his proper station. The ideal human king appointed by Yahweh will be humble, as Yahweh is humble. He will be mindful of his limitations, for it is indeed the Divine Warrior who saved and appointed him.

> THE WORD "MEEK" APPEARS TO LINK THIS FIRST READING WITH THE GOSPEL (MATT. 11:25-30).

Responding to the Text

The Mediterranean cultural context of this reading offers the preacher and worshipers an opportunity to understand Jesus' invitation to learn of him who is meek and humble of heart. How is it possible for a person who makes a whip of cords and causes a disturbance in the temple to describe himself as "meek and humble of heart?"

PSALM 45:10-17 (RCL)

The interpretation of this royal psalm has varied over the centuries. It was probably composed originally for a royal wedding, hence vv. 10-15 acclaim the bride while vv. 16-17 address the king/groom. Subsequently, it was used to describe the mystical union between God and Israel and between the Christ and his church.

SONG OF SOLOMON 2:8-13 (RCL, alt.)

Though it sounds like the words of her lover, these verses represent the beloved's reminiscence of his invitation to her. It also represents her memory of the visit she had evoked. The liturgy adapts the mutual yearning and desire between lovers expressed in these verses to the relationship between God and God's beloved people as well as Jesus and his followers.

PSALM 145 (BCP);
PSALM 145:8-14 (RCL; BCP, alt.);
PSALM 145:1-2, 8-9, 10-11, 13-14 (RC)

This alphabetical psalm of praise highlights God's royal power and status. After the introduction (vv. 1-2), the psalmist lauds God's grandeur (vv. 3-6), goodness (vv. 7-10), kingdom (vv. 11-13), and divine providential care (vv. 14-20). The psalmist's sentiments link the "humble" Warrior King of Zechariah's verses with the "meek and gentle" Jesus of Matthew's verses.

SECOND READING
ROMANS 7:15-25a (RCL);
ROMANS 7:21—8:6 (BCP);
ROMANS 8:9, 11-13 (RC)

Interpreting the Text

After reflecting on union with Christ (Romans 5) and the resulting liberation from sin and death (Romans 6), Paul completes his discussion of Christian freedom with yet another explanation of how believers are freed from the Torah, understood as law. In vv. 14-20, Paul describes the conflict that goes on within a person, but from an Israelite perspective. Tradition taught that there are two drives or urges within each person: a good one and a bad one. They are constantly at war with one another. The Torah (law) is from God's sphere, the "spiritual," and stimulates the good drive. However, experience shows that the "flesh" prevails, that is, the natural self, that dimension of the human person that reverberates with the bad drives or urges. It is the natural playground for the force of sin. Sin is the culprit, not the law (v. 20). The inmost self or mind desires what God wants; the law of sin prompts something else. The answer to Paul's anguished cry, "Who will rescue me from this body of death?" (v. 24) will come in the next chapter.

Chapter 8 of Romans is the climax of the epistle to this point. As Romans 7:7-12 described Paul at the mercy of a force that is not of God, so Romans 8:1-17 describes the workings of God's Spirit unto salvation. Thus, the liberator who will rescue Paul (and all believers) is the Spirit. (This word occurs twenty-nine times in this chapter, though up until this point it has occurred only five times in the letter). The believer comes into contact with this force by living in union with Christ, a union that was initiated in baptism. The person guided by this life-giving Spirit will enjoy both life and peace. Paul uses various descriptions of this Spirit (vv.

THE INDWELLING SPIRIT OF GOD WHO RAISED JESUS FROM THE DEAD WILL ALSO RAISE BELIEVERS IN THE RESURRECTION. FOR THIS WE ARE IN GREAT DEBT TO THE SPIRIT.

9-11): Spirit of God, Spirit of Christ, Christ. All of them express the multifaceted reality of the Christian experience of sharing in divine life. In the end, the indwelling Spirit of God who raised Jesus from the dead will also raise believers in the resurrection. For this we are in great debt to the Spirit.

Responding to the Text

The two drives in the Israelite tradition offer contemporary believers a perspective from which to judge human experiences on a national and global level. To which drive are people responding? Which people, citizens or leaders, give evidence of following the Spirit?

THE GOSPEL
MATTHEW 11:16-19, 25-30 (RCL);
MATTHEW 11:25-30 (BCP, RC)

Interpreting the Text

Verses 16-19 reflect a key Mediterranean cultural value, namely, spontaneity or acting without considering the consequences. It is the exact opposite of the Western preference for planned activity, calculated for a purpose in hopes of tallying and displaying one's achievements. The Mediterranean preference is to respond spontaneously to a cue, just as Mediterranean children respond to cues for specific games: happy games or sad ones. Jesus then chides his listeners for behaving like obstinate children. They refuse to respond to the cue. John gave the cue for penance and asceticism, and he was accused of having a demon. Jesus partied heartily and was accused of being a glutton and drunkard. Hidden in this charge, however, is a serious matter. According to Deut. 21:20, that phrase (glutton and drunkard) describes a stubborn and rebellious son. Was this factual gossip about Jesus' relationship with his family? Or was it calumny?

Jesus' reply to this charge can be found in vv. 25-30. A literal translation of v. 27 makes the familiar proverb stand out all the more: "No one knows a son except a father, and no one knows a father except a son and anyone to whom a son elects to disclose him." In Western culture, the corresponding phrase is: "Like father, like son."

Jesus reminds his audience that his father is like a Mediterranean patron, a godfather. This is the meaning of the title "Father, Lord of heaven and earth," which indicates that Jesus' father is truly in charge of human existence, of all creation. Jesus is a broker for God. Jesus mediates between the patron and the clients. In the Mediterranean world, a patron is someone who freely selects clients and then decides to treat the clients "as if" they are family. Another word for this is "favoritism." A patron plays favorites.

Who are God's "favorites?" Not literally infants but rather the simple or powerless people, those unable to do or obtain anything for themselves, are God's favorites. Children in the ancient Middle East were the weakest and most vulnerable members of society. They had little status within the community or family and, until the age of maturity, the child was considered equal to a slave. In a famine, the elders would be fed before the children.

> WHO ARE GOD'S "FAVORITES?" NOT LITERALLY INFANTS BUT RATHER THE SIMPLE OR POWERLESS PEOPLE, THOSE UNABLE TO DO OR OBTAIN ANYTHING FOR THEMSELVES, ARE GOD'S FAVORITES.

Jesus contrasts these "powerless" ones with the "wise" and the "intelligent." These latter categories of people are much more capable of looking after their own destiny than infants are. In fact, these categories might have the means to be patrons themselves. It would be easy for them, like the greedy farmer with the bumper crop (Luke 12:16-21), to refuse to be patrons and hoard their surplus for their own purposes. Certainly one group of wise and intelligent people Jesus had in mind was the Pharisees.

This image provides Jesus with a natural segue to the topic of "yoke," a word used metaphorically to describe those things that control the lives of people. Peasants always had a yoke. Their lives as tenant farmers were governed by the wills and whims of the landowners. Their lives as rustic folk whose subsistence means allowed them to live only from day to day were controlled by religious leaders who grew fat on tithes that they hoarded in the temple instead of redistributing them to the needy. In the village setting, Pharisees laid the yoke of their 613 commandments upon their followers and others who sought their advice about how to please God. Israelites who recited and lived according to Deut. 6:4ff., "Hear, O Israel: The LORD is our God, the LORD alone. You shall love the LORD your God with all your heart . . ." knew that reciting this prayer expressed a willingness to "bear the yoke of the reign of God." Having offered insight into the nature of God the patron as one who favors the powerless (infants), Jesus the broker invites his peasant listeners to "learn from me; I am your model."

Jesus' invitation echoes that offered by Wisdom in Sirach (51:23, 26): "Draw near to me, you who are uneducated, and lodge in the house of instruction. . . . Put your neck under her yoke, and let your souls receive instruction." Jesus teaches and demonstrates a way of life, a "yoke," that differs markedly from the one other Judean leaders taught. He promises a yoke that is easy and a burden that is light (v. 30). The peasants found this enormously appealing.

Responding to the Text

Modern believers must realize that the Pharisees are not portrayed fairly in the Gospels. Still, no one would deny that their arrogance, pride, and play-acting often cast a shadow on the wise instruction they offered. Modern reformers and spiritual leaders could well take a lesson from Jesus' principal challengers. Spiritual elitism repels many more than it attracts. The best guides are those who practice what they preach.

EIGHTH SUNDAY AFTER PENTECOST

July 10, 2005
Fifteenth Sunday in Ordinary Time / Proper 10

Revised Common	Episcopal (BCP)	Roman Catholic
Gen. 25:19-34	Isa. 55:1-5, 10-13	Isa. 55:10-11
or Isa. 55:10-13		
Psalm 119:105-12	Psalm 65 or 65:9-14	Psalm 65:10, 11, 12-13, 14
or Ps. 65:(1-8) 9-13		
Rom. 8:1-11	Rom. 8:9-17	Rom. 8:18-23
Matt. 13:1-9, 18-23	Matt. 13:1-9, 18-23	Matt. 13:1-23 or 13:1-9

FIRST READING
GENESIS 25:19-34 (RCL)

Interpreting the Text

God's response to Rebekah's inquiry about her pregnancy associates the male twins she is carrying with two peoples (anachronistically translated as "nation" in the NRSV and elsewhere; only after the eighteenth and nineteenth centuries is that word appropriate): Edom (Esau) and Israel (Jacob). The fulfillment of part of this oracle wouldn't occur for almost a millennium, when David (the younger = Israelites) subjugates the Edomites (the older): "all the Edomites became David's servants" (2 Sam. 8:14). The oracle thus reveals three things to Rebekah: she is carrying two peoples, her sons are designated as the eponymous ancestors of these peoples, and the older son will serve the younger. All she wanted to know from God was whether the pain of her pregnancy was worth it.

> CONTEMPORARY PREACHERS AND WORSHIPERS MUST BE CAREFUL NOT TO LOOK ASKANCE AT THE OBVIOUS MISCHIEF, INDEED INJUSTICE, IN THIS STORY. THE TALE IS ABOUT GOD AND HOW GOD GOES ABOUT REALIZING THE DIVINE PLAN.

The boys are contrasts: Esau is an outdoor type, a hunter; Jacob is a "wholesome [NRSV, "quiet"] man," a homebody, a domesticated male. Their parents unwisely play favorites: Isaac favors Esau, perhaps because of his love of venison; Rebekah prefers Jacob, but there is no hint of explanation for her preference. Esau demonstrates poor judgment, to say the least, when he willingly and quickly relinquishes his birthright to allay his exaggerated hunger. That he does it with an oath demonstrates that flaw very well (v. 32). Jacob shows himself to be aggressive and domineering. He takes charge of the situation; he knows what he wants, and he gets it.

Responding to the Text

Contemporary preachers and worshipers must be careful not to look askance at the obvious mischief, indeed injustice, in this story. The tale is about God and how God goes about realizing the divine plan. While God determined the rights of the firstborn (e.g., Deut. 21:15-17), God frequently favors a son other than the firstborn (Abel over Cain, Isaac over Ishmael). Why does God so often appear to ignore the divine arrangements?

ISAIAH 55:10-13 (RCL, alt.);
ISAIAH 55:1-5, 10-13 (BCP);
ISAIAH 55:10-11 (RC)

Interpreting the Text

Chapter 55 is the epilogue to Second Isaiah's entire work (40:1—55:13). In vv. 1-5 (BCP), God invites people to a banquet that provides not only food and life but personal fellowship with the deity. All human beings must eat to live, but God offers something more. God presents an opportunity for establishing and solidifying an intimate bond between all who share in the banquet and in divine companionship. Three times in these brief verses God exhorts people to listen: "listen carefully to me," "incline your ear," "listen." There is more to this banquet than physical nourishment. Second Isaiah plays on two meanings of the word "live" (v. 3), thus illustrating a common theme of the Hebrew scriptures. God gives life by providing nourishment and restores authentic meaning to life by extending to those at the table an opportunity for intimate friendship with the deity, but only if these diners will listen. The covenant that God makes with the chosen people will draw others to them, because God has glorified them.

> GOD'S WORD IS MYSTERIOUS, AN INVISIBLE FORCE THAT STILL BAFFLES CONTEMPORARY BELIEVERS. THE WORD HAS IMMANENT FORCE, SINCE IT SPRINGS FROM GOD'S INNERMOST RECESSES AND REACHES INTO THE VERY DEPTHS OF NATURE AND HUMANKIND.

Verses 10-13 describe the power of God's creative word. Just as the rain-evaporation-condensation-rain cycle in nature produces new life, new growth, and new seeds, so God's word proves to be similarly effective. God's word is mysterious, an invisible force that still baffles contemporary believers. The word has immanent force, since it springs from God's innermost recesses and reaches into the very depths of nature and humankind. Echoes of this word reverberate beyond Israel through all of creation, producing beneficial effects for all of humankind. The infallible and abundant result of God's word is truly amazing. Second Isaiah concludes by repeating the exodus theme (vv. 12-13). The re-establishment of God's chosen people will be an everlasting sign of divine love.

Responding to the Text

The motif of listening and responding to God's word surely binds this reading to the Gospel for today.

RESPONSIVE READING
PSALM 119:105-12 (RCL)

Psalm 119 is an acrostic (alphabetical) psalm in a class by itself. It praises the Torah, God's law, and the joys found in observing it completely and faithfully. Today's verses refer to God's law as God's word, that is, God's self-disclosing speech that also reveals the divine will for those who love God. Verse 115 masterfully bridges the reflections of Second Isaiah with the Gospel parable.

PSALM 65:(1-8) 9-13 (RCL, alt.);
PSALM 65 or 65:9-14 (BCP);
PSALM 65:10, 11, 12-13, 14 (RC)

A prayer of thanksgiving, Psalm 65 has a clear structure: vv. 1-4, God hears prayers and forgives sin; vv. 5-8, the creator God overcomes chaos and sets the universe in secure peace; vv. 9-13, God the giver of rain makes the earth fertile. The verses chosen for today thank God for the abundant winter rains, which have made the earth bear abundant fruit. The anthropomorphic imagery of the psalm has God walking on the earth, breaking up its clods, and showering it with rain. Indeed, God's chariot tracks (v. 11 [NAB v. 12]; see also 2 Kings 2:1-12; Ps. 69:9) now run full of water. The result is an abundant harvest.

SECOND READING
ROMANS 8:1-11 (RCL);
ROMANS 8:9-17 (BCP);
ROMANS 8:18-23 (RC)

Interpreting the Text

For Rom. 8:1-11 (RCL) consult the comments for the Roman Catholic lection for the Seventh Sunday after Pentecost, above. In Rom. 8:9-17, we encounter yet another set of contrasting words that Paul uses to discuss the human condition: flesh and spirit. In the Israelite tradition, human beings were pulled in two different directions or ways by different spirits: good ones and evil ones. The question is, which spirit will be lord over a person? The reader can appreciate the urgency with which Paul exhorts the letter recipients to live by the Spirit.

A very important consequence of being shaped by the Spirit is that one becomes a true child of God. Though this is the first time this concept appears in this letter, it would not catch Paul's audience by surprise. The notion was widely accepted in the ancient world even outside Judaism. In his speech to the Athenians (Acts 17:28), Paul quotes Aratus of Soli, a third-century B.C.E. poet from Cilicia: "For we too are his offspring." In Judaism, Israel

> THE SPIRIT OR FORCE WE HAVE RECEIVED, HOWEVER, IS NOT ONE THAT WOULD CAST US BACK INTO FEAR, EVEN A REVERENTIAL FEAR. RATHER, THIS SPIRIT SAYS WE ARE DEAR TO GOD, WE ARE GOD'S VERY OWN ADOPTED CHILDREN.

was understood as God's child or son (Exod. 4:22-23; Isa. 1:2-4; Hos. 1:10; et al.). The Spirit or force we have received, however, is not one that would cast us back into fear, even a reverential fear. Rather, this Spirit says we are dear to God; we are God's very own adopted children.

While adoption was a widespread legal practice in the Greco-Roman world, it was not a common practice in Israel. Some scholars deny that this option existed in Israel. For this reason, Paul is quite likely not drawing on this legal practice but rather on the notion that grew and developed out of Hos. 1:10 (Heb. 2:1). At one time, God said to Israel, "You are not my people," but later God said to them, You are "children of the living God." Earlier in this letter, Paul lists adoption as one of Israel's privileges (Rom. 9:4).

The idea is startling. As the focal social institution of the ancient Mediterranean world, kinship determined one's primary in-group. All others are the out-group. To be part of God's very own in-group is amazing. Further, not only does the Spirit make this intimate relationship with God possible, the same Spirit gives the ability to recognize and be aware of it. Such people can say with confidence and conviction, "Abba, Father."

The good news gets even better, for children can also inherit. Earlier (Rom. 4:13ff.) Paul noted that Abraham "would inherit the world" because he became right with God on the basis of faith rather than "through [works of] the law." Inheritance, however, entails an obligation to share in the death and resurrection of Jesus, too, for these were an integral part of his life.

Romans 8:18-23 continues Paul's development of the idea that the believer's life is destined for singular and unimaginable honor (glory). Paul now explains how material creation is also included. Because of Adam's sin (Gen. 3:15-17), material nature was cursed, subject to decay itself just like the human beings for whom it had been created. This solidarity in punishment also entails solidarity in redemption. So creation eagerly awaits and groans in labor pains until that final state of glory will be definitively restored.

This reflection has special cultural significance. In general, Mediterranean cultures of antiquity recognized that they had absolutely no control over material creation. They were subject to it; they had to suffer and endure it. Our ancestors in faith believed that because of Adam's sin, human beings had no control over nature, yet the redemption of Adam would include the redemption of material creation as well.

What is the basis for Paul's confidence? He draws insight from the notion of the firstfruits of a harvest. When offered to God, these firstfruits consecrated the entire harvest and became, as it were, down payment, pledge, or guarantee of what was still to come. The Spirit serves this purpose for believers. Since the believer is already son/child of God (Rom. 8:15), the full implementation of this status will include the redemption of the body (v. 23).

Responding to the Text

For anyone who had not been born into and lived as part of the Israelite tradition, Paul's impressive argumentation is quite likely not very impressive or convincing. This is probably as true for contemporary believers as it was for non-Israelites in the past. Paul's ministry was to fellow Israelites living as insignificant minorities in non-Israelite lands. A few non-Israelites were grafted "contrary to nature" into the cultivated olive tree, which is Israel (see Rom. 11:24). What are contemporary non-Israelite followers of Jesus to make of Paul's reasoning?

THE GOSPEL
MATTHEW 13:1-9, 18-23 (RCL, BCP);
MATTHEW 13:1-23 or 13:1-9 (RC)

Interpreting the Text

In the Middle East of antiquity and the present, people often say one thing and mean something else. This is particularly true of parables in the Bible. Jesus says one thing but means something else. His parables are not about fair wages, employer/employee relationships, farming, or any of the apparent topics. They are all about God. They tell what God is like, how God behaves.

In today's parable, the sower poses the first challenge to interpretation. In antiquity, sowing preceded plowing, but this sower is sloppy and wasteful. If the sower is a landowner, the peasant audience would despise him for wasting precious seed. If the sower is a tenant farmer or a day laborer, the peasants would sympathize with the careful sowing that ends up wasting seed anyway because conditions are so difficult.

The impossibly extravagant harvest gives a clue to the identity of the sower. A fourfold or fivefold return on sowing was the average in antiquity. Thirty, sixty, and a hundredfold boggles the imagination. If a wasteful landowner realized such a profit, Jesus' parable is hardly good news to the peasants, who made up 95 percent of his audience. But if the sower were a peasant, then the good news is that the crop will satisfy the landowner, provide seed for next year's sowing, pay all taxes, and still leave enough for the peasant to feed his family. Good news, indeed!

> HIS PARABLES ARE NOT ABOUT FAIR WAGERS, EMPLOYER/
> EMPLOYEE RELATIONSHIPS, FARMING, OR ANY OF THE
> APPARENT TOPICS. THEY ARE ALL ABOUT GOD. THEY TELL
> WHAT GOD IS LIKE, HOW GOD BEHAVES.

In addition, since it is clearly God and not human effort that produces this huge harvest, the "something other" or "something more" that every parable intends is now very clear. The scenario describes sowing and farming, but it really points to a loving and provident God who looks after needy peasants.

The parable reveals yet another dimension of peasant life in the first century. Jesus tells his disciples that parables are "in-group" or "insider" language (see vv. 10-16, lacking in the RCL and BCP lections). Normally, a person's in-group consisted of one's household (including servants and slaves), extended family, and friends. Everyone else, even in the same village, constituted the out-group. Yet the shape of each group was fluid and changed quite often. For example, if a village came under attack from outsiders, the entire village of otherwise distinct and competitive households—that is, a collection of out-groups—banded together as a new in-group.

Verses 18-23 are clearly an allegorical interpretation of the parable, something that is very rare among those who tell parables. Many scholars believe the interpretation was created by second-generation Jesus groups. To understand the interpretation, one needs to know how the nonintrospective people of the Bible judged others. The Deuteronomist acts as a reliable cultural informant in this regard. "The LORD does not see as mortals see; they look on the outward appearance, but the LORD looks on the heart" (1 Sam. 16:7). Our ancestors in faith viewed the human body, that is, the human person, from a purely external perspective as comprised of three zones symbolically interpreted. The mouth, ears, tongue, lips, etc. were the zone of self-expressive speech. The heart and eyes were the zone and center of emotion-fused thought. The hands, arms, legs, and feet were the zone of purposeful human activity. Thus, the point of the allegorical interpretation of the parable is that the person who engaged all three zones in response to the word (seed) was the one who produced a rich return on it.

Responding to the Text

Contemporary psychology is so rooted in Western culture that experts agree it is for all practical purposes useless in the non-Western world. This means that psychological interpretations of the Bible rooted in Western psychology run the risk of misunderstanding and misinterpreting the text. The Deuteronomist has done us a huge favor by pointing out a key element of Middle Eastern psychological perspective. How might the preacher and the worshiper draw insight from this reading and apply it to a distinctly different cultural situation?

NINTH SUNDAY
AFTER PENTECOST

July 17, 2005
Sixteenth Sunday in Ordinary Time / Proper 11

Revised Common	Episcopal (BCP)	Roman Catholic
Gen. 28:10-19a or Isa. 44:6-8 or Wisd. of Sol. 12:13, 16-19	Wisd. of Sol. 12:13, 16-19	Wisd. of Sol. 12:13, 16-19
Ps. 139:1-12, 23-24 or Ps. 86:11-17	Psalm 86 or 86:11-17	Ps. 86:5-6, 9-10, 15-16
Rom. 8:12-25	Rom. 8:18-25	Rom. 8:26-27
Matt. 13:24-30	Matt. 13:24-30, 36-43	Matt. 13:24-43 or 13:24-30

First Reading
GENESIS 28:10-19a (RCL)

Interpreting the Text

This story combines J (vv. 13, 16-17) with E elements (vv. 11-12, 17-18). Perhaps it was originally an etiology (v. 17) explaining the origin of Bethel, a place venerated in Canaan even before Israel's arrival. The heart of the story, however, is God's promises to Jacob as patriarch (vv. 13-15): land, offspring, and blessing to all the earth through him and his offspring. From this perspective, the story is a theophany or, to use social-scientific terminology, it is Jacob's encounter with God in an altered state of consciousness experience (ASC), a level of awareness different from ordinary, waking awareness. Fear (v. 17) is a typical response to an ASC experience in all cultures. The being who appears in an ASC usually allays the visionary's fear and identifies himself or herself. Here God allayed Jacob's fear ("I am with you," v. 15; the storyteller informs that reader that the LORD "stood

> THIS IS AN OPPORTUNITY FOR PREACHERS TO EXPLORE WITH LISTENERS HOW GOD ENCOUNTERS BELIEVERS IN THE MODERN WORLD AND HOW BELIEVERS MIGHT AUTHENTICATE THEIR EXPERIENCE.

beside him" (v. 13) and identified himself ("I am the LORD, the God of Abraham your father and the God of Isaac. . . ," v. 13).

When Jacob names this place "the gate of heaven (v. 17)," he recognizes that over this spot on earth is the hole in the sky through which beings from the realm of God can come to earth, and earth's inhabitants can travel to visit the realm of God. All cultures know of this hole, which ordinarily is located over the earthly abode of the god (in Israel, over the Jerusalem Temple). Of course, at this time God has no fixed abode among the Israelites. The staircase (preferable to ladder) on which beings from God's realm are ascending and descending proves that the hole is there. Jacob recognizes Bethel as a place for encountering God and beings from God's realm (v. 19).

Responding to the Text

While our ancestors in faith linked their experience of God to special places such as Bethel, we their descendants recall that Jesus said place would no longer be critical (John 4:23). This is an opportunity for preachers to explore with listeners how God encounters believers in the modern world and how believers might authenticate their experience.

WISDOM OF SOLOMON 12:13, 16-19 (RCL, alt.; BCP; RC)

Interpreting the Text

The literary genre of the book of Wisdom is a rhetorical exhortation (protreptic). This is similar to the formal, learned introductory lecture that scholars are expected to deliver when they assume a prominent appointment (e.g., an endowed chair) at a prestigious institution of higher learning. The entire book of Wisdom reflects amazing intellectual growth. It very likely represents the fruits of the lifelong reflections of a very serious thinker. The Israelite author was concerned that Greek thought was exerting too strong an influence upon young Israelites. They might be tempted to leave behind their traditions in favor of Greek philosophy.

THE VERSES APPOINTED FOR TODAY REFLECT ON THE TOLERATION AND MODERATION THAT GOD EXHIBITS IN THE EXERCISE OF DIVINE POWER. GOD TEMPERS POWER WITH MERCY AND DOES NOT USE IT AGAINST THE INNOCENT.

Therefore, writing sometime between 100 and 50 B.C.E., he sought to remind these young intellectuals of the relevance of traditional Judaic beliefs and principles which the sacred author was convinced could be compatible with Greek wisdom.

Today's verses are drawn from part three of this meticulously structured book (11:15—16:1a). This purpose of this section was to justify God's conduct toward all human sinfulness. In particular, the verses appointed for today reflect on the toleration and moderation that God exhibits in the exercise of divine power. God tempers power with mercy and does not use it against the innocent. This should serve as a lesson to all human beings to temper justice with mercy and thereby hope to obtain mercy from God. One possible link with the Gospel (Matt. 13:24-30) is that the sower (who in actuality is God) exhibits precisely the same kind of shrewd discernment described by the sage in this first reading.

Responding to the Text

God has left an example to human beings that "the righteous must be kind" (Wisd. 12:19). The wronged farmer in the Gospel did not take revenge but was instead kind toward his enemies. Is it possible to identify contemporary situations in which the righteous (or those who believe themselves to be so) can and should be kind toward enemies?

RESPONSIVE READING
PSALM 139:1-12, 23-24 (RCL)

This personal lament appears to have been composed by a poet who took offense at fellow Israelite apostasy and non-Israelite idolatry. The verses selected for today, however, are purely personal reflections by the psalmist. He hymns God's omniscience (vv. 4-6) and omnipresence (vv. 7-12) and concludes with a prayer that God lead the poet "in the way everlasting."

PSALM 86 (BCP);
PSALM 86:5-6, 9-10, 15-16 (RC);
PSALM 86:11-17 (RCL; BCP, alt.)

This postexilic personal lament weaves a tapestry of texts memorized from other parts of the Bible into a "new" psalm. In times of stress, one can easily recall these memorized passages that reassure the psalmist that the Lord is indeed "good and forgiving." The last stich of v. 16 helps us understand the psalmist's confidence: "save the son of your handmaid." A servant born in the house of his master was deemed more faithful and dependable (see Exod. 21:1ff.). His petitions stood a better chance of being heard expeditiously by the master. This psalm is a prayer well calculated to move God to pity, mercy, and forgiveness.

SECOND READING

ROMANS 8:12-25 (RCL);
ROMANS 8:18-25 (BCP);
ROMANS 8:26-27 (RC)

Interpreting the Text

In Rom. 8:24-27 (RC), Paul notes that three things persuade us of the greatness of the glory or intimate share in God's life that is the destiny of each believer: the testimony of creation (vv. 19-22), the conviction of believers (vv. 23-25), and the testimony of the Spirit (vv. 26-30). In saying that "we do not know how to pray as we ought" (v. 26), Paul seems to contradict what he said just a few verses earlier, namely, that the Spirit prompts us to pray with confidence, "Abba, my Father" (Rom. 8:15). It is possible that Paul offers a corrective here to "enthusiasm," namely, an exaggerated emphasis on the gifts of the Spirit. It is always possible to be overconfident. The truth is that, because of natural human shortcomings, the Spirit adds his intercessions to our inadequate expressions.

Responding to the Text

From a cultural perspective, it is important to notice Paul's indirect reference to God as "the one who searches the heart" (v. 27). Ancient Eastern Mediterranean culture was not only nonintrospective but anti-introspective. Human beings have no ability at all to peer into the inner workings of themselves or others. They can judge only by externals. God alone reads hearts (see 1 Sam. 16:7; 1 Kings 8:39; also Pss. 7:10; 17:3; 139:1). When the Gospels report that Jesus knew what others were thinking (e.g., Mark 2:8), the evangelists are presenting Jesus as an extraordinary Mediterranean human being who does something only God can do. For the evangelist's Mediterranean audience, this was more impressive than working mighty deeds, which, as Jesus himself intimated, many of their own kin were able to do (see Matt. 11:27). In the West, psychology holds a status almost as high as that of religion. People in Western cultures in general feel quite confident they can and do know what others are thinking and why. This is a major difference between ourselves and our ancestors in the faith, one that is evident throughout the Bible.

THE GOSPEL
MATTHEW 13:24-30 (RCL);
MATTHEW 13:24-30, 36-43 (BCP);
MATTHEW 13:24-43 or 13:24-30 (RC)

Interpreting the Text

The parable that opens today's Gospel reflects the agonistic character of Mediterranean society. This culture is conflict-oriented and hostile by nature. An enemy has sowed weeds among the wheat. The fact is mentioned without comment, but the audience understood perfectly. Birth into a family means not only inheriting that family's honor status and its friends but also inheriting that family's enemies. Families become enemies in the ancient world for many reasons, but the consequences are always the same. A state of "feuding" develops and persists over a long period of time. One never knows but must always suspect that a feuding enemy is seeking to "shame" one's family.

In this parable, the "shame" is planted soon after the wheat seeds are sown. However, it does not become full-blown shame until the weeds have matured to the point where they are clearly distinguishable from the wheat. Now the entire village discovers the shame along with the landowner, and they begin to laugh. They laugh even louder when the landowner instructs the servants to allow the weeds to grow alongside the wheat until harvest. The peasants expected retaliation and revenge. Instead, the landowner appears helpless and defeated by his enemies.

But appearances are deceiving. The landowner is shrewd as well as being a savvy farmer. He knows that the wheat is strong enough to tolerate the weeds' competition for nutrition and irrigation. After the harvest, the landowner will not only have grain for his barns, but he will also have extra, unanticipated fuel for his needs. Rather than shaming this landowner, the weed-strategy has backfired and shamed the enemy! The landowner and his servants have the last laugh.

Jesus' peasant audience recognized that this was not a lesson in agriculture. Recall that a parable means something entirely different from what it explicitly states. Perhaps Jesus offered a commentary on his culture's values. The "something other" or "something different" of this parable may well be the landowner's refusal to retaliate, to get even with the enemy. In a society dedicated to revenge, the landowner's success in winning the day by seeming to do nothing is a powerful lesson.

IN A SOCIETY DEDICATED TO REVENGE, THE LANDOWNER'S SUCCESS IN WINNING THE DAY BY SEEMING TO DO NOTHING IS A POWERFUL LESSON.

As with the parable of the sower (Matt. 13:1-23), so too with this parable Matthew reports an allegorical interpretation for the "in-group" (see vv. 36-43).

Second-generation Jesus groups favored allegory in their interpretation of Jesus' parables. This happened, in part, because many early believers no longer shared the peasant worldview or peasant experience. Matthew's community may well have been city people with precious little appreciation for the fine points of farming. Even so, the allegorical interpretation faithfully addresses other basic Mediterranean convictions, especially the overwhelming awareness by the majority of people that they had no control over their lives. They were at the mercy of otherworldly powers: God, the evil one, and the angels. That the righteous often suffered and the wicked often prospered was a common experience. The consolation for the righteous in these allegorically interpreted verses is that in the long run, "God will get" the wicked, and "they'll get theirs" in hell, of course. The righteous will "shine like the sun in the kingdom of their Father."

In vv. 31–33, Matthew's Jesus offers two additional parables that describe the forthcoming theocracy ("the kingdom of heaven") that Jesus announces. The mustard seed is actually a weed that most peasants would pull out. Perhaps the previous mention of weeds suggested this parable as a reasonable sequel. That, however, is not the point of this parable or its partner, the yeast that leavens the flour. Both parables are referring to an astounding expansion beyond the size of what one originally sees. Thus will it be with the forthcoming theocracy.

Responding to the Text

The confidence of the landowner that his grain will survive the effect of the weeds is worth pondering. A trust in goodness that is greater than the fear of wickedness could be a powerful weapon against rampant, senseless violence. The preacher might explain how it has previously worked in history and could work again if given a chance.

TENTH SUNDAY AFTER PENTECOST

<small>JULY 24, 2005</small>
<small>SEVENTEENTH SUNDAY IN ORDINARY TIME /</small>
<small>PROPER 12</small>

REVISED COMMON	EPISCOPAL (BCP)	ROMAN CATHOLIC
Gen. 29:15-28	1 Kings 3:5-12	1 Kings 3:5, 7-12
or 1 Kings 3:5-12		
Ps. 105:1-11, 45b	Ps. 119:121-36	Ps. 119:57, 72, 76-77,
or Psalm 128	or 119:129-36	127-28, 129-30
or Ps. 119: 129-36		
Rom. 8:26-39	Rom. 8:26-34	Rom. 8:28-30
Matt. 13:31-33, 44-52	Matt. 13:31-33, 44-49a	Matt. 13:44-52 or 13:44-46

Today's readings describe the benefits and promise of agreements or covenants made, for example, between people in relationship, and the depths of emotion such agreements may express. The passage in 1 Kings 3:5-12 describes God's ongoing relationship with David's son Solomon, and God's gift of understanding to him. Psalm128 expresses blessings offered through marriage. Each of Matthew's kingdom parables articulates Jesus' imaginative stories describing God's myriad and inexhaustible spread into creation. When human abilities fail to fathom the distance between humanity and God, the Spirit gives voice to human longings for connection in prayer, and Paul articulates at the end of Rom. 8:26-39 that nothing has ever or will ever divide creation from God's love.

FIRST READING
1 KINGS 3:5-12 (BCP; RCL, alt.);
1 KINGS 3:5, 7-12 (RC)

Interpreting the Text

What makes someone wise? Life experience? Age? According to Hesiod's *Theogony* 890, Zeus swallows his wife Métis (wisdom) as she is pregnant with Athene, thus preempting births of her children wiser than he. In so doing, Zeus has in effect become wise. Solomon's wisdom, on the other hand, according to

1 Kings 3:5-12, is a divine gift in response to his request of God. Both examples, however, clarify that men (and gods) must acquire wisdom from an external source. In fact, God is so pleased that Solomon has not made a request for victory over enemies that God promises riches and glory in addition. Once received, Solomon's gift proves beneficial to all as we see in the next story wherein the young king successfully determines (by threatening to saw the child in half) which of the two women is really the child's mother.

Responding to the Text

Solomon's famous wisdom not only gave rise to an entire corpus of wisdom texts in both Hebrew and Greek (Proverbs; Wisdom of Solomon), but his wisdom became legendary and attracted the attention of people near and far (Handel's oratorio *Solomon* included "The Arrival of the Queen of Sheba" to commemorate the visit of a queen of ancient Saba, modern Yemen, to see Solomon's wisdom for herself). Solomon's "listening (discerning) heart" enables him to demonstrate intuitive wisdom. Inventive scribes subsequently wrote different kinds of wisdom literature in his name: proverbs and maxims dependent on cause and effect arguments; stories like Job expressing theological wisdom; and writings like Qohelet (Ecclesiastes) containing skeptical wisdom. All wisdom, however, comes from God, and the reading reminds us that waiting on God is the prerequisite for wisdom and discernment.

> ALL WISDOM, HOWEVER, COMES FROM GOD, AND THE READING REMINDS US THAT WAITING ON GOD IS THE PREREQUISITE FOR WISDOM AND DISCERNMENT.

GENESIS 29:15-28 (RCL)

Interpreting the Text

In Gen. 27:41—28:5, Rebekah has arranged to protect Jacob from his brother's murderous wrath by persuading Isaac to command Jacob to seek a wife from among the family of his maternal uncle Laban in Haran. Rebekah's family has raised deceptive manipulation to an art form, and Jacob has inherited the trait. In this Sunday's text, Laban deceives Jacob by repaying his contracted seven years of service with the wrong sister for a bride, and Jacob agrees to work another seven years for the woman he loves, Rachel. Although Laban gives Rachel in marriage to Jacob only seven days after Jacob has married Leah, Jacob honors his contract for another seven years of work. Subsequently, in Gen. 30:25—31:16, Laban reneges on contracts concerning Jacob's compensation, which amounts to keeping Jacob in servitude. Jacob employs all his animal husbandry skills to protect his property rights, and the sisters repudiate association with their mendacious father in support of Jacob.

Thus Jacob both suffers and gains in the escape from his brother's justifiable wrath. Jacob, who has cheated Esau, becomes the mark for Laban's con games and, like Esau, Jacob consents at first to his own exploitation. But there the comparison ends, for the stakes are widely different: Esau traded his rights and inheritance for a meal; Jacob surrendered a few years of his life for the woman he loved, the establishment of his line, and the property to support them.

Responding to the Text

When we say we love someone, what exactly does that mean? What's at stake for us in our loving? How much are we willing to give of ourselves and our life to be with the person we say we love? Jacob worked fourteen years and suffered the burden and responsibility of a squinty, unattractive, and possibly unpleasant first wife in order to be with the woman he loved. He had no way to know how much depended on his persistence and honor in seeking the woman he loved: the rescue of his entire line through Joseph during the famine, and salvation through the line of Benjamin and David. Jacob went to extreme lengths to seek and secure the love of his life, and refused to be satisfied with anything less. We say we love many things as well as people; to what lengths are we willing to go to seek and find not only the person we can really love and live with all our lives, but also the work that is a passion for us, the vocation through which we can contribute to the world's salvation? In the words of Robert Frost's "Two Tramps in Mud Time":

> TO WHAT LENGTHS ARE WE WILLING TO GO TO SEEK AND FIND NOT ONLY THE PERSON WE CAN REALLY LOVE AND LIVE WITH ALL OUR LIVES, BUT ALSO THE WORK THAT IS A PASSION FOR US, THE VOCATION THROUGH WHICH WE CAN CONTRIBUTE TO THE WORLD'S SALVATION?

> Only where love and need are one
> And the work is play for mortal stakes
> Is the deed ever really done
> For Heaven and the future's stakes.

But what do we do when our own families betray us? The entire Jacob cycle is filled with intra-family deceptions and manipulations. We have seen Jacob the trickster, but here we see Jacob rising above the family system of deception. Following his vision of God at Bethel and God's declaration of commitment to Jacob's future family, Jacob here repays deception with honest labor and fraud with integrity. And God blesses the earth through Jacob.

PSALM 119:129-36 (RCL, alt.);
PSALM 119: 121-36 or 119:129-36 (BCP);
PSALM 119: 57, 72, 76-77, 127-28, 129-30 (RC)

Even greater than Jacob's love for Rachel is the psalmist's love for the observance of God's commandments expressed in this passage (for an extended discussion of Psalm 119, see Proper 18). Jacob received Rachel and Leah and significant property; the psalmist declares God's self to be his allotment (v. 57) and God's law preferable to megamillions in money (v. 72) or the most precious of materials (v. 127). The psalmist's only comfort is God's love, and his life depends on God's mercy (vv. 76-77). His eyes give out because he is looking so hard for God's salvation (v. 123); he is hyperventilating with love of the commandments (v. 131); he weeps to see God's law flouted (v. 136); he urges God to vindicate God's self (v. 126). The psalmist's relationship with God's commandments, which stand for God's very self in his thinking, can only be described in terms of the deepest intimacy. The psalmist is smitten; he is in love with God and therefore with God's law; everything that he is articulates or yearns to articulate that love. For him love of God's law is the meaning of life.

> THE PSALMIST IS SMITTEN; HE IS IN LOVE WITH GOD AND THEREFORE WITH GOD'S LAW; EVERYTHING THAT HE IS ARTICULATES OR YEARNS TO ARTICULATE THAT LOVE. FOR HIM LOVE OF GOD'S LAW IS THE MEANING OF LIFE.

PSALM 105:1-11, 45b (RCL)

This psalm of praise recalls the works of God done for the children of Abraham and Jacob and extols God's judgments, another way of describing God's law. The recitation of the acts of God serves to remind God as much as to remind the people of God, so that God will continue to remember who God's people are and act on their behalf, as implied in v. 9. Although it may seem unsophisticated and unnecessary to remind God of what God has done, God is only as real to us as our prayer life allows God to be, and reminding God of what God has done is a way by which we treat God as real. Should we only talk with God about what *we* have done? That would be boring, both to us and to God. We're never telling God anything God doesn't know already. Let us treat God as a real conversation partner whom

> GOD IS ONLY AS REAL TO US AS OUR PRAYER LIFE ALLOWS GOD TO BE, AND REMINDING GOD OF WHAT GOD HAS DONE IS A WAY BY WHICH WE TREAT GOD AS REAL.

we value. Let us confide in God, but let us first remind God, and ourselves, of what God has done and promised to do in our lives!

PSALM 128 (RCL, alt.)

The psalm opens with a beatitude on all who fear God and walk in God's ways. The specific rewards are described: enjoyment of the fruits of one's labors, happiness, prosperity, a fecund wife, and sturdy sons. A closing blessing invokes lifelong participation in the prosperity of Jerusalem and longevity accompanied by grandchildren.

No honest translation can finesse the patriarchal context and implications in this psalm. The faithfulness of the male yields rewards for the male in the continuation of the lineage of the male. Women constitute a blessing but do not qualify to receive blessings; daughters do not merit mention (despite being a necessary requisite for grandchildren). The psalm reflects and promotes archaic social structures now obsolete in many cultures and modified even in most patriarchal cultures.

SECOND READING
ROMANS 8:26-39 (RCL);
ROMANS 8:26-34 (BCP);
ROMANS 8:28-30 (RC)

Interpreting the Text

Luther thought that the entire chapter of Romans 8 should be written in letters of gold. These passages open with a discussion of the role of the Spirit as aiding us in our weakness, which Paul here defines as not knowing how to pray properly in the circumstances of suffering described in the previous verses. Never mind, says Paul, the Spirit prays fervently (*hyperentunchano*) with inarticulate sighs. The verb, frequently translated "intercedes," appears only here in the New Testament and is a form of the verb *entunchano*, which commonly means "to meet with," "entreat," or "converse with." In participle form in 2 Macc. 2:25; 6:12; and 15:39, it identifies those who read the book as though they were in conversation with it. Here it could be translated "entreats greatly," by contrast with the phrase in the next verse, *entunchano hyper*, which might be translated "entreats on behalf of/in place of" the saints. So it might be well to distance ourselves a little from the commonly understood meaning of "intercede" in Christian ascetic theology when thinking about this passage. This is the Spirit communicating with God as if in our place, not negotiating with God on our behalf (vv. 26-27).

In vv. 28-30, Paul piles on a crescendo of increasingly weighty descriptions of those who love God. They have been foreknown and predestined by God, they are brothers to God's Son, they are the called, they are the acquitted, they are the glorified—despite all appearances of being tried and troubled in this present time of difficulty, which will turn out to be all for the good.

God, says Paul in vv. 31-36, sacrificed his own Son for our sake and will not withhold any other good thing. God has acquitted us, and so there is no one who will dare to condemn us. Paul concludes with a version of his own creed: Christ has died, was raised, is at the right hand of God, and there entreats—*entunchano hyper*—in our defense.

Paul catalogs the difficulties he has experienced in his apostolic work and asserts that none of them can separate us from the love of Christ. Even among those things far beyond mere physical trials and tribulations—the very facts of being either dead or alive, the orders of unseen created beings like angels and powers, the rulers and authorities of this world, things that are or things that will be (the things that have been are already taken care of because we have been acquitted), things that are above the heavens or things that are under the earth (heaven and hell, respectively)—absolutely nothing can separate us from God's love for us that we experience in our Lord Jesus Christ (vv. 35-39). Not even, Paul implies with his citation from Psalm 44, if we forget God's name will God leave us to be separated from God's love.

Responding to the Text

If we are praying people—and we must be, if we aspire to any kind of relationship with God—then we know that when we look around this world we are often rendered speechless in our prayers. What exactly are we supposed to pray for? The authorities of this world, who are supposed to know something about what is going on and what should be done, say one thing one day and another the next. Scientific studies prove something today and disprove it tomorrow. Sometimes all we can do is groan and sigh. And it is enough, because our very inarticulateness, our awareness of the difficulty of prayer, bears witness to the indwelling of the Spirit within us—within *us!*—and to the miracle that God uses and works with even our inchoate longings for good.

For although we cannot know how, we do know that God can transmute anything into good, somehow. God does not merely rescue chestnuts from the fire; God manages to spin straw into gold—providing we are willing to give the straw to God. For what we find so hard to internalize is that everything and everyone is more than precious to God. Paul builds one image upon another of our worth to God: not only do we house within ourselves the praying Spirit of God, to God we are worth the gift of God's Son, we are the called, the justified, the glorified—

we are inconceivably valuable, priceless in the eyes of God. What radical transformations would occur in every parish if each of us could value ourselves and everyone else, every day and in every circumstance, with the worth that God has declared for us!

It is well worth looking at Psalm 44, which Paul quotes in v. 36, to understand the scriptural context out of which Paul asserts that nothing will ever separate us from God's love. Despite their faithfulness to God's covenant, God has permitted the people of Israel to be subjugated to their enemies, to be dispersed, and to be a laughingstock to the nations. The people are even in such dire physical and psychological straits, under "the shadow of death," that they are having trouble remembering who their God is. Nonetheless, they trust that God remembers who they are. When Paul asserts that "nothing . . . in all creation" will separate us from the love of

ALTHOUGH WE CANNOT KNOW HOW, WE DO KNOW THAT GOD CAN TRANSMUTE ANYTHING INTO GOOD, SOMEHOW. GOD DOES NOT MERELY RESCUE CHESTNUTS FROM THE FIRE; GOD MANAGES TO SPIN STRAW INTO GOLD—PROVIDING WE ARE WILLING TO GIVE THE STRAW TO GOD.

God, he speaks from a context in which, to all appearances, even God seems to be trying to separate us from God's love. But it will not happen. We think that we can separate ourselves from the love of God, but Paul refutes that emphatically. Will sin separate us from God? No, for God has forgiven our sin before we have sinned it. Will lack of faith, if nothing else, separate us from God? No, for *God* will never cease to believe in *us*. There is an old saying about heaven and hell: heaven is to be in the presence of God and enjoy it, while hell is to be in the presence of God and hate it. Either way, we are in the presence of God, and nothing will separate us from the love of God.

THE GOSPEL

MATTHEW 13:31-33, 44-52 (RCL);
MATTHEW 13:31-33, 44-49a (BCP);
MATTHEW 13:44-52 or 13:44-46 (RC)

Interpreting the Text

Matthew 13, the parable chapter, forms the third block of Jesus' teaching in the Gospel. Matthew positions the chapter to explain and contain the emergence of opposition to Jesus' ministry in vv. 10-12. While all the parables in today's Gospel explain an aspect of Jesus' message about God's kingdom, these parables are explicitly addressed to the disciples to encourage their discernment and roles: the kingdom's hiddenness (mustard seed, treasure in a field); its surpassing value (pearl of great price); and its universality (dragnet). Parables elsewhere in the chapter and other parables in other Gospels remind the listener that there are other realities conveying different notions of God's realm. The challenge is to preach a particular parable in the context of others. Because of their understanding, to the disciples is given teaching that "every scribe who has been trained [discipled] for the kingdom of heaven is like the master of a household who brings out of his storeroom what is new and what is old" (13:52). Perhaps it describes how Matthew wrote the Gospel.

Responding to the Text

Parables describe God's realm in light of specific human actions or natural phenomena in such a way that causes the hearer to rethink priorities so as to make room for something outside human con-

WHILE ALL THE PARABLES IN TODAY'S GOSPEL EXPLAIN AN ASPECT OF JESUS' MESSAGE ABOUT GOD'S KINGDOM, THESE PARABLES ARE EXPLICITLY ADDRESSED TO THE DISCIPLES TO ENCOURAGE THEIR DISCERNMENT AND ROLES.

trol yet within human potential. The challenge for the modern scribe (or preacher) is to represent them afresh. Either one can rewrite them in contemporary terms or use parables from noncanonical texts like *The Gospel of Thomas* 8:

And Jesus said, A person is like a wise fisherman who cast his net into the sea and drew it up from the sea full of little fish. Among them he discovered a fine large fish. He threw all the little fish back into the sea, and easily chose the large fish. Whoever has ears, let them hear!

Matthew's parable of the dragnet (like the parable of the tares) locates all humanity, good and bad alike, within a large net that has yet to be gathered in and sorted. While it counsels us to leave the sorting to God and angels at the close of the age and thus to forgo judging other fish in our communities, it anticipates the judgment scene of all the nations in Matthew 25. Yet judgment and condemnation must be balanced with Jesus' own self-disclosure as "gentle and humble in heart" at 11:29 together with the heavenly Father's providential care for nature and humans alike in the Sermon on the Mount (5–7).

ELEVENTH SUNDAY AFTER PENTECOST

July 31, 2005
Eighteenth Sunday in Ordinary Time / Proper 13

Revised Common	Episcopal (BCP)	Roman Catholic
Gen. 32:22-31	Neh. 9:16-20	Isa. 55:1-3
or Isa. 55:1-5		
Ps. 17:1-7, 15	Ps. 78:1-29	Ps. 145:8-9, 15-16, 17-18
or Ps. 145:8-9, 14-21	or 78:14-20, 23-25	
Rom. 9:1-5	Rom. 8:35-39	Rom. 8:35, 37-39
Matt. 14:13-21	Matt. 14:13-21	Matt. 14:13-21

As much a comfort to those experiencing a dark night of the soul as an encouragement to preachers struggling with texts, the strange story of Jacob wrestling alone with the angel at the ford of the Jabbok holds out a promise of divine blessings—but at a cost. Isaiah 55:1-5 speaks of the sustenance God freely offers and the promise of God's everlasting covenant. Psalms 17 and 145 assert that in the face of testing, God's promises will not fail. Paul affirms the mystery by which they endure in spite of evidence to the contrary. In the face of the disciples' incomprehension and few resources at hand, Jesus offers God's free nourishment to thousands of people (Matt.14:13-21).

FIRST READING

GENESIS 32:22–31 (RCL)

Interpreting the Text

Jacob's enigmatic encounter with the angel takes place within the context of Jacob's justifiable anxiety about meeting his brother Esau, whom he had defrauded of his birthright with the help of his mother fifteen years earlier. Jacob sends his wives, children, and possessions ahead to appease Esau while he remains alone. The unidentified man he encounters at night is surely a supernatural being who reflects his anxiety. Perhaps it is his conscience. Sir Jacob Epstein's 1940–41 sculpture "Jacob and the Angel" depicts Jacob's collapse into the supporting angel's arms, which some have seen in the context of Jewish struggles to survive. Out of respect for Jacob's struggle, food restrictions come into being, although they are not written down until Sinai.

Responding to the Text

Jacob is given no choice about his encounter with God until he begins to prevail and God seeks to withdraw. No one struggles with the supernatural and survives without wounds. Even Jacob's new name as Israel's eponymous ancestor, "someone who struggles with God," indicates Israel's identity. Our encounters with God take on the characteristics of a struggle, because God constantly challenges us and, in responding to that challenge, we change. Elie Wiesel writes, "The mysterious aggressor? The other half of Jacob's split self. The side of him that harbored doubts about his mission, his future, his raison d'être."[1] What are our struggles of identity and marks of blessing from God? How can we wrest a blessing from our doubts and weaknesses?

ISAIAH 55:1-3 (RC);
ISAIAH 55:1-5 (RCL, alt.)

Deutero-Isaiah depicts God offering three things: rich food, promise of a covenant, and relation to an unknown nation. The offer is conditional: by hearing and obeying (Heb: *Shema*, "Listen and do!" Septuagint: *akouo*, which connotes hearing and obeying), the people benefit materially and spiritually, receiving food and drink as the result of a covenant relationship to God, and they get to be convener of a nation. For the RC lection, the feeding is contingent on obeying, since the verse describing Israel as convener of the nations is omitted.

Water, wine, food, and milk are offered without cost to the listeners. However, it turns out that the nourishment God offers is the sustenance of instruction, torah. Is this a bait and switch? Perhaps. But what is offered is what truly satisfies: the choicest food and the richest repast (v. 2). Where once the covenant was promised to David, now the nation as a whole is a recipient of the Davidic covenant. Their blessings in turn yield benefits for all of humanity.

NEHEMIAH 9:16-20 (BCP)

Interpreting the Text

This contrary text describes a prayer now incorporated into the morning prayer of Jewish liturgy that recapitulates salvation history (Neh. 9:6-37). Communal confession describes the Israelites' hardhearted rejection of God's commandments. They wanted to return to slavery. God nevertheless forgave them and gave them manna in the wilderness.

The passage's paschal imagery is brought out in the "Catechetical Homily" of John Chrysostom, which, in Eastern Orthodox Churches at the Vigil of Easter, replaces the sermon and is always heard by the people while they stand. Chrysostom says, "Rejoice today both you who have fasted and you who have disregarded the fast: the table is full-laden; feast you all sumptuously. The calf is ample; let no one go hungry away. Enjoy all the feast of faith; receive all the riches of loving-kindness. Let no one bewail his poverty, for the universal kingdom has been revealed. Let no one weep for his iniquities, for pardon has shone forth from the grave." The challenge this reading poses is that if God will be merciful to all, what's the point of fasting or other religious practices? One answer is that of reciprocal love: you do it because God loved you. But there are other responses you may wish to invoke.

> THE CHALLENGE THIS READING POSES IS THAT IF GOD WILL BE MERCIFUL TO ALL, WHAT'S THE POINT OF FASTING OR OTHER RELIGIOUS PRACTICES?

RESPONSIVE READING
PSALM 17:1-7, 15 (RCL)

This section of Psalm 17 is a protestation of innocence predicated on vindication by God as judge. The psalmist appeals to God as the arbiter of what is just: "Hear a just cause, O LORD, attend to my cry; give ear to my prayer; . . ." (v. 1); "from you let my vindication come; let your eyes see the right" (v. 2). Testing and probing have found nothing amiss. Appeals to God for answers and requests for protection from assailants are met with the assurance of the concluding verse: "As for me, I shall behold your face in righteousness; when I awake I shall be satisfied, beholding your likeness" (v. 15), although it can be taken as expressing a wish or desire, perhaps expressing a yearning fulfilled in a vision like Ezekiel's (Ezekiel 1). As is well known, notions of life after death appear in the Hebrew scriptures only in later texts, like Daniel 12.

PSALM 145:8-9, 15-16, 17-18 (RC);
PSALM 145:8-9, 14-21 (RCL, alt.)

This section of Psalm 145 is a statement of confidence in God's mercy and compassion. To be sure, the opening assertions constitute a reminder to God to be just. It is not the first time nor will it be the last that God is shown in the dual roles of judge and accuser at the same time. In vv. 14-16, the Lord is depicted as a benevolent ruler dispensing food to the oppressed and starving. In vv. 18-19, the Lord is ready to hear all who pray to him sincerely. The conclusion in v. 21 expresses the psalmist's praise of the Lord and the assurance that all human beings, perhaps even all creation, shall bless God's holy name forever.

PSALM 78:1-29 or 78:14-20, 23-25 (BCP)

Psalm 78 is addressed to the people rather than to God. The opening verses echo wisdom literature (Sir. 51:16, "I inclined my ear a little and received [wisdom]"), and v. 2 has been translated, "I will open my mouth in a parable" (RSV). The whole psalm is a lengthy recitation of salvation history that starts with a promise to tell future children of Israel's infidelities by recalling how the people of God did not remember God's deeds of deliverance from Egypt and provision of manna in the wilderness: "They forgot what he had done, and the miracles that he had shown them" (v. 11). Within the body of the psalm are two distinct narratives: miracles in Egypt, the deliverance at the Red Sea, and subsequent wilderness events (vv. 12-39); and the movement from Egypt to Canaan (Ps. 78:40-72). The structure of both is parallel: act of deliverance (Ps.78:12-16, 40-55), rebellion (Ps. 78:17-20, 56-58), divine punishment (Ps.78:21-31, 59-64), God's willingness to forgive because human life is transitory (Ps. 78:32-39, 65-72).

Second Reading

ROMANS 9:1-5 (RCL)

Interpreting the Text

Paul anguishes about his Jewish brothers and sisters, acknowledging the love he has for them. This follows immediately on Paul's assertion in Rom. 8:39 that nothing can separate us from the love of God. Nonetheless, Paul would be willing to be so separated if it could bring about full reconciliation with the Israelites. Paul has no doubt about God's incorporation of Israel into the promises already made. The great gifts of God—adoption as children, the scriptures, the worship, the covenants, the glory—are all given to Israel as their own inheritance, and Jesus is ethnically an Israelite.

> WHEN WE FEEL THAT OUR FELLOW CHURCH PEOPLE, THOSE WHO SHARE OUR CREED AND POLITY, OUR FAMILY MEMBERS, OR OUR FELLOW CITIZENS ARE SEPARATING THEMSELVES FROM US AND FROM GOD, WE CAN AFFIRM THAT GOD WILL NOT BE SEPARATED FROM THEM.

Paul grieves over what he believes to be the unfaith of his own people but affirms the ability of God to include them because of God's love. Just so, when we feel that our fellow church people, those who share our creed and polity, our family members, or our fellow citizens are separating themselves from us and from God, we can affirm that God will not be separated from them. Our ability to be separated from God does not lie in our own hands but in God',s and God does not choose to exercise this prerogative.

ROMANS 8:35-39 (BCP);
ROMANS 8:35, 37-39 (RC)

In the context of seeking to understand how God's covenant promises made to his Jewish compatriots obtain, the Jewish Paul asks rhetorically whether "anything can separate us from the love of God." The answer he gives is that nothing past, present, or still to come, nothing in heights or depths, nothing in all creation can separate us from God's love. Is there any more powerful text in the New Testament?

For more extended discussion of this passage, see the comments on the Second Reading for the Tenth Sunday after Pentecost, Proper 12, above.

THE GOSPEL
MATTHEW 14:13-21 (RCL, BCP, RC)

Interpreting the Text

Jesus has withdrawn (Greek: *anachoreo*) when he hears of the death of John the Baptist. He distances himself from hostility, but when the crowd hears of Jesus' action (Greek: *akouo*) they follow. God's plan, seen from chapter 2 onward in the use of the verb *anachoreo*, turns isolation and avoidance into an occasion manifesting divine blessing. The crowds in Matthew come to hear Jesus, and they and the disciples receive God's free food offered by Jesus, which "all ate and were filled" (v. 20). Although there is no explicitly stated teaching (in Matthew, Jesus teaches in discreet blocks of material), the fact that the crowds hear and follow implies that Jesus is teaching as does the fact that no one leaves during the entire day's events.

THE HOMILETIC CHALLENGE IS TO PRESENT A CONVINCING RATIONALE FOR ADHERENCE TO GOD'S TEACHING IN LIGHT OF GOD'S UNQUALIFIED MERCY. IF GOD FEEDS FOLLOWERS WITHOUT DEMANDING ANYTHING ELSE, WHAT IS THE INCENTIVE TO OBEY?

The same problem obtains for the Gospel reading as for Neh. 9:16-20, namely, the feeding of the crowds is not contingent on their obedience. They hear and follow but make no other continuing commitment. The *ochloi* (crowds) at this point in Matthew are essentially neutral. The homiletic challenge is to present a convincing rationale for adherence to God's teaching in light of God's unqualified mercy. If God feeds followers without demanding anything else, what is the incentive to obey?

Note

1. Elie Wiesel, *Messengers of God: Biblical Portraits and Legends*, trans. Marion Wiesel (New York: Summit, 1985).

TWELFTH SUNDAY
AFTER PENTECOST

AUGUST 7, 2005
NINETEENTH SUNDAY IN ORDINARY TIME / PROPER 14

REVISED COMMON	EPISCOPAL (BCP)	ROMAN CATHOLIC
Gen. 37:1-4, 12-28	Jon. 2:1-9	1 Kings 19:9a, 11-13a
or 1 Kings 19:9-18		
Ps. 105:1-6, 16-22, 45b	Psalm 29	Ps. 85:9, 10, 11-12, 13-14
or Ps. 85:8-13		
Rom. 10:5-15	Rom. 9:1-5	Rom. 9:1-5
Matt. 14:22-33	Matt. 14:22-33	Matt. 14:22-33

Cries of anguished humans in dire circumstances reach God's ears. Salvation furthers God's purposes. Joseph is saved not only by Reuben, his elder brother, but through the providence of God in being sold to passing traders who sell him in turn to Potiphar, a courtier of Pharaoh's household. In Egypt, he flourishes. From the belly of the great fish, Jonah is vomited out onto dry land only to hear for the second time God's command to preach in Nineveh. Peter is saved from drowning by Jesus' grasp so that he may shortly confess Jesus to be the Son of the living God through divine revelation.

FIRST READING
GENESIS 37:1-4, 12-28 (RCL)

The favoritism that plagued Jacob's life brought blessing through trickery but enmity between him and his brother, Esau. Now it repeats itself again a generation later through his children. Jacob loves his son Joseph better than all Joseph's brothers. Joseph is hated by them on account of his father's favoritism. So begin the Joseph stories that continue in the RCL for another week. The anger of his brothers results in Joseph's being sold as a slave to traders going to Egypt. From there he will not only survive but thrive. But at this point in this story it must seem as though he has lost control of his life.

In these stories, we see God working behind the scenes to guide Joseph's life toward prosperity in Egypt and to eventual reconciliation with his old father and envious brothers. The irony of his brothers' selling Joseph into slavery is that soon they will all end up as slaves in Egypt. The one who enslaves another ends up enslaving himself.

JONAH 2:1–9 (BCP)

Jonah's attempts to ignore the call of God to proclaim God's judgment in Nineveh now result in his entombment in a whale's belly for three days and nights. Jonah's prayer to God is spoken in psalmlike phrases, articulating anguish and fervent pleas for deliverance.

Psalm prayers are often placed into the mouths of humans. Psalm 51, for example, is traditionally believed to express David's anguished guilt over his adultery with Bathsheba and the death of her husband, Uriah. Jonah's plea for deliverance is almost a plea from a place of death as far as Jonah is concerned. But God uses natural resources like the whale and the storm to bring Jonah to his senses. What threatens to overcome him turns out to be the hand of God.

We might consider the approach of Phyllis Trible.[1] From the psalm's opening lines, we hear one thing and remember something different in the narrative: Jonah says, "I called to the LORD" (v. 2), but when the ship was swamped by a storm, he was in fact fast asleep. It was the sailors who called God. They are more pious than he, even though he represents them as idol worshipers (v. 9). "You cast me into the deep," Jonah says (v. 3), but it is not the Lord who did the casting. Jonah dwells on his plight: "The waters closed in over me, the deep surrounded me, weeds were wrapped around my head . . . I went down . . ." (vv. 5–6). The first person singular as subject, object, or possessive occurs twenty-six times; Jonah is far more interested in himself than in God. Jonah speaks of having been delivered, but there he is praying from the belly of a fish. If Jonah is self-righteous and his words false, when God speaks to the fish and it spews Jonah up onto dry land, perhaps it is because Jonah's prayer makes God sick. The psalm reflects the self-delusion in which he is still trapped and because of which the narrative is on hold. However, the good news is that God can use even forced piety, self-serving prayers, and delay as a means to the end God has in mind.

> THE GOOD NEWS IS THAT GOD CAN USE EVEN FORCED PIETY, SELF-SERVING PRAYERS, AND DELAY AS A MEANS TO THE END GOD HAS IN MIND.

1 KINGS 19:9a, 11–13a (RC); 1 KINGS 19:9–18 (RCL, alt.)

The prophetic call to Elijah identifies him in isolation from all other prophets who have been put to death. The revelation of God to Elijah is not in the sound of a great and mighty wind that splits rocks, nor in an earthquake nor in the fire, but in "a sound of sheer silence" (NRSV; *Jewish Study Bible*: "a soft murmuring sound"). The Hebrew "sound" (*qol*) can also denote "voice." The Hebrew root of the verb means being silent, still, or waiting, while the noun in our passage, *demama*, often connotes catastrophe and mourning. Silence is in apposition to sound. The sound is silence.

God's revelation to Elijah is unique and enigmatic. It establishes that he is alone and not alone. In Job 4:16, silence is followed by a voice. Elijah's sound is silence (Greek: the voice of a thin breeze). The silence that Elijah experiences suggests both presence and absence.

RESPONSIVE READING
PSALM 105:1-6, 16-22, 45b (RCL)

The psalmist issues an invitation to praise the Lord and "make known his deeds among the peoples" (v. 1), particularly those identified as offspring of Abraham and descendants of Jacob (v. 6). Such people are the fulfillment of the covenant with Abraham (Gen.15:3-6). They are enjoined to "remember the wonderful works he has done, his miracles and the judgments he has uttered" (v. 5), perhaps recalling the deliverance of the Israelites at the Red Sea and the giving of the law at Sinai. Verses 16-22 are a recitation of the sending of Joseph into slavery in Egypt with details of his enslavement: "His feet were hurt with fetters; his neck was put in a collar of iron" (v. 18). These details are not recorded in Genesis and serve to emphasize the contrast in Joseph's status from slavery to high office. Freed by Pharaoh in Egypt, Joseph was made lord of Pharaoh's household and possessions with powers to discipline princes and to "teach his elders wisdom" (v. 22). Finally, v. 45b advocates adherence to God's laws and teachings.

PSALM 85:9, 10, 11-12, 13-14 (RC);
PSALM 85:8-13 (RCL, alt.)

Commentators interpret this psalm as an exilic or postexilic prayer for the restoration of Israel to its land. In this selection, the land is mentioned in v. 9: "His salvation is at hand for those who fear him, that his glory may dwell in our land"—a reference that it would be all too easy to ignore. Yet the request from God is for a restored place to live wherein "faithfulness will spring up from the ground, and righteousness will look down from the sky" (v. 11). The selection concludes with an affirmation that God's bounty is manifest in produce of the land (v. 13). The RC lection's inclusion of v. 14 indicates that the means of redress will be just. To be sure, this psalm can be read as a promise of future salvation. But the psalmist affirms that God's presence will be in the midst of the people and all creation will experience peace.

PSALM 29 (BCP)

The psalm invites the members of the heavenly court to acknowledge God's supremacy by ascribing glory and might to God alone: "Ascribe to the LORD, O heavenly beings, ascribe to the LORD glory and strength . . .";"in his temple all say, 'Glory!'" (vv. 1-2a, 9b). "Heavenly beings" are literally "sons of God," i.e., members of the divine court (cf. Pss. 82:1; 89:6-8). Divine glory and might ("the voice of the LORD") are dramatically visible through thunderclaps in seven ways: over the waters; in power; in majesty; breaking cedars; kindling flames of fire; convulsing the wilderness; and causing hinds to calve (vv. 3-9a). The closing verse (v. 11) is a prayer that the Lord grant strength to his people and bestow well being (peace) on them. The whole psalm resonates with the vision of Elijah to articulate contrasting aspects of the voice of the Lord.

SECOND READING
ROMANS 10:5-15 (RCL)

This passage from Paul's letter to the Romans is an extended meditation on the internalization of the word of faith and the need to evangelize. Paul cites the meditation on the command of God in Deut. 30:11ff. and interprets it with respect to faith in Jesus Christ. Here as in so many places, Paul demonstrates how scripture must be understood anew and interpreted freshly in new and changing circumstances.

Paul uses Deuteronomy 30 to assure us that salvation is not something "we get" after a long search. Rather, Christ has drawn near to us through the gospel. Christ is with us—in us—here and now wherever and whenever the gospel is preached. Moreover, salvation belongs to all the faithful. Everyone who calls out to God for help can and will be heard.

ROMANS 9:1-5 (BCP, RC)

For a discussion of this passage, see the comments on the Second Reading for the Eleventh Sunday after Pentecost, Proper 13, above.

THE GOSPEL

MATTHEW 14:22-33 (RCL, BCP, RC)

Interpreting the Text

Following the feeding of thousands, Matthew records Jesus' dispatch of the disciples into a boat. After dismissing the satisfied crowds, Jesus hopes for time alone to pray by himself on a mountain. Shortly afterward, the disciples' boat appears to be in difficulty from the headwind. Jesus comes to their rescue in the middle of the night walking on water. The disciples, although fisherfolk, are afraid of the storm and then even more of the apparition that is Jesus.

Peter appears to recover first and proposes that he come to Jesus on the water. Becoming frightened, he begins to sink. In his anguish he cries out, "Lord, save me!" Jesus catches him and they both get into the boat. He speaks directly to Peter: "You of little faith [one word in Greek: little-faith-person], why did you doubt?" In the boat all disciples worship him as Son of God.

Responding to the Text

The theme of water that threatens to overwhelm human life runs through the Jonah passage and today's Gospel. Water is always potentially chaotic to ancient Israel, a landlocked nation that had no navy until the time of Solomon.

THE THEME OF WATER THAT THREATENS TO OVERWHELM HUMAN LIFE RUNS THROUGH THE JONAH PASSAGE AND TODAY'S GOSPEL.

Jesus seeks to make it possible for others to conquer ancient fears and also walk on water. Peter's cry of help is confessional: "Lord, save me!" He has a prominent role in the Gospel. Like all the disciples, his faith is small, but there are grounds for hope in its growth. In Matthew a theophany is always accompanied by doubt and fear (28:16-17); here, however, the end result is a recognition of Jesus' divine abilities and status as "Son of God."

Note

1. Phyllis Trible, *Rhetorical Criticism: Context, Method, and the Book of Jonah* (Minneapolis: Fortress, 1994).

THIRTEENTH SUNDAY AFTER PENTECOST

AUGUST 14, 2005
TWENTIETH SUNDAY IN ORDINARY TIME / PROPER 15

REVISED COMMON	EPISCOPAL (BCP)	ROMAN CATHOLIC
Gen. 45:1-15	Isa. 56:1 (2-5) 6-7	Isa. 56:1, 6-7
or Isa. 56:1, 6-8		
Psalm 133 or Psalm 67	Psalm 67	Ps. 67:2-3, 5, 6, 8
Rom. 11:1-2a, 29-32	Rom. 11: 13-15, 29-32	Rom 11:13-15, 29-32
Matt. 15:(10-20) 21-28	Matt. 15:21-28	Matt. 15:21-28

God cares deeply about saving all human life. Humans have to learn to mirror divine concern for each other. Joseph's deep love for his father, from whom he has been forcibly separated, overrides any thoughts of revenge on his brothers. He understands that he has been sent by God to Egypt to save his family in Israel from famine. Psalm 133 celebrates the unity of brothers. God does not reject his own people but is merciful (Romans 11). One must, however, be a determined parent, as in the case of the Canaanite woman who had to remind Jesus in Matt.15:21-28 that the contours of his mission might be larger than the borders of Israel and that her daughter did not lie incurable beyond the pale.

FIRST READING

GENESIS 45:1-15 (RCL)

At an end of the RCL's selective use of the Joseph saga, this reading highlights reconciliation between Joseph and his brothers that ensures their survival through famine and separation. In the end, Joseph will be restored to his father before Jacob dies. Joseph initiates everything: he declares his identity before his brothers recognize him at the Egyptian court; he reminds them that they sold him into slavery but immediately declares that this was God's plan to ensure their survival through the famine; he identifies himself through God's providence as lord of Pharaoh's household and ruler over Egypt. His brothers are dumbstruck at these revelations. It is only after he and Benjamin weep together with arms around each other's neck that his brothers are able to speak.

Fraternal reconciliation evokes the reconciliation of Jacob and Esau in Genesis 33–34. In fact, it effectively heals generational rift. Joseph has learned that there are more important things than revenge for his shameful treatment. His success at the hand of God in Egypt sanctions divine blessing that can generously be bestowed on others. Shortly, Jacob's family will go down into Egypt to avoid the continuing famine, and there in Egypt they will survive and thrive.

ISAIAH 56:1, (2-5) 6-7 (BCP);
ISAIAH 56:1, 6-7 (RC);
ISAIAH 56:1, 6-8 (RCL, alt.)

Interpreting the Text

The prophet declares benefits to a people in exile that will accrue from keeping God's laws. The optional text describes first the blessing (*ashre*; Latin: *beatus*, which gives us the English word "beatitude") that accrues to the individual who keeps the Sabbath and refrains from doing evil. The prophet assures people returning from Babylon, among whom are foreigners and eunuchs (probably officials at the Babylonian court, possibly even including some Jews), that through observance of the covenant they are full members of the community and that their name will be more remembered than those of children they are prevented from having. The set text preserves the second effect of doing justice, namely, inclusion of foreigners (lit., "sons of strangers") in worship of God so that "My house shall be called a house of prayer for all peoples" (v. 7) and the gathered diaspora will be more than they have ever been.

WORSHIP OF GOD AND KEEPING THE COVENANT IS NOW MADE ACCESSIBLE TO ALL AS A NATURAL CONSEQUENCE OF "OBSERVING WHAT IS RIGHT AND DOING WHAT IS JUST."

Responding to the Text

Isaiah instructs the exiles in their attitudes to outsiders. Worship of God and keeping the covenant is now made accessible to all as a natural consequence of "observing what is right and doing what is just." It may be important to include the optional text concerning foreigners and eunuchs. While discussion of eunuchs may seem anachronistic or even archaic, many of the issues pertaining to eunuchs arise in discussions around the inclusion of gay and lesbian persons in congregations today.

RESPONSIVE READING
PSALM 133 (RCL)

The psalmist affirms the benefits of fraternal relations and likens them to the overflowing of oil used for anointing the high priest Aaron (Exod. 30:22-33) and the dew on Mount Hermon in the northern region of Israel falling on the mountains (possibly mountain) of Zion in the south. It is unusual to see a description of fraternal relations in psalm texts.

PSALM 67 (BCP; RCL, alt.); PSALM 67:2-3, 5, 6, 8 (RC)

The psalmist prays for continuation of good harvests as a blessing from God. Verse 2 speaks of the "shining face of God" as a visible expression of God's benevolence. All nations of the earth are invited to acknowledge and praise God in response to God's guidance.

SECOND READING

ROMANS 11:1-2a, 29-32 (RCL); ROMANS 11:13-15, 29-32 (BCP, RC)

Interpreting the Text

Readings from Romans 9–11 continue, and in chapter 11, Paul specifically considers, then rejects, the notion that God has abandoned his own people. He describes himself as an Israelite of the tribe of Benjamin. Paul cites the example of Elijah's poignant cry to God that in his struggle against foreign religion he is alone and isolated (1 Kings 19:1-8; see RCL Proper 14), which meets with divine assurance that there is a remnant chosen by grace. God will not abandon Israel. To the Gentiles (vv. 13-15), Paul says that just as he has used his Jewish identity to demonstrate God's salvation of Israel, so now he uses his identity as apostle to the Gentiles to shame a few fellow Jews into changing their minds. He knows that God's grace has come to foreigners in part because of Jewish rejection. If any accept, it will be as if the dead have come back to life! Finally, Paul concludes (vv. 29-32) that Gentiles, having been afforded God's promises because of Jewish

> PAUL SAYS THAT JUST AS HE HAS USED HIS JEWISH IDENTITY TO DEMONSTRATE GOD'S SALVATION OF ISRAEL, SO NOW HE USES HIS IDENTITY AS APOSTLE TO THE GENTILES TO SHAME A FEW FELLOW JEWS INTO CHANGING THEIR MINDS.

disobedience, should now recognize that God's mercy extends in turn to those once disobedient. God intends to be merciful to all.

Responding to the Text

In this extraordinary passage, we see the limits and possibilities of an intractable issue, the inclusion of those Jews for whom God's promises were first intended. Paul presumes to express the mind of God when he declares that God's promises are not contingent upon human behavior. In fact, all are disobedient. Paul infers God's merciful plan for humanity from his own experience and the example of Elijah. The story continues next week.

The Gospel

MATTHEW 15:(10-20) 21-28 (RCL);
MATTHEW 15:21-28 (BCP, RC)

Interpreting the Text

Jesus once again withdraws from confrontation with some Jerusalem scribes and Pharisees. This time he withdraws outside the boundaries of Israel into a house. However, he is pursued by a woman stranger and winkled from his shell. She is identified as a "Canaanite woman," i.e., slave proselyte. The *Mishnah's* regular use of the word to identify a slave proselyte (*m. Ma'aser Sheni* 4.4; *m. Erub.* 7.6; *m. Kid.* 1.3; *m. B. Qam.* 8.3, 5; *m. B. Metzia* 1.5; *m. 'Arak.* 7.4) provides the most reasonable explanation for Matthew's designation, particularly in light of the servant/slave language Matthew inserts into Mark's shorter version (Mark 7:25-31): "Lord," vv. 22, 25; "crumbs that fall from the masters' tables"; the psalmic language of prayer she uses, "Have mercy on me, Lord" (Septuagint Pss. 6:3, 9:14; 31:9; 56:1; 86:3), and "Help me!" the language of Septuagint Ps. 53:6; 93:18; addressing Jesus as "Son of David"; 15:25, "she kneels before him," from *Proskyneo,* "kneeling, falling down, or worshiping," a verb that occurs frequently in Matthew, particularly to describe the respectful attitude of outsiders to Jesus (2:2, 8, 11; 4:9; 8:2; 9:18; 14:33; 15:25; 18:26; 20:20; 28:9, 17).

Responding to the Text

No one, not even Jesus, and possibly not even God, understands the infinitely expandable dimensions of God's open arms. In the face of Jesus' initial silence and the hostility of the disciples, the woman's persistence begins to change Jesus' attitude to outsiders. Where he declared to the disciples ("Go nowhere except to the lost sheep of the house of Israel," Matt. 10:6) his own understanding of an exclusive mission (15:24), it is this anonymous woman proselyte who changes his mind. While Jesus might be excused from not having noticed that the magi ("wise men") of chapter 2 were the only ones celebrating his birth unreservedly, he surely would have read and reflected upon both the narratives of Joseph's reconciliation with his brothers and Elijah's vision.

> NO ONE, NOT EVEN JESUS, AND POSSIBLY NOT EVEN GOD, UNDERSTANDS THE INFINITELY EXPANDABLE DIMENSIONS OF GOD'S OPEN ARMS.

However, Jesus changes his mind during the course of Matthew's Gospel. At the great commission of 28:16-20, he commissions the disciples to "make disciples of all nations." As we in turn reflect on these texts, what boundaries do we and our communities need to look beyond?

DEIRDRE J. GOOD

FOURTEENTH SUNDAY AFTER PENTECOST

AUGUST 21, 2005
TWENTY-FIRST SUNDAY IN ORDINARY TIME /
PROPER 16

REVISED COMMON	EPISCOPAL (BCP)	ROMAN CATHOLIC
Exod. 1:8—2:10	Isa. 51:1-6	Isa. 22:19-23
or Isa. 51:1-6		
Psalm 124 or Psalm 138	Psalm 138	Ps. 138:1-2, 2-3, 6, 8
Rom. 12:1-8	Rom. 11:33-36	Rom. 11:33-36
Matt. 16:13-20	Matt. 16:13-20	Matt. 16:13-20

The revolution that became the emancipation of the Israelite slaves from Egypt originated with the actions of the Hebrew midwives Shiphrah and Puah, Moses' mother, and Miriam, Moses' sister, acting in accountability to a higher authority than Pharaoh. Individual roles play an important part in biblical tradition. Paul in Romans 12 imagines insight through the renewing of human minds. Jesus concurs with Peter's designation, "You are the Son of the living God" (Matt. 16:16), in distinction from the report of the same event in every other Gospel. Perhaps the call that we have is to accept the call that identifies who we really are rather than who we might like to be.

> PERHAPS THE CALL THAT WE HAVE IS TO ACCEPT THE CALL THAT IDENTIFIES WHO WE REALLY ARE RATHER THAN WHO WE MIGHT LIKE TO BE.

FIRST READING
EXODUS 1:8—2:10 (RCL)

Interpreting the Text

The rise of a new Egyptian dynasty that knows nothing of Joseph's connection to the royal court puts the Israelite nation into a marginal situation, and they are enslaved for making bricks in service of a vast building program. But Gen. 47:25 demonstrates that like the Israelites, Egyptians themselves were enslaved to Pharaoh. However, the more oppressed the Israelites were, the faster they grew. Through the intervention of the Hebrew midwives, an entire generation of Israelite slaves was saved, and one of them, Moses, was rescued by the pity of Pharaoh's daughter. Having been watched secretly by his sister Miriam, Moses' mother is offered as a wet nurse to her son. Eventually Moses is taken to Pharaoh's court and raised there. *Moses* is in fact an Egyptian name, explained in the text as though the Hebrew form of it, *Mosheh*, were related to the Hebrew verb "to draw out" (of the water).

Responding to the Text

For George V. Pixley and Robert R. Barr, the central characters of Exodus are the "sons of Israel," demonstrating the transition from a family saga of the patriarchs and their brothers to a nation.[1] The Hebrew midwives Shiphrah and Puah are entirely extraneous to the story. Are they Gentile women, as the Greek translation of the Hebrew Scriptures and their remarks (Exod. 1:19) imply? Verses 17 and 20 are not necessarily references to the Hebrew God. Or are they (less likely) Hebrew women with careers in midwifery? The fact that they are named is surely significant. Their example of civil disobedience sets emancipatory wheels in motion. Perhaps it serves as an example to Moses' mother, who hides her son in the bulrushes. Are there times when one puts obligations to one's God above those to secular authorities?

ISAIAH 51:1-6 (BCP; RCL, alt.)

Interpreting the Text

Second Isaiah (Isaiah 40–55) was written by an anonymous prophet during Israel's exile in Babylon. The two paragraphs in this reading, vv. 1-3 and 4-6, both begin with the word "Listen" and are followed by comforting promises of God. The faithful audience is characterized as those who pursue righteousness and seek Yahweh. Grounds for confidence may be found in Israel's ancestors Abraham and Sarah, here compared to a rock or a quarry.

> WE LOOK TO THE PAST TO FIND HOPE FOR THE FUTURE: AS GOD NEVER ABANDONED THEM, SO GOD WILL NEVER ABANDON US.

Though they were only one couple, they became a numerous people. Similarly the exiles, few in number, could count on the solidity of a divinely sanctioned population increase.

"Comfort" is a theme word in Second Isaiah, beginning with 40:1. Comfort means much more than sympathy; it means God-worked transformation. Zion's waste places and wilderness will become luxuriant, like the Garden of Eden. The transformation will be marked by appropriate human rejoicing: joy, gladness, thanksgiving, and singing (v. 3).

The second paragraph, vv. 4-6, is written in the first person as the words of Yahweh. God is the source of teaching that goes forth. This is the promise of salvation. The conclusion (v. 5) promises imminent triumph by means of the metaphor of God's powerful arm.

Responding to the Text

In a time of exile, despair would have been a close companion. Images of Abraham and Sarah as rocks or quarries from which subsequent generations were born is a solid and comforting image particularly when the prophet couples it to a picture of the restored Zion as a garden of the Lord wherein gladness and joy exist. To a contemporary congregation in times of despair, exhortations to look back to one's spiritual ancestors, to those forefathers and mothers in the faith is often helpful. We look to the past to find hope for the future: as God never abandoned them, so God will never abandon us.

ISAIAH 22:19-23 (RC)

This passage reports the designation of Eliakim as the one to whom the keys of the house of David are given to open and shut. He is invested with God's authority. A metaphor describes Eliakim as a tent peg and, although the lection extends only to v. 23, subsequent verses declare that the tent peg shall give way, and by the word of the Lord, the weight it supports will be destroyed.

Obviously the passage is selected for its resonance with Matthew 16, given the use of words like "key." The Isaiah text is a salutary reminder that initial confidence in a leader is often affirmed or undermined by subsequent events.

RESPONSIVE READING
PSALM 124 (RCL)

The psalmist expresses confidence in divine support through a thanksgiving, which teaches that Israel's very existence is owed to God who rescues them. In the first part ,Israel's enemies are imaged through verbs: "they would have swallowed us" (v. 3), "the flood would have swept us away" (v. 4), and "Blessed be the LORD, who has not given us as prey to their teeth" (v. 6). The quasi-personification of a sea monster held particular terrors for a nonnautical nation and conjures a picture of the mythic sea dragon (Ps.124:2b-3a; cf. Jer. 51:34) and the flood (Ps. 124:3b-5). The psalm heightens the malice of human enemies by linking them to the primordial enemies of God's creation. Israel is a bird freed from the trapper's snare (Ps. 124:6-8)—freed originally from Pharaoh and now from the current danger. The psalm ends on a note of confidence, reminding the worshiper of God's omnipotence: "Our help is in the name of the LORD, who made heaven and earth" (v. 8).

173

FOURTEENTH
SUNDAY
AFTER PENTECOST
―――――――
DEIRDRE J. GOOD

PSALM 138 (BCP; RCL, alt.); PSALM 138:1-2, 2-3, 6-8 (RC)

The entire psalm expresses praise to God for an individual's deliverance from enemies. The conceit is that it is David (as Calvin's commentary reminds us) who remembers the help God has always afforded him. On the basis of gratitude and from what he knows of divine faithfulness, David anticipates a continuance of the same mercy. If dangers must be met, he confidently looks for a happy issue: "Though I walk in the midst of trouble, you preserve me against the wrath of my enemies" (v. 7). Verse 2 alludes to worship in the temple.

SECOND READING
ROMANS 12:1-8 (RCL)

Interpreting the Text

Paul exhorts the Romans to whom the letter was written to view human bodies as a place for the power of God to be manifest. He speaks about the transformation of minds not conformed to this world in order to discern the will of God (v. 2). One such transformation is evident in "not to think of yourself more highly than you ought to think" (v. 3) but to think communally in a manner that takes into account diverse spiritual gifts. Within every community, different spiritual gifts will be evident. Paul suggests ways of employing them consonant with these gifts: prophecy in proportion to faith; ministry in ministering; the teacher in teaching; the exhorter in exhortation; the giver in generosity (lit., "zeal"); the leader in diligence; the compassionate in cheerfulness. Curious is the correlation of giving aid with zeal and doing acts of mercy with cheerfulness. Perhaps these correlations suggest more about Paul's personality.

Responding to the Text

It would be easy to think highly of oneself as the recipient of a particular spiritual gift. Although we have a unique equal value, we function differently in the community. Comparisons are odious. Liturgical traditions transform this possible distortion of Paul's words into a corporate prayer. In Eucharistic Prayer 1 of the BCP, for example, the priest says on behalf of the congregation: "Here we offer and present unto thee, O Lord, ourselves, our souls and bodies to be a reasonable, holy, and living sacrifice unto thee. . . ." In this prayer, our persons, our bodies and our lives participate in the redemptive offering of Christ.

ROMANS 11:33-36 (BCP, RC)

Paul's rhetorical questions seem to function as a coda to his insight that God shows mercy to everyone, Jew and Gentile alike. God's mysterious ways do not disclose how promises made to the Jews will be held. Thus, interpretations are inaccessible.

How often do we engage in ecstatic utterance or spontaneous prayer?

An 1854 hymn text by Frederick W. Faber summarizes Paul's rhetorical insight:

> There's a wideness in God's mercy like the wideness of the sea;
> There's a kindness in God's justice, which is more than liberty.
> There is welcome for the sinner, and more graces for the good!
> There is mercy with the Savior; there is healing in his blood.
> For the love of God is broader than the measure of our mind,
> and the heart of the Eternal is most wonderfully kind.
> If our love were but more simple, we should rest upon God's word,
> and our lives would be illumined by the presence of the Lord.

THE GOSPEL
MATTHEW 16:13-20 (RCL, BCP, RC)

Interpreting the Text

Peter's confession by means of insight ("revelation") that Jesus is "Son of the living God" (cf. "our living Lord" in 2 Macc. 7:33; 15:4; Dan. 6:27) marks a high point of comprehension in the Gospel and is blessed in turn by Jesus. Knowledge of the heavenly Father is a central teaching of the Gospel and is disclosed only to the disciples by Jesus (cf. 5:16, 45; 6:1, 9; 7:11; et al.) but revelation and the comprehension of it are rarely described except here and by implication in 11:25. The blessing to Peter: "You are Πέτρος [stone] and on this rock [πέτρα]. . ." are of course a wordplay in Greek. However, the noun Πέτρος (stone) was not a personal name at the time of the Gospel's writing and thus cannot be translated "Peter." In both Greek and English, God's intentions are not entirely clear. To what does "on this rock" refer? To Πέτρος (the traditional interpretation)? If so, then why a change in noun? Πέτρα is a feminine singular noun. Or should we use an antecedent feminine noun, e.g., "revelation," the verbal form of which is in v. 17, thus paraphrasing "on this revelation I will build. . ."? Certainly the latter has internal and external support.

The NRSV translation "church" is anachronistic. The word *ekklesia* denotes "community" or "assembly," here with the notion that the Matthean community is coming into being (cf. 18:18). Matthew 7:24, 26 uses the same verb, "building a house on a rock," metaphorically for hearing and doing Jesus' words. The notion of bind and loose probably derives from the rabbinic terms התיר / אסר Aramaic (שרא / אסר), meaning "forbidding" and "permitting" with a decision about the law (*b. Shab.* 81b). Just as Peter is given the power to regulate in the present passage, so in 18:18 the community binds and looses.

"From that time on" (v. 21) is an important transitional moment (cf. 4:16); it introduces the culmination of Jesus' story, his death and resurrection. Jesus' enthusiastic response to Peter's declaration is tempered by Peter's immediate refusal in v. 22 (to be read next week) to countenance the suffering and the death of Son of Man.

Responding to the Text

In Matthew's Gospel, it is only through insight that disciples like Peter recognize Jesus to be "Son of God." Insight comes not through human effort but from a higher authority. Is this not similar to our own experience in recognizing Jesus as Lord? It is a recognition that happens to us if we are guileless enough to permit it. Perhaps Pascal's famous argument known as "Pascal's wager" is relevant. For Pascal, faith was not logical. His philosophy was the result of a lifetime dedicated to science that could not explain his own religious faith. If God does not exist, the skeptic loses nothing by believing in him; if God does exist, the skeptic loses everything by not believing in him but wins everything (eternal life) by believing in him. The rational gambler must therefore choose to believe in God.

> IN MATTHEW'S GOSPEL, IT IS ONLY THROUGH INSIGHT THAT DISCIPLES LIKE PETER RECOGNIZE JESUS TO BE "SON OF GOD." INSIGHT COMES NOT THROUGH HUMAN EFFORT BUT FROM A HIGHER AUTHORITY.

Note

1. George V. Pixley and Robert R. Barr, *On Exodus: A Liberation Perspective* (Maryknoll, N.Y.: Orbis, 1987).

FIFTEENTH SUNDAY AFTER PENTECOST

AUGUST 28, 2005
TWENTY-SECOND SUNDAY IN ORDINARY TIME /
PROPER 17

REVISED COMMON	EPISCOPAL (BCP)	ROMAN CATHOLIC
Exod. 3:1-15	Jer. 15:15-21	Jer. 20:7-9
or Jer. 15:15-21		
Ps. 105:1-6, 23-26, 45c	Psalm 26 or 26:1-8	Ps. 63:2, 3-4, 5-6, 8-9
or Ps. 26:1-8		
Rom. 12:9-21	Rom. 12:1-8	Rom. 12:1-2
Matt. 16:21-28	Matt. 16:21-27	Matt. 16:21-27

Disclosure of God's identity and purpose is always entirely other to a human point of view. God's name disclosed to Moses in Exod. 3:14 is YHWH, which connotes "I am who or that I am" or "I will be what I will be." It suggests that God's nature is disclosed in God's actions. Thus, God's strangeness and difference reflected in the human response of Peter in the Gospel: "God forbid it, Lord!" ensures that we are not merely projecting our mental landscapes onto the biblical text. The text's alienness always confronts our expectations and imagination. This is a measure of its truth.

FIRST READING

EXODUS 3:1-15 (RCL)

Interpreting the Text

Moses is dutifully tending the flock of his father-in-law, Jethro, priest of Midian, on Horeb, the mountain of God. Out of the blue a burning bush catches his eye. It is ablaze but is not consumed. Moses moves closer to examine this strange phenomenon when out of the burning bush a voice addresses him: "Moses! Moses!" God tells Moses that the plight of Israelite slaves in Egypt has been noticed. God intends to rescue them and bring them to "a land flowing with milk and honey," to which end Moses is sent

GOD'S IDENTITY IS NOT DISCLOSED FOR ITS OWN (OR MOSES') SAKE BUT TO DEMONSTRATE CARE FOR HUMAN SUFFERING ENOUGH TO EFFECT THE LIBERATION OF SLAVES.

to Pharaoh to free God's people from Egypt. God's identity is not disclosed for its own (or Moses') sake but to demonstrate care for human suffering enough to effect the liberation of slaves.

Responding to the Text

To Moses the prophet and visionary, God's identity and purpose are revealed for the sake of human anguish. Perhaps the only thing that makes any difference in the world is that we should care about someone else enough to do something, as Elie Wiesel often reminds us. Indifference effects nothing and offers no hope. God declares to Moses, "My identity will be manifest in my actions." At the heart of the text's revelation of God is compassion for others, and this has shaped Jewish and Christian theological traditions, albeit in different ways.

JEREMIAH 15:15-21 (BCP; RCL, alt.)

Jeremiah's lament recalls to God his suffering and anguish as a mirror image of the suffering of Jerusalem experienced because of a drought. Jeremiah's prophetic insight saw the drought as a symbol of divine judgment against the nation. This is why he speaks of "a deceitful brook" and "waters that fail" (v. 18). God then promises that if Jeremiah turns back, God will in turn take him back and support him even against all the people.

True prophets like Moses, Jeremiah, and the seer of Revelation receive uncomfortable visions difficult to report. The seer of Revelation alleges that the prophetic word given to utter was sweet to taste but a bitter pill to swallow (Rev. 10:9-11). Alas, there is sometimes no option but to speak the truth.

JEREMIAH 20:7-9 (RC)

In this poetic expression of further persecution and lament, Jeremiah accuses God of deceiving him. God gave him prophetic words to articulate and promised support, yet uttering them caused Jeremiah shame and disgrace. Although he tried not to speak out, yet God's word was "within me . . . something like a burning fire shut up in my bones; I am weary with holding it in, and I cannot" (v. 9). Of course, no one wants to hear that Jerusalem will fall and the people will be carried off into exile in Babylon.

> LIKE JEREMIAH, WE HAVE AN OBLIGATION TO HOLD GOD ACCOUNTABLE FOR THE CALL WE RECEIVE AS WELL AS TO ASK GOD TO SUPPORT OUR FIDELITY TO THAT CALL EVEN IF IT IS HARD FOR OTHERS AND OURSELVES TO HEAR.

The experience of having a vocation that is costly and shameful is not uncommon. In fact, its cost is probably a hallmark of authenticity. However, it is indeed burdensome. Like Jeremiah, we have an obligation to hold God accountable for the call we receive as well as to ask God to support our fidelity to that call even if it is hard for others and ourselves to hear.

RESPONSIVE READING
PSALM 105:1-6, 23-26, 45c (RCL)

This psalm praises God on the basis of God's covenant with Abraham to give his descendants the Promised Land. Verses 23-26 allude to the experience of slavery in Egypt and the role of Aaron and Moses in facilitating the escape of the Israelite slaves. The section closes with an exhortation to obey the traditions that are the subject of the psalm itself.

PSALM 26 or 26:1-8 (BCP);
PSALM 26:1-8 (RCL, alt.)

The psalmist appeals to God on the basis of innocence for divine justice and vindication. God is addressed in imperatives: "Vindicate me" (v. 1), "Prove me . . . and try me; test my heart and mind" (v. 2). The psalmist expects a favorable response since his (or her) life has been lived according to God's requirements. This is a confident appeal all religious persons might emulate.

PSALM 63:2, 3-4, 5-6, 8-9 (RC)

The psalmist declares a vision of God's might and glory in the sanctuary. This gives rise to blessing God as if sated with a gourmet meal. Attachment (Hebrew: *davkah*) of the soul to God is intense and shows closeness and longing (v. 9).

SECOND READING
ROMANS 12:9-21 (RCL);
ROMANS 12:1-8 (BCP);
ROMANS 12:1-2 (RC)

Interpreting the Text

After concluding the theological discussion of God's promises to both Jews and Gentiles in Romans 11, Paul exhorts readers of his epistle to certain kinds of moral conduct both in minds and bodies. He appeals for love to be the ground of community relationships and counsels rejoicing in hope, patience in suffering, and perseverance in prayer. To outsiders he advocates hospitality and financial giving. In general Paul commends peaceable behavior to persecutors and evildoers. Revenge belongs to God. To hungry enemies Paul suggests giving food and drink "for by doing this you will heap burning coals on their heads" (v. 20).

Responding to the Text

"Let love be genuine," a central precept of Romans 12:9, is not only sage advice for community relations, but it is the foundation for true religious life. Leading away from self-absorption and toward humility, it is the motivation for care and self-giving resulting in acts of charity and hospitality. Since unresolved anger cannot coexist with love, resistance to anger and nonretaliation became a way of life for the desert fathers and mothers living by biblical precepts in the third and fourth centuries. Prayer (Romans 12:9) is "the seed of gentleness and the absence of anger," said Abba Evagrius.[1] In the twentieth century, methods of nonviolent resistance were employed by Tibetan monks, Gandhi, and Martin Luther King Jr. through the application of power without the use of physical violence to achieve sociopolitical goals by means of symbolic protests, economic or political noncooperation, and civil disobedience.

THE GOSPEL
MATTHEW 16:21–28 (RCL);
MATTHEW 16:21–27 (BCP);
MATTHEW 16:21–27 (RC)

Interpreting the Text

The prediction by Jesus of the suffering and death he would undergo at the hands of Jewish leaders in Jerusalem almost eclipses the note about resurrection. Peter's self-assured response reflecting his new leadership role but his attempt to take charge now evokes critical dismissal from Jesus. Like Jeremiah, Jesus faced Peter's ridicule and his dismissal of Jesus' prophetic witness. Thus Jesus not only has to overcome this reaction from one of his closest followers who had just shown considerable aptitude but also to hold to the dreadful fate that he and others now know would befall

> THE CHALLENGE OF THIS WEEK'S GOSPEL IS TO TAKE SERIOUSLY THE PROPHETIC ADMONITION OF JESUS ON DISCIPLESHIP FOUND IN ALL THREE GOSPELS, "TAKE UP YOUR CROSS AND FOLLOW ME," EVEN IF IT MEANS TO DEATH, AS IT MOST CERTAINLY DID IN PETER'S CASE.

him in Jerusalem. More challenging still are Jesus' words about those who would be followers: they have to deny themselves and take up their cross and follow Jesus. For Matthew, Jesus' fate will become their fate.

Responding to the Text

The challenge of this week's Gospel is to take seriously the prophetic admonition of Jesus on discipleship found in all three Gospels, "Take up your cross and follow me," even if it means to death, as it most certainly did in Peter's case. Suffering as a model of discipleship is a reality for persecuted Christians in parts of the world today as it has been at certain periods of Christian history. And yet there is an equal challenge in living quiet, selfless, heroic lives for others without seeking to suffer for suffering's sake.

Note

1. *Patrologia Graeca*, ed. J.-P. Migne; 162 vols., vol. 65 (Paris: 1857–86): 305b.

SIXTEENTH SUNDAY AFTER PENTECOST

September 4, 2005
Twenty-third Sunday in Ordinary Time / Proper 18

Revised Common	Episcopal (bcp)	Roman Catholic
Exod. 12:1-14	Ezek. 33:(1-6) 7-11	Ezek. 33:7-9
or Ezek. 33:7-11		
Ps. 149 or Ps. 119:33-40	Ps. 119:33-48	Ps. 95:1-2, 6-7, 8-9
	or 119:33-40	
Rom. 13:8-14	Rom. 12:9-21	Rom. 13:8-10
Matt. 18:15-20	Matt. 18:15-20	Matt. 18:15-20

Today's readings offer prescriptions for community life to our highly individu-alized Western mind-set. All members of religious communities create and engage in ritual (Exodus) and self-regula-tion (Matthew). Regulations for Passover are stipulated for insiders and strangers alike. The invitation to restore a sinner back to the community (Ezekiel and Matthew) is

> TODAY'S READINGS OFFER PRESCRIPTIONS FOR COM-MUNITY LIFE TO OUR HIGHLY INDIVIDUALIZED WEST-ERN MIND-SET.

present for a while. However, for the good of the whole, steps must be taken by the community itself to expel a willful offender who refuses to repent (Matthew).

FIRST READING
EXODUS 12:1-14 (rcl)

Today's reading records preparations for the exodus from Egypt in antici-pation of release. A meal is prepared and eaten in haste while the tenth plague causes the sudden death of all firstborn Egyptians. Is this the retaliation for the slaughter of Israelite males that is reported in Exod. 1:22? Israelite children were spared: Passover connotes protection and deliverance. The sacred significance of the meal requires that nothing of it remain (Exod. 12:10).

That the Israelites were to assume they would be released by Pharaoh by preparing their final meal in Egypt is an act of faith in God's power. An unblemished lamb was cooked and eaten by people present at the meal. This meal became the model for the postbiblical seder at which the exodus from Egypt is retold each year at Passover. A difficulty for interpreters is that Israel's liberation from Egypt is at the expense of Egyptian children and livestock.

Exercise of one group's rights frequently seems to require curtailment of another's. Our mission should be to try to find ways not just to liberate the oppressed but also to liberate the oppressor from the need or desire to oppress.

> OUR MISSION SHOULD BE TO TRY TO FIND WAYS NOT JUST TO LIBERATE THE OPPRESSED BUT ALSO TO LIBERATE THE OPPRESSOR FROM THE NEED OR DESIRE TO OPPRESS.

EZEKIEL 33:(1–6) 7–11 (BCP); EZEKIEL 33:7–9 (RC); EZEKIEL 33:7–11 (RCL, alt.)

As did other prophets, Ezekiel received a prophetic call to be a watchman for the house of Israel, watching over the city. Verses 1-6 make clear the watchman's responsibility: if he sounds no warning of impending danger, then he alone bears responsibility for the fate of the people and his life is forfeit. On the other hand, if he utters a warning and no one attends, the watchman's responsibility ends and his life is spared. Those warned must take responsibility for their repentance. To those who ask, "How can we survive?" (v. 10), the prophet is to say that God does not desire the death of the wicked but that the wicked repent and turn back to God.

The passage clarifies mutual responsibility within a religious community: the prophet must warn, and the wicked must heed the warning and turn back to God. That the wicked are offered through the warning a chance to repent is an indication of God's mercy.

RESPONSIVE READING
PSALM 149 (RCL)

In this psalm of praise the psalmist bids the faithful (vv. 1, 5, and 9; Hebrew *hasid*) "sing to the LORD a new song," dance, and praise God with musical instruments, namely, timbrel and lyre. All who celebrate God in worship are invited to do so in myriad ways.

PSALM 119:33-48 (BCP);
PSALM 119:33-40 (BCP, alt.; RCL, alt.)

Psalm 119 is the longest psalm partly because it is an acrostic that uses the Hebrew alphabet, which consists of twenty-three consonants. Each line of the twenty-three sections of eight verses or lines begins with the same letter. It is an extended mediation in the first person singular on the relationship of the faithful to God's commandments. To the Israelite, words for law are like words for snow are for the Eskimo. Within vv. 33-40, for example, there are different Hebrew words for laws (*choq*, "statutes," v. 33) "teaching" (*torah*, v. 34), "commandments" (*mitzvah*, v. 35), "decrees" (*eduth*, v. 36), "ways" (*derek*, v. 37), "promise" (or "speech," *imrah*, v. 38), "rules" (*mishpat*, v. 39), and "precepts" (*piqud*, v. 40). Reciting this psalm together regularly is a method of community formation wherein the community articulates its love of God's law through verbs like "keep," "observe" (v. 34), "delight" (v. 35), "turn my heart" (v. 36), "desire" (v. 40), "trust" (v. 42), "hope" (v. 43), "delight" and "love" (v. 47), "lift up my palms to," "love," and "meditate upon" (lit., "talk about" v. 48). The relationship of the faithful believers with the law reflects the relationship of God to the community.

PSALM 95:1-2, 6-7, 8-9 (RC)

This is an exhortation to the community to come together in worship to hear the voice of God. The word "for" in verses 3 and 7 indicates the source for the people's praise: "for the LORD is a great God" and "for he is our God." Images for God include "rock," "maker," and "shepherd."

SECOND READING

ROMANS 13:8-14 (RCL);
ROMAN 13:8-10 (RC)

Paul's central notion is that love fulfills the law (v. 8). This is interpreted as "Love your neighbor as yourself" (v. 9) and "Love does no wrong to a neighbor" (v. 10). Paul's appeal is urgent because of the notion of an imminent end (vv. 11-12), an idea found in several Pauline letters in which the eschatological perspective gives an urgency to exhortations to ethical behavior (1 Cor. 7: 29-31; Phil. 4:4).

While there are seasons of the church calendar (Advent, Lent) in which the notion of preparation for imminent change is prominent, Paul's eschatology of an imminent end is, for the most part, not ours. Nevertheless, the centrality of love for one's neighbor as foundational in community life was the experience of the Israelites, early Christian communities of the second century, and the fourth century desert fathers and mothers. John Colobos said to his disciples: "A house is not built by beginning at the top and working down. You must begin with the foundation in order to reach the top. The foundation is our neighbor, whom we must win and this is the place to begin. For all the commandments of Christ depend on this one."[1]

THE CENTRALITY OF LOVE FOR ONE'S NEIGHBOR AS FOUNDATIONAL IN COMMUNITY LIFE WAS THE EXPERIENCE OF THE ISRAELITES, EARLY CHRISTIAN COMMUNITIES OF THE SECOND CENTURY, AND THE FOURTH CENTURY DESERT FATHERS AND MOTHERS.

ROMANS 12:9-21 (BCP)

See the comments above on the Second Reading for the Fifteenth Sunday after Pentecost, Proper 17.

THE GOSPEL
MATTHEW 18:15-20 (RCL, BCP, RC)

Interpreting the Text

The presence of community regulations in Matthew's Gospel indicates that there was a coherent Matthean community that prayed the Lord's Prayer together (Matt. 6:9-13). The proposed steps in Matthew 18 make every attempt to invite the errant brother (or sister) back into the community. Peter's authority to "bind and loose," i.e., legislate within the Matthean community (Matt. 16:16) as "first amongst equals," is complemented by the community's ability to do the same thing (Matt. 18:18). Jesus' teaching about the heavenly Father continues to be given to insiders, here the Matthean community. Finally, Jesus' statement, "Where two or three are gathered in my name, I am there among them" (Matt. 18:20), evokes Matthew's post-resurrection Christology (28:20: "I am with you [plural] always"), behind which may lie texts like Isa. 12:6 (the Holy One in the midst of Zion); Judith 11:19 (the throne in the midst of Jerusalem); and Ps. 46:5. Gathering in Jesus' name is shorthand for making what is essential to Jesus' character manifest.

Matthew 18 presents a communal approach to dissent in which the individual has at least three opportunities to rethink offense against another. If the community is saying Psalm 119 together, the assumption of innocence is important, because everyone is on the same page. It is surely necessary to gather a larger group together to work out together how to regulate persistent disagreements within a community. Jesus is present in the middle of a group as the interface between community brothers and sisters. At the same time, two or three people must act together in a way that is consistent with who Jesus is.

The writings of the desert fathers and mothers apply Matthew's community regulations to another community in a different time and place. Abba Bitimius questioned Abba Poemen one day: "If someone has a grievance against me and I ask his pardon but cannot convince him, what is to be done?" Abba Poemen answered, "Take two other brothers with you and ask his pardon. If he is not satisfied, take five others. If he is still not satisfied by them, take a priest. If even so he is not satisfied, then pray to God without anxiety, that God may satisfy him, and do not worry about it." As Douglas Burton-Christie points out, Poemen develops and extends Matthew's instruction on forgiveness in intriguing ways.[1] Poemen transforms Matthew's scenario from one in which I have an issue with my brother or sister to one in which my brother or sister has an issue with me that I must find a way to satisfy. In the Matthean text, there is a point of no return after which the offending individual is to be treated as a pagan or tax collector, namely, shunned. Poemen, from the perspective of the one being shunned, proposes that if I have done all I can and the work of reconciliation has failed, the work should nevertheless continue in a different manner: I should pray to God without anxiety that God (alone) may satisfy my accuser.[3] "Poemen's resolution of the problem shows a greater level of detachment and compassion than the Gospel text itself and indicates how he envisioned such a text might be put into practice."[4]

> IF I HAVE DONE ALL I CAN AND THE WORK OF REC-
> ONCILIATION HAS FAILED, THE WORK SHOULD NEVER-
> THELESS CONTINUE IN A DIFFERENT MANNER: I
> SHOULD PRAY TO GOD WITHOUT ANXIETY THAT GOD
> (ALONE) MAY SATISFY MY ACCUSER.

The practice of the desert fathers in this interpretation of Matthew 18 suggests a methodology that we can apply usefully to any text: turn it around. If Matthew says: "If my brother sins against me . . . ," ask the question, "How does this work if I am the sinner against my brother?" The Matthean Jesus enjoins, "And if anyone forces you to go one mile, go also the second mile" (Matt. 5:41). Ask what it means to be the person forcing another to go the extra mile. Ask what it means to hear the Lord's Prayer from God's perspective.

Note

1. *Patrologia Graeca*, ed. J.-P. Migne; 162 vols., vol. 65 (Paris: 1857–86): 217a.

2. Douglas Burton-Christie, *The Word in the Desert: Scripture and the Quest for Holiness in Early Christian Monasticism* (Oxford: Oxford Univ. Press, 1993), 277.

3. *Patrologia Graeca*, 360cd.

4. Burton-Christie, 277.

SEVENTEENTH SUNDAY AFTER PENTECOST

SEPTEMBER 11, 2005
TWENTY-FOURTH SUNDAY IN ORDINARY TIME /
PROPER 19

REVISED COMMON	EPISCOPAL (BCP)	ROMAN CATHOLIC
Exod. 14:19-31 or Gen. 50:15-21	Sir. 27:30—28:7	Sir. 27:30—28:9
Psalm 114 or Exod. 15:1b-11, 20-21 or Ps. 103:(1-7) 8-13	Psalm 103 or 103:8-13	Ps. 103:1-2, 3-4, 9-10, 11-12
Rom. 14:1-12	Rom. 14:5-12	Rom. 14:7-9
Matt. 18:21-35	Matt. 18:21-35	Matt. 18:21-35

September 11, 2001, is a day engraved on the memory of the world. Four years later, the world is a different place. Today's readings speak of miraculous deliverance by the hand of God from enemies (Exodus) and the limitless compassion and forgiveness of the heavenly Father (Ps. 103:13 and Matthew). Paul speaks of the need to be careful of the consciences of "weak" community members.

FIRST READING

EXODUS 14:19-31 (RCL)

Interpreting the Text

As God declared an identity to Moses in Exod. 3:14, suggesting, "My name will be present in my actions," so this reading shows the foundational act of God in Israelite history: the deliverance of the Israelite slaves from the Egyptians. Verses 19-20 describe a pillar of cloud as divine manifestation. The cloud stands between the Israelites and the Egyptians. Moses raises his hand and the Red Sea separates to enable the Israelites to pass through on dry ground. The Lord looks down on the Egyptian army from the cloud and they spin their wheels in the mud. They turn around and God instructs Moses to stretch out his arm and drown the Egyptians. The same sea immediately closes up over the entire Egyptian army, and they are drowned.

God's mighty deeds attest control of nature. The Israelites are saved through a miracle. Yet this is liberation at a cost. Jewish haggadah, service books for the Passover seder, include a midrash describing the angels singing a hymn while the Egyptians are drowning. God rebukes their offensive behavior: "My creatures are drowning in the sea and you want to sing a song?" (*b. Sanh.* 39b).

Qur'anic traditions also report the Exodus (*Sura* 10:90-92), perhaps even indicating that Pharaoh is saved. God is speaking:

> We took the Children of Israel across the sea. Pharaoh with his hosts pursued them in rebellion and hostility till, when the fact of his drowning overtook him, he said: I believe there is no God except the God in whom the Children of Israel believe. I am of those who submit themselves to Him. God said: 'What? Now! Thou hast rebelled and caused depravity. This day We save thee in thy body so that thou mayest be a sign for those who come after thee.' But verily, many among mankind are heedless of Our signs.

For Christians, the symbols of Passover are foundational for the liturgical celebration of Easter. Exodus traditions function in the liturgy as marking the passage from old life to new life. Hence Jews, Muslims, and Christians are brothers and sisters, all people of the book sharing exodus traditions. What are the implications of sharing this tradition?

JEWS, MUSLIMS, AND CHRISTIANS ARE BROTHERS AND SISTERS, ALL PEOPLE OF THE BOOK SHARING EXODUS TRADITIONS.

GENESIS 50:15-21 (RCL, alt.)

Joseph has forgiven his brothers, but they do not comprehend his forgiveness. They act out of guilt and fear and invent a final word of their dying father imploring Joseph's forgiveness for the sins of his brothers. They even offer to be his slaves, just as they had once sold him into slavery. The principle under which Joseph operates is that "although you intended me harm, God intended it for good, so as to effect the survival of many people" (v. 20).

Joseph knows the difference between himself and God. He is not going to function as a judge for his brothers. Joseph doesn't even say he forgives them; this is not his job. He operates on a different principle: that God can bring good out of evil.

ECCLESIASTICUS (SIRACH) 27:30—28:7 (BCP); 27:30—28:9 (RC)

Ecclesiasticus, or The Wisdom of Jesus ben Sira, is a Jewish text written in Greek and classified as wisdom literature, in which there is much practical advice. This particular section decries retributive anger (28:2), in part because it does not promote health or self-esteem. To move beyond retaliation, the text argues, one must think of larger issues: the end of life and, since there is no notion of afterlife in this text, death and decay.

This reading could be understood as a commentary on the unease of Joseph's brothers. They have been locked in a cycle of guilt and revenge ever since they sold Joseph into slavery, to the extent that when they meet Joseph in Egypt, they cannot even speak a word of greeting. They cannot see reality. How can they (or any one of us) break out of this cycle? Look

> THIS READING COULD BE UNDERSTOOD AS A COMMENTARY ON THE UNEASE OF JOSEPH'S BROTHERS.

beyond their immediate circumstances of fear and anticipation of retributive anger from Joseph to see the anguish of their father separated from his beloved son and famine that threatens their lives.

RESPONSIVE READING
PSALM 114 (RCL)

This imaginative psalm commemorates the exodus. The deliverance of Israel is sympathetically echoed by a description of the sea fleeing from God's power and mountains and hills skipping like sheep. Nature is charged with the grandeur of God's deliverance, as the Jesuit poet Gerard Manley Hopkins might have said. Verses 1-2 refer to the northern and southern kingdoms: Israel and Judah. "A people of strange language" refers to a classification of Egyptians by language, not race. In vv. 7-8, the psalmist imagines the earth trembling at God's presence because God's power over nature is so vast that water can be wrought out of stone and a fountain from flinty rock.

EXODUS 15:1b–11, 20–21 (RCL, alt.)

The so-called Song of the Sea (*Shirat Hayam*) celebrates God's triumphant deliverance of the Israelites from the might of the pursuing Egyptians at the Red Sea. As Everett Fox writes, the Song of the Sea "sets off the Egypt traditions from those of Sinai and the wilderness and brings to a spectacular close the saga of liberation."[1] The song begins in the first-person singular: "I will sing to the Lord." and continues, "this is my God and I will praise him; my father's God, and I will exalt him" (Exod. 15:1-2). Why? "Out of his own insight," Abraham Joshua Heschel relates, "a person must first arrive at the understanding: 'This is my God, and I will glorify Him,' and subsequently he will attain the realization that 'He is the God of my father and I will exalt God.'"[2] Access to the universal experience comes only through the rich particularity of our own personal experiences of God. The Song of the Sea challenges us to have our own understanding of past, present, and future and to use that understanding on a path to God. When we make a place for God in our hearts, we are not only nurturing our own spiritual lives—we are in fact building the essence of community. A community whose members recognize this value is indeed a community worthy of a redemptive song.

The miracle was the dividing of the sea for the Israelites, who were able to walk through unharmed on dry land. This imagery conjures up two solid walls of water on either side of the fleeing Israelites (Exod. 15:8-9) visualized by the brick-like formation in the layout of the Hebrew poem creating its own walls. In Torah scrolls, the song must be written in thirty lines and must be laid out in this way with no deviations, or the scroll is *pasul* (invalid).

THE SONG OF THE SEA CHALLENGES US TO HAVE OUR OWN UNDERSTANDING OF PAST, PRESENT, AND FUTURE AND TO USE THAT UNDERSTANDING ON A PATH TO GOD.

Although the song was attributed to Moses (Exod. 15:1), Exod. 15:20-21 retains what scholars now understand to be the vestiges of an older tradition that could not be entirely suppressed, namely, one that attributed the song to Miriam. Washington Allston's portrait of Miriam singing on the shores of the Red Sea, now in the Farnsworth Museum in Rockland, Maine, and Franz Schubert's "Mirjam's Siegesgesang" keep this tradition alive in art and music.

The song has passed into Christian liturgical tradition. It is sung on the Vespers of Holy Saturday in Eastern Orthodox tradition, the eve of the resurrection commemorated at Easter. When the reader reaches 15:1, the reader and the congregation sing the Song of Moses. The reader takes the main verses and the people sing the refrain between each set of verses. The translation follows the Septuagint, and the breaking of verses begins as follows:

Reader: Let us sing to the Lord
People: For he has been clothed with Glory!

In monastic tradition the Song of Moses is sung at Lauds on Thursday. This passed into the Daily Office of the BCP as Canticle 8, one of the canticles sung during Morning Prayer.

PSALM 103 or 103:8-13 (BCP);
PSALM 103:1-2, 3-4, 9-10, 11-12 (RC)
PSALM 103:(1-7) 8-13 (RCL, alt.)

The psalmist extols God's qualities of compassion and graciousness, how God is slow to anger and abounding in steadfast love. God does not nurse a grudge or retain anger for all time. God's righteous acts are most evident in the exodus events (v. 7) when the Israelites saw mighty deeds and experienced liberation. Finally, in v. 13, God is portrayed as a compassionate father who loves his children. Compassion displaces anger and is at the heart of sound relationships.

Second Reading

ROMANS 14:1-12 (RCL);
ROMANS 14:5-12 (BCP);
ROMANS 14:7-9 (RC)

Interpreting the Text

The Roman community to whom Paul wrote contained both weak and strong members. Who might these be? Perhaps, argues Mark Nanos, those "able" to believe (i.e., "strong" ones) are Christ-believers, while the "stumbling" or "weak" are not, and it is along this difference that the line is drawn in Paul's rhetoric. Nanos brilliantly critiques the "almost universal agreement" that both weak and strong were Christians, and that the "weakness" in question was an inadequate appreciation on behalf of Jewish Christians of their freedom from Torah observance. He shows how Christian interpreters have routinely fallen into "Luther's trap," characterizing the Torah-observant "weak," in patronizing or pejorative terms. This interpretation completely ignores Paul's clear acknowledgment that the weak are "fully convinced" that their observance is "for the Lord" (Rom. 14:6) and contradicts Paul's injunctions that the strong not judge the weak. The result is "a theological double standard": Gentiles may

ANYONE WHO HAS BEEN A PART OF RELIGIOUS COMMUNITIES KNOWS THAT WELCOMING DIVERSITY IS A PARTICULAR CHALLENGE.

come to faith in Christ without becoming Jews, but Jews must give up Jewish identity to become Christian. The "weak" of Romans 14 are not Jewish Christians who keep the law. Showing that in the Septuagint and Qumran literature alike, "weakness" was parallel to "stumbling," Nanos concludes that "the "weak" of 14:1—15:12 are the "stumbling" of 9:30-32. Thus the weak and the stumbling are clearly non-Christian Jews; indeed, they are Jews who have "stumbled" over the confession of Jesus as Messiah. Nevertheless, Paul insists they have faith that must be respected by the strong, "even if that faith is characterized as 'weak.'" The "strong" on the other hand, hold "the kind of Gentile prejudices toward Jews" that were prevalent in Rome. The result of Nanos's argument is a truly new perspective that respects "the integrity of Paul as a Jew."[3]

Anyone who has been a part of religious communities knows that welcoming diversity is a particular challenge. Outsiders are likely to gravitate to communities with values similar to theirs. A wonderful example of this in the seminary where I live and work is the inscription on the steps of the seminary chapel, the Chapel of the Good Shepherd: "Blessed are they that enter in through the gates into the City." The chapel opens onto a path that leads out of the seminary property through iron gates to the street. Presumably the blessing (from Rev. 22:14) was intended for those who entered and exited the chapel through the seminary gates onto the street. Today the street gate is locked and the key available only to members of the community. Only seminary insiders can get in and out. To whom does the blessing pertain? A community must, as Paul knew, be intentional and practical in seeking diversity. However, because we are accountable to God in the end, who alone is judge, we cannot indulge in judgment of each other.

THE GOSPEL

MATTHEW 18:21-35 (RCL, BCP, RC)

Interpreting the Text

Peter's question, "Lord, if another member of the church sins against me, how often should I forgive?" continues the discussion of community relations. Jesus' response in Matt. 18:22 can be translated "seventy-seven times" (cf. Gen. 4:24) or seven times seventy. As Plutarch (*Moralia* 245d) indicates, the number 7777 denotes an incalculable number. To the parable that follows, a conclusion is attached: "So my heavenly Father will also do to every one of you, if you do not forgive your brother or sister from your heart" (Matt. 18:35). Forgiveness of others must be driven by a new orientation of compassion, characteristic of God's own steadfast love that Psalm 103 describes. Matthew 18:27 depicts the compassion of the king who forgave the servant's debts. Compassion has been modeled by Jesus throughout the Gospel in active ways—his own compassion for the crowds (9:36; 14:14; 15:32) and individuals whom he heals (20:34) and his ardent yearning for the inhabitants of Jerusalem, his own brothers and sisters (23:37). Thus members of religious communities are to be characterized by the attitudes of mercy and forgiveness toward others. "For if you forgive others their trespasses, your heavenly Father will also

> FORGIVENESS OF OTHERS MUST BE DRIVEN BY A NEW ORIENTATION OF COMPASSION, CHARACTERISTIC OF GOD'S OWN STEADFAST LOVE THAT PSALM 103 DESCRIBES.

forgive you. But if you do not forgive others, neither will your Father forgive your trespasses" (Matt. 6:14-15). The reciprocity of mercy is the theme of 5:7, "Blessed are the merciful, for they will receive mercy" (see 9:13 and 12:7), and consequently the basis of appeal to Jesus in 9:27; 15:22; 17:15.

Lastly, we should note the particularities of the Matthean teaching of God the heavenly Father. While the compassionate care of the Father was evident in Matthew 6, here the heavenly Father is punitive. Dire consequences pursue an unforgiving heart.

Responding to the Text

Mercy and forgiveness are crucial in relationships and community life. A new convert to Christianity asked the desert father Abba Poemen the question, "If a brother is involved in sin and is converted, will God forgive him?" Poemen responded with a question of his own, "Will not God, who has commanded men to act thus, do as much himself and even more? For God commanded Peter to forgive till seventy times seven (Matt. 18:22)." Poemen cites Matthew to assure the brother of the certainty of God's forgiveness, while linking this assurance of God's mercy to the need for humans to forgive each other. If God commands humans to forgive each other to such an extent, how much more will God forgive human beings?[4]

Notes

1. Everett Fox, *The Five Books of Moses* (New York: Shocken), 354.

2. Fritz A. Rothschild, ed., *Between God and Man: An Interpretation of Judaism from the Writings of Abraham J. Heschel* (New York: Free Press, 1959), 242.

3. Mark D. Nanos, *The Mystery of Romans: The Jewish Context of Paul's Letter* (Minneapolis: Fortress, 1996), 154.

4. *Patrologia Graeca*, ed. J.-P. Migne; 162 vols., vol. 65 (Paris: 1857–86): 341d.

EIGHTEENTH SUNDAY AFTER PENTECOST

SEPTEMBER 18, 2005
TWENTY-FIFTH SUNDAY IN ORDINARY TIME /
PROPER 20

REVISED COMMON	EPISCOPAL (BCP)	ROMAN CATHOLIC
Exod. 16:2-15 or Jon. 3:10—4:11	Jon. 3:10—4:11	Isa. 55:6-9
Ps. 105:1-6, 37-45 or Ps. 145:1-8	Psalm 145 or 145:1-8	Ps. 145:2-3, 8-9, 17-18
Phil. 1:21-30	Phil. 1:21-27	Phil. 1:20c-24, 27a
Matt. 20:1-16	Matt. 20:1-16	Matt. 20:1-16

What claims on God do God's people have? Are God's children entitled to anything at all? Do they have a right to expect certain standards? Today's readings remind hearers that God's justice is often not measurable by human standards. The Israelites in the wilderness feel entitled to a lifestyle they had in Egypt. Jonah too expects God to behave in a certain way toward the pagan Ninevites. He is angry at God's generosity. The early workers in the vineyard in Matthew's Gospel grumble at God's generous determination of the wages of latecomers. The prophet Isaiah reminds us that God's ways are not our ways.

FIRST READING
EXODUS 16:2-15 (RCL)

Interpreting the Text

About a month after their journey through the wilderness begins, the Israelites declare their dissatisfaction with provisions on their journey. They complain, recalling how life in Egypt was good (selectively forgetting that they were slaves). God patiently tells Moses of food about to appear and instructs Moses to tell the people how to collect it. Moses and Aaron tell the people that the provisions reveal God's providence and glorious presence. Then Moses and Aaron invite the people into God's presence: "Draw near to the LORD, for he has heard your complaining" (Exod. 16:9). God notes the complaints and repeats the promise for provisions. They appear miraculously. The narrator describes the provisions. The people wonder what they are, and Moses tells them, "It is the bread that the LORD has given you to eat" (Exod. 16:15). Commentators note that the manna provided is solid crystallized tamarisk sap excreted from insects that is found in parts of the Sinai in June and July. If this is the manna described in the text, the miracle is that it appeared both in and out of season and twice as much on the sixth day.

Responding to the Text

Sometimes it seems as if humans are never satisfied. Once free from slavery the Israelites felt they were entitled to expect a certain lifestyle at least commensurate with their Egyptian experience—without the slavery. However, feeling entitled to something means that without it one is aggrieved. The alternative is the "gratitude attitude" (thank you, Oprah!). Embracing gratitude is spiritually and psychologically liberating. Gratitude is the recognition that life owes me nothing and all the good I have is a gift. My health is a gift. So are my friends, my clothes, my job, and my every breath. This is a major shift from the entitlement mode. Recognizing

> GRATITUDE IS THE RECOGNITION THAT LIFE OWES ME NOTHING AND ALL THE GOOD I HAVE IS A GIFT.

that everything good in life is ultimately a gift is a fundamental truth of reality. To try to remind the Israelites of this truth, God provided food only one day at a time, except once a week when a double portion meant that the food did not have to be gathered on the Sabbath. The only response to God's provender is thanks.

The story of Bruria is told in the Talmud. Bruria and her husband, Rabbi Meir, had two sons who both died one Friday afternoon before Shabbat. Bruria decided not to tell her husband of the tragedy until after Shabbat since, according to Jewish law, one is not permitted to have a funeral on Shabbat or to openly mourn. There was nothing they could do until after Shabbat, so she kept the information to herself and allowed her husband to enjoy the day. Explaining where the boys were was the least of her challenges.

When Shabbat was over, this is how Bruria broke the horrible news to her husband. She asked him a legal question: "What is the proper course of action if one person borrows two jewels from another and then the original owner requests the return of the jewels?" He replied with the obvious answer that one is obligated to return the loan upon demand. She then took her husband to where their two dead sons lay and said, "God has requested that we return the loan of our two jewels."[1]

JONAH 3:10—4:11 (BCP; RCL, alt.)

Interpreting the Text

In Jon. 3:1 the word of the Lord comes to Jonah a second time, and this time he goes at once to Nineveh, the capital of Assyria, as the Lord commands. Perhaps to Jonah's astonishment, the people of Nineveh repent, and the reading opens with God's decision to forgo the planned punishment of the city dwellers (v. 10). This displeases Jonah. He expects God to behave differently. What was the point of preaching repentance in Nineveh if God is going to forgo punishment? He sits in a booth overlooking the city and tells God how he feels (4:5). God causes a shady plant to grow up and shelter him (v. 6). The next morning God causes a worm to appear that ate the plant so that it withered, leaving Jonah exposed to scorching sun and a sultry east wind that God also provided. Jonah wants to die (v. 8). God asks if he really cares for the plant whose existence he had nothing to do with (v. 10). "Should I not be concerned about Nineveh, that great city, in which there are more than a hundred and twenty thousand persons who do not [yet] know their right hand from their left, and also many animals?" (v. 11). Jonah seems to be learning that God's compassion encompasses the non-Jewish and the natural worlds, for which Jonah has shown no great interest.

Responding to the Text

What is Jonah's problem? He has received God's mercy and God's providence in the form of shade from the sun's heat, and yet he would deny that mercy to the Ninevites. His expectations of God's behavior are not met. But is he persuaded? That the reading ends with God's and not Jonah's words leaves Jonah's response unknown. Readers can thus supply their own reaction. Some interpreters think that Jonah's attitude indicates his awareness that Assyria will later conquer Israel and take her inhabitants off into exile. It is hard to sit with an open-ended text.

ISAIAH 55:6-9 (RC)

Isaiah enjoins Israelites in exile to seek the Lord in order to repent. God is near. To people who repent, God will indeed issue pardon. However, God's ways and designs are not human ways and designs.

We cannot be reminded too often that God's ways are inscrutable and often incomprehensible to humans. The biblical portrait of God can delude us into thinking of God as a conversation partner with whom we can always be in dialogue. Yet God's otherness too must be a part of our spiritual life. How are we open to the mystery of the divine presence that transcends every human faculty? There are many ways to be mindful of this. We can read translations of the Bible like those of Everett Fox that stress the otherness of the text. We can engage the Christian mysticism of John of the Cross and Meister Eckhart, the silence of the Quaker Meeting, the poetry of R. S. Thomas, and the emptiness of Zen Buddhism, all of which are distinctly apophatic spiritualities. "Apophatic spirituality has to start at the point where every other possibility ends. Whether we arrive there by means of a moment of stark extremity in our lives or (metaphorically) by way of entry into a high desert landscape, the sense of inadequacy remains the same. . . . Prayer without words can only begin where loss is reckoned as total."[2]

RESPONSIVE READING
PSALM 105:1-6, 37-45 (RCL)

The psalmist enjoins praise by invoking first the wonders the Lord has done (v. 5) and then, more specifically, the exodus traditions, including leading Israel out with silver and gold (v. 37). God provided food and water for the Israelites. Mindful of the promise to Abraham, he led his people out in gladness and gave them the lands of nations in order that they might keep his laws.

PSALM 145 (BCP);
PSALM 145:1-8 (RCL, alt.; BCP, alt.);
PSALM 145:2-3, 8-9, 17-18 (RC)

Psalm 145 is an alphabetic acrostic in praise of God sung in the three daily prayer services. It portrays God as king whose qualities are goodness, compassion, kindness, and mercy. Not only does the psalmist praise God every day (v. 1), but praise of God continues from one generation to another in an unbroken fashion (v. 4). The psalm assumes God's beneficence toward the created order and echoes the ending of Jonah.

> NOT ONLY DOES THE PSALMIST PRAISE GOD EVERY DAY (V. 1) BUT PRAISE OF GOD CONTINUES FROM ONE GENERATION TO ANOTHER IN AN UNBROKEN FASHION (V. 4).

SECOND READING
PHILIPPIANS 1:21-30 (RCL);
PHILIPPIANS 1:21-27 (BCP);
PHILIPPIANS 1:20c-24; 27a (RC)

Interpreting the Text

Paul's letter to the Philippians was probably composed in prison. Paul has great affection for the Philippians. However, in spite of this good relationship and the note of joy that pervades the reading (v. 25), v. 20 poses the exaltation of Christ, whether through life or death. Verse 21 replaces these nouns with articular infinitives: "To live is Christ; to die is gain" (NRSV: "living" and "dying"). Verse 22 explains that living in the flesh offers fruitful labor, presumably the "bold proclamation" of vv. 18 and 20. How then is it gain to die? Instead of an explanation, we have a deliberation: "I am hard pressed between the two" (v. 23) followed by a restatement that being with Christ in death is better. Clayton Croy proposes that Paul here is using a rhetorical trope known as "feigned perplexity."[3] Paul expects to continue working for the Philippians, but he presents the issue as a serious quandary: he describes himself as in a quandary in the resolution of which he demonstrates his commitment to them. He thus presents himself as someone who exemplifies the qualities he advocates in the letter, forgoing personal advantage for the sake of others (cf. 2:5-11).

Responding to the Text

For the purposes of the lectionary readings in which inscrutability of God's ways is a theme, perhaps highlighting the "progress and joy in faith" (v. 25) of the Philippians is helpful. The verb *prokopto*, translated as "progress," connotes particularly in philosophical writings moral and spiritual growth here of the Philippian community. Taking stock of the spiritual growth of a congregation is a ministerial or priestly responsibility. Today's readings, stretching listeners to recognize the limitations of human knowledge about God, would seem to be a good occasion to do this.

TAKING STOCK OF THE SPIRITUAL GROWTH OF A CONGREGATION IS A MINISTERIAL OR PRIESTLY RESPONSIBILITY. TODAY'S READINGS, STRETCHING LISTENERS TO RECOGNIZE THE LIMITATIONS OF HUMAN KNOWLEDGE ABOUT GOD, WOULD SEEM TO BE A GOOD OCCASION TO DO THIS.

THE GOSPEL

MATTHEW 20:1-16 (RCL, BCP, RC)

Interpreting the Text

Matthew's version of the parable of the laborers in the vineyard presents particularly Matthean themes: an interpretation of what is just or right (as opposed to what is unjust or wrong) for both hired workers in the parable and disciples in a context of Peter's question: "Look! We have left everything and followed you. What then will we have?" (19:27); a notion of a community of equals in God's kingdom (under one heavenly Father) in which the newcomers are treated as equal to those who came first. The landowner declares an operating principle at the outset; to the second group of hired workers he declares, "I will pay you whatever is right" (v. 4). Discovering themselves to have been paid the same amount as workers hired late in the day, and not having heard the principle spoken to the second group, those hired first object: "These last worked only one hour and you made them equal to us who have borne the burden of the day and the scorching heat" (v. 12). This prompts the landowner to articulate the principle of justice to one of them, "Friend, I am doing you no wrong," or, more literally, "I am not doing you an injustice." Why? Because you agreed to be paid the usual daily wage. The principle receives further elaboration: "[Or] is it not lawful for me to do what I want with what is mine?"(v. 15). The NRSV, "Am I not allowed to do what I choose. . . ?" gives undue weight to the first person singular form of the verb "to wish," implying by "I choose" the independent volition so prized by modern Western societies. The principle by which the householder (God) specifies justice dispensed is one generally allowed, not arbitrarily chosen. "What I wish" is the counterpart of what is just, not unjust. At stake is the distribution not only of wages but of inheritance. What the householder wishes is what is just, but it is not the only principle by which inheritance is bequeathed.

Responding to the Text

Like the Israelites in the desert and Jonah evaluating God's conduct, the first laborers hired in the vineyard have expectations about how the landowner will pay their wages. Thus the story is applied to the first followers of Jesus, like Peter, who think they are entitled to something (19:27). Similarly, modern listeners as faithful churchgoers might be arguing "equal work for equal pay." However, this is an attitude of entitlement. In Matthew's community, disciples who followed Jesus from the start, such as Peter, are treated equally with newer disciples or proselytes. Indeed, newer followers may even come first (v. 16). The wonderful perspective this parable affords is a glimpse into God's notion of recompense: generosity to those newer laborers and fairness to all. John Chrysostom understood this principle:

> THE WONDERFUL PERSPECTIVE THIS PARABLE AFFORDS IS A GLIMPSE INTO GOD'S NOTION OF RECOMPENSE: GENEROSITY TO THOSE NEWER LABORERS AND FAIRNESS TO ALL.

> If any have labored from the first hour, let them receive today their rightful due. If any have come at the third hour, let them feast with thankfulness. If any have arrived at the sixth hour, let them in no wise be in doubt, for in no wise shall they suffer loss. If any be delayed even until the ninth hour, let them draw near, doubting nothing, fearing nothing. If any have tarried even until the eleventh hour, let them not be fearful on account of his lateness; for the master, who is jealous of his honor, receives the last even as the first. He gives rest to him who comes at the eleventh hour, as well as to the one

who has labored from the first hour; and to the last he is merciful, and the first he pleases; to the one he gives, and to the other he bestows; and he receives the works, and welcomes the intention; and the deed he honors, and the offering he praises. Wherefore, then, enter all of you into the joy of your Lord; both the first and the second, receive your reward.[4]

Notes

1. Quoted in "Mastering the Gratitude Attitude," by Rabbi Dov Heller: www .aish.com/spirituality/growth/Mastering_The_Gratitude_Attitude.asp).

2. Belden C. Lane, *The Solace of Fierce Landscapes: Exploring Desert and Mountain Spirituality* (Oxford: Oxford Univ. Press, 1998).

3. Clayton Croy, "To Die Is to Gain: Phil. 1:19-26," *Journal of Biblical Literature* 122, no. 3 (2003): 517–31.

4. John Chrysostom, *Catechetical Homily at Easter;* see also the comments on the Eleventh Sunday after Pentecost, Proper 13, above.

NINETEENTH SUNDAY AFTER PENTECOST

SEPTEMBER 25, 2005
TWENTY-SIXTH SUNDAY IN ORDINARY TIME /
PROPER 21

REVISED COMMON	EPISCOPAL (BCP)	ROMAN CATHOLIC
Exod. 17:1-7 or Ezek 18:1-4, 25-32	Ezek. 18:1-4, 25-32	Ezek. 18:25-28
Ps. 78: 1-4, 12-16 or Ps. 25:1-9	Ps. 25:1-14 or 25:3-9	Ps. 25:4-5, 6-7, 8-9
Phil. 2:1-13	Phil. 2:1-13	Phil. 2:1-11 or 2:1-5
Matt. 21:23-32	Matt. 21:28-32	Matt. 21:28-32

These readings lead us to consider our responsibility before God and humanity. They offer a number of perspectives on the question of humanity's relationship with God. What does God expect of us, and what can we expect of God?

FIRST READING
EXODUS 17:1-7

Interpreting the Text

This is the story of God's demonstration, through Moses, of the divine presence with the Israelites in the wilderness. They question God's way: why rescue us from slavery and then let us die in the wilderness? The marvel of bringing water out of the dry, hard stone does two things in the story. First, it reminds the complainers of God's marvelous leadership across the Nile through Moses' staff. There Moses struck the Nile and made it undrinkable (Exod. 7:21, 24). However, second, it provides the nourishment the people need now. As Yahweh had provided food for them in the previous chapter, now they are given water to drink.

The whole passage is structured around a parallelism, which may be lost in the place names. The pair of terms in v. 2, "quarreled" and "test," are parallel to the names in v. 7, Massah ("quarrel") and Meribah ("test"). Together these characterize the impatience and the faltering nature of the people's faith.

This reading shows us the necessary link between the past and our present, between what God has already done for us and what the divine grace is doing in our present. Moses' staff is the symbol of God's grace then and now. However, the implicit question is the common human complaint that God is unjust. For God to bring the people out of Egypt and then allow them to die made no sense. It is the same question that looms large when we are trying to make sense of the tragic dimension of life. Elie Wiesel, along with many others, asks how the Holocaust was possible if God is just.[1] Many of us asked how God could allow the atrocity of 9/11. Lots of us test God and quarrel with God as a result of these tragedies. The texts, of course, do not answer that question but actually accentuate it. Because for now, at least, there is no answer!

EZEKIEL 18:1-4, 25-32 (BCP; RCL, alt.); EZEKIEL 18:25-28 (RC)

Interpreting the Text

This confronts the question of divine justice head on. Ezekiel 18:2 quotes what seems to have been a popular saying about how God punishes the sinner. Deeply rooted in Hebraic religion is the corporate unity of the people, so that sin in one generation has results in later ones. Like Jeremiah (31:30), Ezekiel rejects the saying in favor of individual responsibility (v. 4). Later in the chapter, attention is focused on the underlying issue: "The way of the LORD is unfair" (v. 25). God turns the statement around, saying that it is humanity's way that is unfair.

Responding to the Text

The massive number of lawsuits in our society today causes one to ask about the individual's responsibility for her or his actions. Is the café responsible when I spill coffee on myself and it is hot enough to burn me? Can we hold the tobacco companies liable for lung cancer or the alcohol producers for suicides among drinkers? These are difficult questions and ones through which we seem to winding our way in North American society.

BOTH JEREMIAH AND EZEKIEL WANT TO PRESERVE A SENSE OF AN INDIVIDUAL'S RESPONSIBILITY FOR HER OR HIS OWN ACTION.

The Hebrew people believed very strongly that future generations are punished for the sins of earlier generations. So this quaint saying: "The parents have eaten sour grapes, and the children's teeth are set on edge." Ezekiel speaks for God in saying, "It is only the person who sins that shall die."

How shall we establish who is responsible for what? Both Jeremiah and Ezekiel want to preserve a sense of an individual's responsibility for her or his own action.

RESPONSIVE READING
PSALM 78:1-4, 12-16 (RCL)

The Psalms are mirrors of human life, both in the past and in the present. The speaker in psalm 78 is not identified, although he or she is a religious leader. That unnamed voice affirms God's care for the people and their ancestors. In vv. 3-4, ancestors, children, and future generations are mentioned. In the enumeration of God's caring actions in the past, both the exodus and the splitting of the rock are mentioned. In the face of human sin and failure, the instruction is a recitation of God's saving activity.

When we find ourselves trapped in sin and broken relationships, it is so easy to believe that God has utterly abandoned us. Our common and popular perspective is that God is in the lives of those who are obedient and faithful but utterly absent in the lives of those who have neither faith nor love. Yet this psalmist assumes just the opposite. God is present for those who are sinners. Perhaps we should look at those who seem hopelessly lost and confused for the presence of divine leadership.

The movie *Lost in Translation* features two lonely and lost people who find themselves in Tokyo. There is no purpose or meaning in life for either of them, and the plot grinds on and on so that we finally feel both their boredom and their alienation. Yet gradually their relationship with one another begins to offer a glimmer of hope. For some of us, that story pictures the way in which God guides even the most lost and hopeless and may well use others who are lost and hopeless to do so.

PSALM 25:1-14 or 25:3-9 (BCP);
PSALM 25:4-5, 6-7, 8-9 (RC);
PSALM 25:1-9 (RCL, alt.)

Psalm 25 is a prayer for the strength to remain faithful. The individual prays for God to teach and lead him or her (v. 4-5). The psalmist confesses sins from the past but also affirms God's presence throughout his life (v. 7). Most interesting, perhaps, is the claim that God is active even in the lives of those who are sinners (v. 8). Again we find the reading trying to articulate God's presence and love in the past as well as the present.

Something curious struck me while reading this psalm. Notice how the psalmist prays by reminding God of God's mercy, steadfast love, goodness, and justice. To eavesdrop on this prayer one might think that the psalmist is telling God who God is, or, perhaps the psalmist is trying to hold God responsible for what God has promised. Is that not the nature of our prayers? We are actually reminding ourselves of the nature of the one to whom we pray. Think for a minute about how much of our praying is really a kind of affirmation of faith.

PHILIPPIANS 2:1-13 (RCL, BCP); PHILIPPIANS 2:1-11 or 2:1-5 (RC)

Interpreting the Text

This well-known passage is rich beyond our reach. Paul (or whoever the author might have been) first articulates a way of life that seems impossible for us (vv. 1-4). "Do nothing from selfish ambition . . . ; regard others as better than yourselves." That's asking a lot of the readers. Thankfully the reading does not end with v. 4. We are invited to "let the same mind be in you that was in Christ Jesus." The word translated "mind" raises problems but seems to refer to disposition, frame of mind, attitude, or contemplation. The point is that the Christ story provides us with a power and attitude that makes the life described in vv. 1-3 possible.

The Christ hymn in vv. 6-11 is an account of both Christ's and God's acts. There are two stages in the hymn: (1) What Christ did (vv. 7-8) and (2) what God did in response to Christ's activity (vv. 9-11). The point of the first stage is Christ's utter self-surrender. Emptying himself of his divine status, he took up life as a human and as God's servant. God's response is to elevate Christ to the status of one to be worshiped. The self-emptying (kenōsis) stands at a pivotal place in the hymn with all of the consequences following that.

Responding to the Text

The Philippians hymn articulates the essence of what faith in Christ pulls from us. The startling message is that receiving requires giving, and serving results in being served.[2] Dying and losing life is the means by which we find ourselves. However, the message of the hymn is gospel not law. The story of what God has done for us in Christ brings about a new way of thinking of ourselves and of life. Above all, this message entails the scandal of the Christian message.

DYING AND LOSING LIFE IS THE MEANS BY WHICH WE FIND OURSELVES.

In her 1964 short story "Revelation," Flannery O'Connor paints a vivid portrayal of Mrs. Turpin, a self-righteous southern woman who despises all blacks and "whitetrash." Her life centers not only in what she believes is her righteousness before God but in the preservation of a way of life. As she is cleaning out the pig-pen one day, she has a vision. There in the sky is a long line of souls moving toward heaven. But at the front of the line are the despised white trash, followed by black folks in white robes. Next come the mentally deranged—the crazies of the community. At the very end of this procession, she sees people like herself, and their faces are filled with shock and horror as a result of what they are experiencing.[3]

"He humbled himself and became obedient to the point of death—even death on a cross. . . . Therefore God also highly exalted him."

THE GOSPEL
MATTHEW 21:23-32 (RCL)
MATTHEW 21:28-32 (BCP, RC)

Interpreting the Text

The power of the Philippians hymn is doubled in this lesson. The RCL includes the setting for the parable, while the reading in the other two lectionaries is comprised of the parable itself, which is usually called the parable of the two sons. Not only is the Matthean ordering of these materials forceful, but coupling this story with the Philippians hymn is a stroke of genius.

Verses 23-27 present a simple conflict story in which Jesus outwits his opponents, "the chief priests and the elders of the people." They demand to know by what authority he ministers and preaches. Jesus responds with his own question about John, which puts the chief priests and elders in a no-win situation so that they dare not answer.

The parable in vv. 28-32 is the first of a series of three parables in Matthew 21 and 22, each of which challenges Jesus' opponents. There is a textual problem with this passage resulting in three different versions of the parable, but the version on which the NRSV translation is based is surely the best of the three.[4] In this case, Jesus asks his opponents his question. The story of the two brothers and their responses to their father's command poses a clear distinction but also creates a dilemma. Given the importance of honor and shame in the society of Jesus' times, it is curious that *both of the sons shame their father*: the first, of course, by not obeying his father, and the second by initially saying no to his father's request.[5] The meaning of such a dilemma may well be that neither son is without fault.

The question "what do you think?" immediately involves the listeners. They will be asked to make a decision at the end of this story. In Matthew Jesus uses the same question on a number of occasions (e.g., 17:25; 22:17, 42; and 26:66). You cannot be only an observer of Jesus' ministry. Something is demanded of you. By saying that it is the first son who is obedient, the chief priests and elders claim that actual service rather than profession is important. The story is followed immediately with two declarations by Jesus (vv. 31b and 32), each of which directly condemn the religious leaders.

Some have interpreted the parable as an allegory, taking God as the father, the vineyard as Israel, and the two sons as the obedient and disobedient Israelites. However, it is probably better that we avoid the allegorical character and search for a single direct message.

Responding to the Text

Many of us could probably write our own version of this parable. Those of us who have or are raising children are not shocked by the child who says, "Yes, dad, I'll take out the garbage," but then never does it. Perhaps, too, we have known a son or daughter who says no to one of our requests but then later thinks better of it and changes her or his mind. Verbal answers are not always the most important thing. What you say may not be what you do. Who of us can claim innocence on that score?

We probably should never pretend that we fully understand any of Jesus' parables, for they continue to stir up further reflections long after we have first considered them. The chief priests and elders, however, seem wise in this case. We have enough who count themselves as believers and servants of God but never get around to service, so we find a contemporary flavor to the parable. However, both sons are less than pure; neither is a model of obedience or faith. Both bring shame upon their father by their behavior. The parable suggests that none of us is a perfect servant of God, for in one way or another we do less than honor God. Maybe the point is that it is not what we say or even what we do that finally matters. What finally matters is that God has come into our world with an offer of a new relationship with our Creator.

IT IS NOT WHAT WE SAY OR EVEN WHAT WE DO THAT FINALLY MATTERS. WHAT FINALLY MATTERS IS THAT GOD HAS COME INTO OUR WORLD WITH AN OFFER OF A NEW RELATIONSHIP WITH OUR CREATOR.

Bernard Brandon Scott makes this interesting observation about one of the themes of Jesus' parable in general and the parable of the two sons in particular: "The parable ironically employs the metaphor of the kingdom as a family because this family is not perfect but ordinary, rife with the tensions of normal families."[6] To live in the reign of God does not mean that we are without our faults, sins, and shortcomings, but it does mean to live with God, other people, and ourselves as accepted and responsible humans.

If you are able, I invite you to read O'Connor's story, "Revelation," and reflect on how it addresses each of us, regardless of our particular prejudices.

Notes

1. See Elie Wiesel's classic *Night,* trans. Stella Rodway (New York: Bantam Books, 1960).

2. Gerald F. Hawthorne, *Philippians,* Word Biblical Commentary 43 (Dallas: Word, 1984), 95.

3. Flannery O'Connor, "Revelation," *The Complete Stories* (New York: Farrar, Straus and Giroux, 1971), 508.

4. For a discussion of the textual problem see Arland J. Hultgren, *The Parables of Jesus; A Commentary,* The Bible in Its World, David Noel Freedman, ed. (Grand Rapids: Eerdmans, 200), 218–20.

5. Bernard Brandon Scott, *Hear Then the Parable: A Commentary on the Parables of Jesus* (Minneapolis: Fortress Press, 1989), 84.

6. Ibid.

TWENTIETH SUNDAY AFTER PENTECOST

<small>OCTOBER 2, 2005</small>
<small>TWENTY-SEVENTH SUNDAY IN ORDINARY TIME /</small>
<small>PROPER 22</small>

REVISED COMMON	EPISCOPAL (BCP)	ROMAN CATHOLIC
Exod. 20:1-4, 7-9, 12-20	Isa. 5:1-7	Isa. 5:1-7
or Isa. 5:1-7		
Ps. 19 or 80:7-15	Ps. 80 or 80:7-14	Ps. 80:9, 12, 13-14, 15-16, 19-20
Phil. 3:4b-14	Phil. 3:14-21	Phil. 4:6-9
Matt. 21:33-46	Matt. 21:33-43	Matt. 21:33-43

Parents sometimes find themselves between a rock and a hard place. One couple we know have a precocious four-year-old son who is so bright and capable that it sometimes frightens his parents. The problem is this: should he be put in a school in which he would be with other children who are equally bright as he is or should he be exposed to a more representative group of peers who are, so-to-speak, "normal"? If you expect too much, do you squash his growth in other ways? If you expect certain things of him, does he begin to feel he has had no choice?

Expectations of others are always dangerous. How then do we understand God's expectation for us? In a sense, these readings continue some of the concerns of those for the previous Sunday. However, most of the readings contribute to that question, not so as to answer it, but complicate it!

FIRST READING
EXOD. 20:1-4, 7-9, 12-20 (RCL)

Interpreting the Text

The two lections for the First Reading are very different, while each contributes something to our understanding of God's expectation of humans. The first is comprised of some parts of the Ten Commandments in the Exodus form (compare these with Deut. 5:6–21). The most striking and important thing about the Exodus version of the commandments is the introduction. In 20:2, God identifies God's self and refers to what God has done for the people of Israel. Because of God's saving actions, the people are to have no other gods. The implication, of course, is that there is a multitude of gods whom people could worship. The earliest strains of Pentateuchal stories assume a multitude of gods, but Israel's God is supreme.

The first four commandments, as is often noted, have to do with our relationship with God, while the last six deal with relationships among humans. Moreover, each of the first five includes a sanction, or a reason why the commandment is made and should be obeyed. Verses 5b-6, 7b, 11, and 12b all explain the reason for the commandment. While the will of God is absolute and unquestionable, these give a rationale for obedience.

Responding to the Text

In parts of the United States, a legal battle is being waged about the propriety of displaying the Ten Commandments in public buildings. Both sides of the debate recognize that these are important and formative. Whatever the outcome of the debate might be, the Jewish and Christian religious traditions value these as fundamental to what our Creator expects of us. Obviously they are inadequate for moral guidance today, since they do not cover all the bases, as it were. Moreover, Christians recognize that in his teachings, Jesus superseded the commandments with assertions of the deeper and wider sovereignty of God. (See the Matthean "antitheses" in 5:21-48.)

The inadequacies of the commandments constitute one of their powers. We are not given a giant collection of law books that provide precedent for every situation we may face. Instead, we are left with the task of determining how, if at all, these divine expectations bear on the decisions we have to make every day. God does not let us off the hook by telling us every little thing we should and should not do, no more than parents provide their children with encyclopedias of moral expectation. The struggles to understand God's will for abortion, homosexuality, preemptive war

> WE ARE LEFT WITH THE TASK OF DETERMINING HOW, IF AT ALL, THESE DIVINE EXPECTATIONS BEAR ON THE DECISIONS WE HAVE TO MAKE EVERY DAY.

and so many more issues are left for us to decide within the context of the community of faith.

ISAIAH 5:1-7 (BCP, RC, RCL, alt.)

Interpreting the Text

This famous "love song" has long been appreciated both in its own right and as a foundation for the parable of the evil tenants of a vineyard in Matt.

21:33-46; Mark 12:1-12; and Luke 20:9-19. The voice in Isa. 5:1-7 belongs to one who sings for a "beloved" who owns the vineyard. "Vineyards" seem to have been a frequent metaphor for a lover, as sections of the Song of Songs demonstrate (e.g., 7:6-13; 8:12). The details of the owner's care for the vineyard in v. 2 demonstrate how important it is for him and makes it all the more tragic when the vines yield no fruit. There is pathos in the two questions in v. 4: What more could I have done? The owner must now take drastic action, again portrayed vividly in the details of vv. 5-6. Finally, without warning, the metaphor is made clear—the Lord is the owner and the vineyard the people of Israel and Judah. God expected justice and righteousness but saw only blood and heard nothing but a cry (v. 7).

Responding to the Text

We have all experienced the disappointment of unfulfilled expectations. The parents who lavish love on a child, only to have the child betray them. The employees who labor long and hard at their jobs only to be passed over for promotion. The friends who have been betrayed by one whom they tried to love and care for. Unfulfilled expectations are painful. And here in this song, God is pictured in that very pain. However, the pain is the good news of God's salvation, not an effort to make us feel guilty. That another should care so deeply for us as the owner cared for his vineyard is the wonderful news of the extent to which God's love goes for us.

Another lover betrays his beloved wife and has a series of affairs with other women. Soon the betrayal becomes common knowledge, and he sees his wife devastated and broken. What does the wayward husband see? He sees among other things how very much his wife loves him and how deeply his unfaithfulness grieves her.

> THAT ANOTHER SHOULD CARE SO DEEPLY FOR US AS THE OWNER CARED FOR HIS VINEYARD IS THE WONDERFUL NEWS OF THE EXTENT TO WHICH GOD'S LOVE GOES FOR US.

RESPONSIVE READING
PSALM 19 (RCL)

This psalm is a model of how Hebraic faith seamlessly connects creation and the law. It begins with a declaration of God's glory in the created order, peppered with provocative and compelling metaphors, such as the sun's coming from a tent like a bridegroom and a strong man (vv. 4b-6). Then, without a transition of any sort, the psalm shifts to the praise of the law. First the created order, then the law. God's expectations of humans are as natural and functional as the sun's passage through the heavens. Verses 7-10 emphasize the character and status of the law. Then, vv. 11-13 accentuate the importance of the law to an individual (or more likely the community spoken of as an individual). "Hidden faults," "insolence," and "great transgression" are the dangers facing one who would be obedient. This psalm ends in v. 14 with a prayer.

One of the amazing things about this psalm, and the Jewish faith in general, is the appreciation of the law. For many of us, law is a negative phenomenon. Okay, we need law to allow us to live in a society without destroying one another. But who among us has ever thought of laws as "sweeter also than honey, and drippings of the honeycomb"? The psalmist finds a beauty and an unsurpassed value in God's expectations of us. In our conviction that law functions to break us of our independence and bring us on our knees to the Gospel, we have perhaps missed something important. Think of how God's expectations of us work harmoniously with each other to produce a meaningful and unified life. The law provides for the poor, represses the greedy, and honors the honest. Does it not "revive the soul" and make "wise the simple"?

PSALM 80 or 80:7-14 (BCP); PSALM 80:9, 12, 13-14, 15-16, 19-20 (RC); PSALM 80:7-15 (RCL, alt.)

Parts of this psalm sound as if it is to be read with the destruction of Jerusalem and the laying waste of the lands of Judah and Israel in mind. The walls are "broken down" and "the boar from the forest ravages it" (vv. 12-13). Clearly, Psalm 80 has been chosen because of its connection with the parable of the tenants of the vineyard, and it supplements the love song of Isaiah 5. As a whole, it is a prayer for restoration (e.g., v. 3) and reiterates the plea, "How long, LORD" (v. 4).

The vineyard metaphor is sketched in vv. 8-13, which sounds much like the Isaiah image. However, the psalmist stretches the metaphor with v. 8, "You brought a vine out of Egypt." The picture deviates from the Isaiah image or the parable in complaining that it is God who has destroyed the vineyard (v. 12) but then changes in v. 16. Verses 3 and 19 provide bookends between which the complaint is made.

It is painful and puzzling to see something that seemed to be God's constructive work in the world suddenly destroyed. Some of you may feel that the work God started in your congregation years ago has been destroyed now. Members have died or moved away. The new building of years ago is now in desperate need of repair. The successors of a beloved pastor back in the "good old days" have been woefully inadequate. The vineyard is in disarray. There is a note of nostalgia in this psalm, not unlike that which we hear in the voices of some of our elderly members, and we join the prayer, "Restore us, O Lord!" The question is whether or not we can discern something new being done among us today—perhaps quite different from what some remember as the best years of the congregation. Let us join the psalmist in the prayer for the future: "But let your hand be upon the one at your right hand, the one whom you made strong for yourself. Then we will never turn back from you; give us life, and we will call on your name" (vv. 17-18).

SECOND READING
PHILIPPIANS 3:4b-14 (RCL);
PHILIPPIANS 3:14-21 (BCP)

Interpreting the Text

Our journey through Paul's letter to the Christians in Philippi brings us to this famous passage filled with the pathos of one who knows his future may be limited. There seems to be a break or at least abrupt transition between vv. 1a and 1b. The tone of what follows 3:1b is considerably different. Paul warns his readers of the dangers that await Christians in the world and defends himself against an implicit threat to his integrity. The reading is comprised of two related parts. In the first (vv. 1b-11), Paul evaluates his life before Christ and after. Verses 3:12—4:1 appear to be his anticipation of the future and an invitation for the readers to imitate his life.

In vv. 4b-6, Paul describes his life as a Jew and takes pride in it. Then in 7-14 he claims he has surrendered all his accomplishments with a righteousness Christ gives him, and he now stretches out into the future for the prize of "the heavenly call of God in Christ Jesus" (v. 14). He does not repudiate his life as a Jew but rather calls it "righteousness under the law" (v. 6). This, along with other passages, such as Romans 9–11, have lead some Pauline scholars to speak not of Paul's conversion but of his new calling. However that may be, here Paul makes clear that he does not claim his past as any sort of credit. Rather, he puts it aside in favor of life in Christ. He counts it mere rubbish when compared to his Christian life (v. 8). (The word translated "rubbish" here means garbage or human fecal matter.) Verse 10 states Paul's goal (knowing Christ and sharing his sufferings), and vv. 12-14 are Paul's disclaimer of having achieved his goal.

Responding to the Text

What do you see when you stop and look back over your life to this point? Some of us, of course, have more to look back over than do others! It may include some major accomplishments or achievements, but it may also include some devastation and loss. Sooner or later, however, we are pressed to decide of what value our past life has been. Does it really "win" us anything? Does it actually promise that the future will be even better?

It is that kind of self-evaluation Paul does in this portion of Philippians. Some of us may be tempted to cling to what we have accomplished in the past, and indeed, for some those accomplishments are important. However, Paul suggests that, for him, at least it is the future that is important. He speaks of some heavenly prize.

We humans need a future. We need the anticipation that there is something ahead of us that is important and for which we strive. Paul is a good example. He hopes to "make Jesus Christ" his "own." But note, too, that his own striving is possible only "because Christ Jesus has made me his own." When we look to the future in confidence that Christ has claimed us as his own, we are no longer trying to achieve something. We are not trying to win enough "Brownie points" to get into heaven. Christ has given us all we need, and with that we too can press on into the future.

PHILIPPIANS 4:6-9 (RC)

Interpreting the Text

Paul has reached the conclusion of his letter to the Philippians, and in this reading we hear a part of his general exhortations to the readers. There are two parts to the reading. In the first (vv. 6-7), he encourages prayer and thanksgiving, the results of which will be God's peace. The second portion (vv. 8-9) summarizes the values he believes Christians should seek and then his admonition to continue to imitate what they have seen in him. It is a practical, down-to-earth conclusion to his efforts to strengthen the readers in their faith.

> WE HUMANS NEED A FUTURE. WE NEED THE ANTICIPATION THAT THERE IS SOMETHING AHEAD OF US THAT IS IMPORTANT AND FOR WHICH WE STRIVE.

Responding to the Texts

In these earlier years of the twenty-first century in the United States, values are up for grabs. Take almost any traditional value, and you will find those who oppose it. In this sort of a cultural setting, we sometimes wonder how we get our moral compass properly set. Of course, this is not the first time in history that there has been a revolution in values. The Philippian Christians probably felt that their new faith had upset all the values of their culture. Paul gave them some simple suggestions, which aren't bad for our own time. Seek what is worthy of praise, and God's peace will be with you. It is not as easy as Paul makes it sound, but with the support and conversation of the community of faith, it sets direction for us.

THE GOSPEL
MATTHEW 21:33-46 (RCL);
MATTHEW 21:33-43 (BCP, RC)

Interpreting the Text

This is the second in a series of three parables in Matthew 21–22, and one which, on the surface at least, seems simple enough. (For Synoptic parallels of this parable, see Mark 12:1-12 and Luke 20:9-19.) The difficulty with this parable is the question of how far we should go in reading it as an allegory (i.e., each character and action in the story represents contemporary figures and/or occurrences). It has frequently been interpreted as a condemnation of Israel for their failure to care for what God had given them and has been attributed not to Jesus but to the early church. While we probably should not so quickly and easily dismiss the possibility that Jesus sometimes uses allegory, once again it is best first to try to make sense of the story without allegory.

Like so many of Jesus' parables, this one has a solid basis in contemporary life in first century C.E. Palestine. Rome awarded conquered land to worthy warriors and statesmen, and hence absentee owners and tenant farmers were common. The fact that the tenants would rebel in an effort to win the land for themselves is also quite realistic. Furthermore, their hope that by murdering the owner's son the land would become ownerless and they could claim it as their own is probably quite reasonable.

As ruthless as the tenants seem to us, their behavior is more believable than that of the owner. That the owner would persist in sending representatives to claim his rightful share of the harvest makes some sense, but does it make any sense that after the murder and beating of two groups of his slaves, he would then send his own son thinking, "They will respect my son" (v. 37)? With this act, the focus of the story shifts from the dastardly tenants to the unbelievably patient owner. Only after his son is killed does his patience weaken. Like a number of parables, this one ends with a question to the listeners (v. 40): "Now when the owner of the vineyard comes, what will he do to those tenants?" The passage, then, may be among those attributed to Jesus that shock readers with the nearly inexhaustible patience of God.[1]

Verse 42 is a quotation of the Septuagint version of Ps. 118:22-23, and v. 43 is likely a Matthean construction. The problem the latter poses is the question of who is meant by "you" in the statement "the kingdom of God will be take away from *you!*" Does it threaten the religious leaders of the time and perhaps refer to Rome's defeat of the Jewish revolution? That certainly seems the sense of the conclusion of the chapter in vv. 45-46. However, could it be addressed to you and me?[2]

Responding to the Text

Who owns the farm? The parable asks that question and dares us to answer it. In the last decade, we heard a great deal about CEOs and other leaders making enormous amounts of money at the expense of the stockholders and ordinary employees of large corporations. Leaders have "cooked" the books of their companies and made the companies their personal "piggy banks." It sounds rather like a contemporary version of those greedy tenants in the parable who want to take ownership of the vineyard. So, who owns the farm?

A constant temptation in congregations is getting and keeping the answer to that question right. We may forget that we are servants who have been entrusted with the responsibility of being the church. We may forget that we are little more than tenant farmers responsible for what God has given us.

But that is not the whole story of the parable for us today. The parable asks us to remember why we are here, but God knows that we can never be as faithful as we should be. So God keeps sending us messengers to remind us of who owns the farm. In the parable, the owner sends one group of his servants, then another, and finally his own son. We know that we cannot of our own power be faithful tenants of the church and our world. We must rely totally on God's ceaseless and patient love for us.

> WE CANNOT OF OUR OWN POWER BE FAITHFUL TENANTS OF THE CHURCH AND OUR WORLD. WE MUST RELY TOTALLY ON GOD'S CEASELESS AND PATIENT LOVE FOR US.

Dwelling with the Text

As a youth, I grew up in the Methodist church, and I learned the prayer of "humble access" used at each Communion service. I still find it helpful, not only in preparation to take the sacrament, but whenever I need to remember my dependence on God's continuing grace.

We do not presume to come to this thy table, O mercifully Lord, trusting in our own righteousness, but in thy manifold and great mercies. We are not worthy so much as to gather up the crumbs under thy table. But thou art the same Lord, whose property is always to have mercy. Grant us, therefore ,gracious Lord, so to partake of this Sacrament of thy Son Jesus Christ, that we may walk in newness of life, may grown into his likeness, and may ever-more dwell in him, and he in us. Amen."[3]

Notes

1. See the provocative discussion of the parable in John R. Donahue, S.J., *The Gospel in Parable* (Philadelphia: Fortress Press, 1988), 52–57, 89–92.

2. M. Eugene Boring, *The Gospel of Matthew: Introduction, Commentary, and Reflections,* New Interpreter's Bible (Nashville: Abingdon, 1995), 8:414–15.

3. *The United Methodist Hymn: Book of United Methodist Worship* (Nashville: United Methodist Publishing House, 1989), 30.

TWENTY-FIRST SUNDAY AFTER PENTECOST

October 9, 2005
Twenty-eighth Sunday in Ordinary Time /
Proper 23

Revised Common	Episcopal (BCP)	Roman Catholic
Exod. 32:1-14	Isa. 25:1-9	Isa. 25:6-10a
or Isa. 25:1-9		
Ps. 106: 1-6, 19-23	Psalm 23	Ps. 23:1-3a, 3b-4, 5-6
or Psalm 23		
Phil. 4:1-9	Phil. 4:4-13	Phil. 4:12-14, 19-20
Matt. 22:1-14	Matt. 22:1-14	Matt. 22:1-4 or 22:1-10

These lections lead us back and forth between grace and works or, more precisely, what God does for us and what we are to do for God. As usual, the passages do not resolve that tension but give it new vitality.

First Reading

EXODUS 32:1-14 (rcl)

Interpreting the Text

In terms of the narrative, this story brings to another climax the insecurity and fear of the people wandering in the wilderness. It also represents the way in which law seems to be given to be broken. As recently as twelve chapters earlier, God commanded that the people should not make idols and worship them (20:4; repeated again in 20:23). The people's anxiety arises as a result of what they think is Moses' abandonment of them and their being left without a leader. So, they turn to Aaron, the one who was appointed to speak for Moses (Exod. 4:14-16) and who has served as Moses' chief assistant, especially in his absence (Exod. 24:14). Yet Aaron, too, is taken up in the anxiety of the moment and orders the people to make the golden calf. Having done so, they eat and drink and revel.

Moses takes a priestly role to intercede for his people to convince Yahweh not to "consume" them. He asks Yahweh to remember the covenant made with Abraham Isaac, and Israel, and "the Lord changed his mind about the disaster that he planned to bring on his people" (v. 14).

We can understand how the absence of a leader creates desperation, and so we ought not be quick to condemn Aaron and the people. We know what it is like to feel out of touch with God, as the people did that day. For them Moses was their contact with God, and like it or not, they had been forced to trust him. Feeling alienated from God leads many of us to seek another power. In 2004 a survey found that church attendance had increased in the United State in the wake of the destruction of the twin towers in New York City. Fear, confusion, and uncertainty drove people to seek some transcendent power that would care for them. In those cases, one might ask if some god became a "golden calf."

> FEELING ALIENATED FROM GOD LEADS MANY OF US TO SEEK ANOTHER POWER.

ISAIAH 25:1-9 (BCP; RCL, alt.); ISAIAH 25:6-10a (RC)

Interpreting the Text

This passage makes a sharp turn in v. 6, so that the preceding five verses seem to constitute one unit and vv. 6-10 another. Together these parts are confusing because each speaks of a city but apparently not the same one. The city mentioned in v. 2 may be a representation of the region of unbelievers ("the palace of aliens is a city no more," v. 2), while the city on the mountain is surely Jerusalem. First, God is praised and the divine actions lauded. The city is destroyed by God, the prophet claims, even though God shelters the poor and homeless. Finally, God shelters all those who suffer loss.

The second phrase of the passage speaks of "the mountain" and has a strong eschatological tone. God prepares a feast on "this mountain" (i.e., Mount Zion). However, the mountain is also the site of God's re-creation of the people (vv. 7-8). God destroys the shroud and sheet, swallows death, wipes away all tears, and rescues the people from disgrace. The meanings of "the shroud" and "the sheet" are not clear; although the proclamation of the end of death in v. 8 makes it possible to believe they are related to burial clothes. This great transformation and salvation of the human condition will elicit rejoicing and praise, as well as the continued presence of God on this mountain.

> GOD DESTROYS THE SHROUD AND SHEET, SWALLOWS DEATH, WIPES AWAY ALL TEARS, AND RESCUES THE PEOPLE FROM DISGRACE.

Responding to the Text

We cannot be sure of the meaning of v. 7, which speaks of the end of death. Paul quotes v. 7 in his famous declaration of the promise of the resurrection of the dead at the end of time (1 Cor. 15:54b). It may be too much to assume that Isaiah means the end of death in any literal sense. However, as one commentator says, "The prophetic voice declares that life, not death is what God endorses."[1] Life, not death! We may be tempted to think that God desires the death of some, even that God causes the death of some. When we are confronted with an enemy, like the terrorists who threaten us, we may want to say that God wants them all dead. However, our God is life-affirming. We may think that it is not necessary to say this, but let's acknowledge that there is a temptation at least to sometimes question it.

RESPONSIVE READING
PSALM 106:1-6, 19-23 (RCL)

The first part of the reading (vv. 1-6) expresses thanks to God for faithfulness and forgiveness (v. 1-3), followed by the psalmist's confession and plea for mercy (vv. 4-5). Finally, the psalmist unites with ancestors who have all sinned (v. 6). The psalm details the way God has forgiven the people (vv. 7-15) and then turns to the people's experience in the wilderness (vv. 16-18). Verses 19-23 comprise a poetic image of the golden calf incident, climaxing with Moses standing "in the breech" between God and the people. Several themes are worth noting. The first is the psalmist's confession that he or she is part of a tradition of sin and wickedness. Too often we may be hesitant to acknowledge our inheritance of sin. The second theme once again is God's history of steadfast love and mercy.

The individualism of our culture sometimes prevents our comprehension of the impact of our ancestors on our lives. Psychologists and sociologists continue to point out that we are all products of our culture, but we seem to want (need?) to take full responsibility without acknowledging our heritage. We should not evade responsibility. However, we want to understand ourselves better; and to do that, we need to see from where we have come.

PSALM 23 (BCP; RCL, alt.);
PSALM 23:1-3a, 3b-4, 5-6 (RC)

This beloved psalm begins with a statement of who God is. The image of the shepherd is difficult for urban dwellers today, since few of us are acquainted with sheep and shepherds. The result is that we have tended to romanticize the shepherd. To name God shepherd is to identify God with the way the shepherd cares for his sheep, his precious possessions. It implies the protection against dangers, which the shepherd provides. The reference to "still waters" alludes to the fact that sheep are often frightened by moving waters.

What God does, then, is integral to who God is. God fulfills our basic needs as a shepherd does for his sheep. However, life with this shepherd-God is no fairy-tale land, for we are led through suffering and seated at meal with our enemies. God's protection does not guide us away from suffering and pain or from enemies.

It is difficult to preach on a well-known and beloved passage like Psalm 23. People are tempted to think they already know what it means and don't want the preacher to disturb their sense of comfort in believing they already know all they need to know about it. Because of the romanticizing of this image of God as a shepherd, it has lost its power. In biblical times, shepherds were not idealized. They were itinerant, never putting down roots in one place, and for that reason they often aroused suspicion. They were known for robbing the villages at night, and by the next morning they were gone on to another site. So, using the shepherd as an image for God (cf. Ezek. 34:11-16) had a certain shock value.[2] The other thing about this psalm is its realistic appraisal of what God does. Even though God leads us, we pass through valleys of suffering and must deal with our enemies. It is interesting that the divine Shepherd prepares a meal for us with our enemies? Rather than helping us avoid them, God leads us to deal with them directly. Perhaps that message is one especially relevant for us today, as our culture seems to become more and more polarized.

> LIFE WITH THIS SHEPHERD-GOD IS NO FAIRYTALE LAND, FOR WE ARE LED THROUGH SUFFERING AND SEATED AT MEAL WITH OUR ENEMIES.

SECOND READING

PHILIPPIANS 4:1-9 (RCL);
PHILIPPIANS 4:4-13 (BCP);
PHILIPPIANS 4:12-14, 19-20 (RC)

Interpreting the Text

This is the conclusion of what is perhaps Paul's most personal letter. His reference to the two women who "have struggled beside" him is both touching and instructive of how women were involved in the ministry of the early church. There follows a number of exhortations, some of which are very familiar (e.g., v. 7). (See the previous Sunday for a brief discussion of 4:6-9.) In vv. 10-20, he thanks the Philippians for their support but is hesitant to say that he is in any need (vv. 16-18). He expresses a remarkable contentment (one that sounds even Stoic) since he has found that God fulfills all his essential needs. He has already lavished praise on Epaphroditus (2:25-26) and now indicates that he carried the Philippians' gift to Paul. As is often the case in the conclusions of his letters (e.g., see Romans 16), Paul acknowledges other members of his missionary team.

Responding to the Text

Paul's contentment is remarkable. My father-in-law was a Norwegian immigrant to the United States and managed to scrape little more than a bare living out of land he farmed. Yet Martin was the most contented person I have ever known. You could hardly buy him a gift at Christmas and his birthday because he so deeply believed that he didn't need a thing. His contentment arose in part out of his background of bare necessities. How-

PAUL'S CONTENTMENT IS REMARKABLE.

ever, one could hardly miss the fact that his peace was rooted in his faith. He believed that God had already given him the most important things in life—love, grace, and care. Why would he need more?—he seemed to say. He sounds like a contemporary Paul. Would that more of us could discover that kind of contentment in the Gospel!

THE GOSPEL

MATTHEW 22:1-14 (RCL, BCP, RC);
MATTHEW 22:1-10 (RC, alt.)

Interpreting the Text

This parable has at least four scenes or movements. In the first, we learn of a king who has prepared a wedding banquet and sends his slaves out with invitations to the affair. However, no one would accept the invitation, and some even mistreated his slaves. This enrages and embarrasses the king, so in the second scene, he sends his army to destroy these impolite people. The third scene opens with the king declaring that those who had been invited "were not worthy," and he again sends his slaves out to find peo-

MATTHEW HAS MODIFIED THE THEME OF GRACE IN THE EARLIER PORTIONS OF THE PARABLE WITH AN INSISTENCE THAT THE LIFE OF FAITH ENTAILS OBEDIENCE.

ple to fill the wedding hall. He orders them to go "into the main streets and invite everyone you find to the wedding banquet." We are told that they succeeded "and gathered all whom they found, both good and bad."

Unfortunately, the story doesn't end on this joyful note. In the next scene, the king inspects how his guests are garbed. He finds some guests inappropriately dressed and orders that they be bound and thrown "into the outer darkness, where there will be weeping and gnashing of teeth." The story ends with the narrator's statement that many will be called but only a few chosen.

What a strange story this is, especially because of vv. 11-14. When compared to the similar parable in Luke 14:16-24, we may even be offended by the wedding garment incident. It sounds as if Matthew has soured a parable about the open invitation of grace with a works-righteousness insertion. Again this allegorical parable needs to be handled carefully. The issue seems to come down to the question of what the absence of a wedding robe means. Is it indeed a wedding robe that is the issue? Joachim Jeremias argued that the garment is soiled, and by wearing it, the guest has insulted his host.[3] As convenient as that sounds, the Greek offers no hint that such interpretation is sound. It is perhaps simpler to take the garment as a metaphor for the guest's moral life. If this is the case, then Matthew has modified the theme of grace in the earlier portions of the parable with an insistence that the life of faith entails obedience. Such a modification seems entirely consistent with the first Gospel as a whole. Obedience follows grace.

Responding to the Text

On their second trip out inviting people to the wedding, the slaves "gathered all whom they found, *both the good and the bad*" (v. 10). The initial invitation has no moral prerequisites. You do not have to show your credentials as a good person to be invited to God's banquet. We may be taken aback by this explicit inclusion of all kinds of people, for we are often tempted to set moral standards for life in the community of faith. Some are scandalized by the possibility that "bad people" might be part of the Christian household. However, Matthew knows exactly what he or she was doing with the phrase, "both and the good and the bad." Grace has no prerequisites, no conditions, and no preparation. Pure grace ignores the moral life of those who truly seek it.

But wait! What does it mean, then, that some quests are thrown out because they are not wearing a wedding robe (a tuxedo?). Isn't that the imposition of a standard? The garment in question is most likely a metaphor for obedience and righteousness. So does it not ruin the grace-filled story of the wedding banquet? Matthew seems to be saying that after the acceptance of grace, one is called to live a life appropriate to the reign of God. But notice that obedience *follows the acceptance of grace and does not precede it*. When God fills our lives with grace, love, and acceptance, then we want to obey our Benefactor. Our gratitude for what God has done for us leads us to faithful living.

The relationship of faith and good works is not an easy one and has a history of dividing the church. I have tried to follow the simple idea articulated first (I think) by Martin Luther. "For faith is followed by works as the body is followed by its shadow."[4] Maybe we should once in a while glance down to see if our behavior follows the grace God has given us.

Find yourself in these readings. Look back over all of the passages to see if you can find one character with whom you most closely identify. What difference does your identification with this person make in the way you read the passage?

Notes

1. Gene M. Tucker, *The Book of Isaiah 1–39: Introduction, Commentary, and Reflections,* The New Interpreter's Bible (Nashville: Abingdon, 2001), 6:217.

2. See Kenneth Ewing Bailey, *Poet and Peasant: A Literary-Cultural Approach to the Parables in Luke* (Grand Rapids: Eerdmans, 1976), 147.

3. Joachim Jeremias, *The Parables of Jesus,* rev. ed.; trans. S. H. Hooke (New York: Charles Scribner's Sons, 1972), 187–88.

4. Quoted by George Wolfgang Forell in *Faith Active in Love: An Investigation of the Principles Underlying Luther's Social Ethics* (Minneapolis: Augsburg, 1954), 56.

TWENTY-SECOND SUNDAY AFTER PENTECOST

OCTOBER 16, 2005
TWENTY-NINTH SUNDAY IN ORDINARY TIME /
PROPER 24

REVISED COMMON	EPISCOPAL (BCP)	ROMAN CATHOLIC
Exod. 33:12-23	Isa. 45:1-7	Isa. 45:1, 4-6
or Isa. 45:1-7		
Psalm 99	Ps. 96 or Ps. 96:1-9	Ps. 96:1, 3, 4-5,
or Ps. 96:1-9 (10-13)		7-8, 9-10
1 Thess. 1:1-10	1 Thess. 1:1-10	1 Thess. 1:1-5b
Matt. 22:15-22	Matt. 22:15-22	Matt. 22:15-21

Threaded through all (or nearly all) these readings is the theme of human leadership. Moses needs an assistant to help him be a good leader. The Persian general Cyrus is God's agent for freeing Israel. God is thought of in royal images. Jesus responds to the issue of loyalty to the emperor and loyalty to God.

FIRST READING
EXODUS 33:12-23 (RCL)

Interpreting the Text

Following on the heels of Moses' communicating with God in the tent of meeting outside the camp, it sounds as if Moses is seeking reassurance from God and wants an assistant chosen by God. Apparently he finds Joshua ineffective. The conversation is peppered with the words "see," "know," and "face." God reiterates the promise that the divine presence will go with Moses, just as God had promised on Sinai (Exod. 3:12), but Moses wants some way to certify that he is God's agent (v. 16). Then Moses asks to see God's "glory" (meaning God's aura, the particular invisible atmosphere that followed the divine presence). Instead, God speaks of the divine goodness and the impossibility of Moses' seeing God's face. Moses stands in a cave while God passes by, guarding against being seen by Moses. Then, Moses may see God's back!

The anthropomorphic language used of God is not unusual in the Old Testament, but this story seems extravagant, supposing that God has a "back." The point of the story is that even Moses, God's special agent, is not able to see God face-to-face.

Responding to the Text

The story is an odd one. On the one hand, it stresses the absolute mystery of God's being, and on the other, it attributes a backside to God. Does that not characterize our own situation? Like Moses we wish that we could have some visual evidence of God's being, for how else can we make our faith seem well founded? Others ask us how we know God, and we have no "hard evidence." Deprived of sensory perception, we have no choice but to believe even though we cannot see. At least until another comes who has been in God's own heart (John 1:8)

ISAIAH 45:1-7 (BCP; RCL, alt.); ISAIAH 45:1, 4-6 (RC)

Interpreting the Text

This reading is taken from that portion of Isaiah often attributed to "Second Isaiah," a prophetic figure who lived during the period of the exile. In this case, the message is simply that God has a plan whereby the people will be released and freed to return to their homeland. God calls Cyrus to be the agent of liberation. Cyrus was a king and warrior of Persia, and it is he who leads the Persian army to topple Babylon, thus freeing the people in exile to return home (539/538 B.C.E.). The story of the Hebrew people is dotted with times God used a human agent and not necessarily one who was a believer. They attribute the fall of Jerusalem to God's hand working though Nebuchadnezzar to punish the people and carry them off into exile (587 B.C.E.). Isaiah 40:2 indicates that the people thought their fate was a result of their sin. The reading, however, contains the passage in which Cyrus is called God's "anointed," a title reserved for the kings.

Verses 2-3 suggest that God would work in such a way that Cyrus would know that it was Yahweh who was enabling his victories. Yet v. 4 indicates that Cyrus would never know Yahweh. The last sentence of the reading is important: "I the LORD do all these things."

Responding to the Text

How does God work in our world? Where can we observe the activity of God today, or can we ever know it is God behind events? In recent history, especially, it seems that some of the major developments in world history have appeared to be purely the result of human action. It took the church considerable time to realize that the freedom movement among African Americans was a working out of divine will. The church resisted the woman's movement almost until it had no choice but to join it. The point is clear that God does not work in our world exclusively through the believing community.

Such was the case for the people of Israel in exile and yearning for the freedom to return to their homeland. Their liberation came through a Persian general/ king, Cyrus—one who hardly knew who the God of the people of Israel was. However, the prophet who appeared among them to announce God's liberation declared that God had chosen Cyrus. This unnamed prophet even declared that Cyrus was God's messiah, or anointed one. Fortunately, God's plan for the world comes not only or exclusively through Christians. So we watch and become sensitive to what might be happening in our world.

GOD DOES NOT WORK IN OUR WORLD EXCLUSIVELY THROUGH THE BELIEVING COMMUNITY.

RESPONSIVE READING
PSALM 99 (RCL)

This is one of the so-called enthronement psalms, which include 47, 93, and 95–99. Scholars have long thought that these psalms were used on occasions that celebrated God's kingship, which in some cases involved the inauguration of a new human king. Psalm 99 is a song of praise and a celebration of God's holiness. Note the repetition of the word "holy" in vv. 3, 5, and 9. (In this case, holiness means the utter otherness of God, whose being is beyond human limitations.) Amid this emphasis on the otherness of God, one is impressed by the characteristics attributed to God beyond the divine rule and exaltation. God is a "lover of justice and righteousness" (v. 4) and "a forgiving God." The king of Israel was more than a mighty being; this king is the epitome of moral virtue.

You have heard the stories of the discovery of the new Buddha in Tibetan Buddhism. After the death of the ruling Buddha, the new one enters the world secretly and may be born to any one of the inhabitants of the land. It is the task of the wise men of the religion to know when the new Buddha has been born. So they walk into a humble home and look for a newborn infant to exhibit signs of his real identity. If he does show such signs, he is taken away to begin his rule of the land.

We need a king, a leader, a master, and when there is a void, we look where we can for a replacement. The reason royal families continue to be important in our world is that everyone knows where the new king will be born. When you have a king or queen, you celebrate and submit yourself to him or her. Israel regularly celebrated the kingship of Yahweh, not because the celebration made Yahweh any more powerful—indeed this king needs no more power. His subjects rejoice that they have a king who is mighty, justice and holy. We Christians should celebrate the kingship of Christ simply because it is a joyful thing to have a leader.

PSALM 96:1-9 (10-13) (RCL, alt.); PSALM 96 or 96:1-9 (BCP); PSALM 96:1, 3, 4-5, 7-8, 9-10 (RC)

This is another of the enthronement psalms honoring God's royal status. In this case, Yahweh's royalty is contrasted with the idols and elevated above all the gods of the world (v. 5). Yahweh's salvation and creative activity set this God off from all others. Furthermore, the whole of creation rejoices with the people in Yahweh's stature. Note that the heavens, earth, sea, field, and trees all join in the ceremony (vv. 11-13). The song ends with a declaration that Yahweh is coming to judge the world.

In C. S. Lewis's *The Lion, the Witch, and the Wardrobe,* the children climb through a wardrobe to find the whole new secret world of Narnia. But this new world is ruled by evil people, and consequently it is always winter and spring never comes. The children discover, however, that many are expecting the Lion Aslan to return and take back the rule of Narnia—a rule that is really his anyway. Aslan does return, and everywhere he walks, there suddenly appear flowers and fresh grass around his paws. Everyone knows that he will drive the wicked rulers out of the land and spring will come.

The true ruler of the universe brings spring, flowers, and fresh grass, and we recognize him for who he is. We can worship Jesus' God because we know this King is real and brings life where there had been only death.

SECOND READING

1 THESSALONIANS 1:1-10 (RCL, BCP); 1 THESSALONIANS 1:1-5b (RC)

Interpreting the Text

By some estimates, the Thessalonian letters may be the first Paul wrote, at least of those that survived. This simple document indicates the basic contents of letters in the Greco-Roman world and therefore begins with a greeting that names the senders and a declaration of peace and grace followed by a statement of thanksgiving. The latter wins the readers' attention and rehearses the history between them and the letter's author. Interestingly, of all the Pauline letters in the

New Testament, there is only one that does not have a thanksgiving, for Paul was angry enough that he could not write praise for the Galatians. Our reading includes only the salutation, the peace, and the thanksgiving, the latter being the longest. Paul is part of a missionary team at this time, and the letter comes from all three of them—Paul, Silvanus, and Timothy. They praise the Thessalonians' steadfastness in the Christian message they received from this team. The message came to them accompanied by the Spirit (v. 5), a sign for the first Christians that God was working through them. Verse 6 indicates that the readers have experienced some persecution, although we know nothing more about it. The readers are praised for having "turned to God from idols" (v. 9) and await Christ's return. Unfortunately, such thanksgivings as this one tell us little about the recipients except that they embraced the missionaries' message.

Responding to the Text

Imagine what it might have been like in the city of Thessalonica when the Christians there received this letter from Paul and his companions. Gluing together the little information we have, we know they had not been Christians long but apparently attracted the attention of some other churches in the region. We can imagine that it was not easy for them. They must have wondered: Who is this Jesus person about whom the missionaries had talked? How is he different from the other gods we worship? When they embraced this new religion, their neighbors immediately became suspicious of them. What was in it for them? How would they act now that they had embraced this Jesus faith?

> WHO WAS THIS JESUS PERSON ABOUT WHOM THE MISSIONARIES HAD TALKED? HOW WAS HE DIFFERENT FROM THE OTHER GODS WE WORSHIP?

It wasn't long before old friends who were cherished by the young Christians refused to associate with them anymore. The cordial village spirit that had made life in Thessalonica bearable was withheld from them. They were ostracized, made fun of, and treated as if they had some sort of disease. The young Christians had not expected this. In their jubilant enthusiasm for their new faith, they could not imagine they would be isolated from their home town. Then, a letter from Paul, Silvanus, and Timothy arrived, and reading their praise for the Thessalonian Christians strengthened the resolve of the young Christians to remain faithful.

Most of us have never experienced this sort of persecution. Our Christian faith never made us seem to be odd or weird. Perhaps we should think about those first Christians and try as best we can to pick up some of their enthusiastic resolve.

MATTHEW 22:15-22 (RCL, BCP);
MATTHEW 22:15-21 (RC)

Interpreting the Text

This reading tells the story of the first of another three attempts on the part of the religious leaders to entrap Jesus and discredit him with others. The question of paying taxes to Rome was a thorny one in Jesus' day, and this story may have been remembered and repeated because taxation continued to trouble the young Christian community. The opponents this time are the Pharisees and Herodians. The latter group was comprised in all likelihood of supporters of the Herodian rulers (e.g., Herod, the Great, Herod Antipas). The Pharisees, we need to remember, were lay Jews who

> THE QUESTION OF PAYING TAXES TO ROME WAS A THORNY ONE IN JESUS' DAY, AND . . . TAXATION CONTINUED TO TROUBLE THE YOUNG CHRISTIAN COMMUNITY.

had taken upon themselves to obey the whole of the biblical law, including even those parts required only of the priests. They were devout Jews who tried to be as faithful to the law as they possibly could be.

When they asked Jesus whether it was "lawful to pay taxes to the emperor or not," they thought they might trap him into saying something offensive, either about the Romans or about his Jewish faith. Matthew tells us that Jesus knew very well what they were up to. A group of rebellious Jews were toying with the idea of withholding taxes from Rome and believed that it was fundamentally evil to support such an evil regime. If Jesus said no, it is not lawful to pay the Roman tax, he would be aligned with the rebellious minority. If, on the other hand, he were to say yes, his loyalty to the Jews and Jerusalem would be questioned.

Receiving a coin from one of them, Jesus asked whose inscription was on it. A denarius of that time would have had the image of the emperor's head, along with the inscription, "Tiberius Caesar, son of the Divine Augustus." His opponents, probably a bit puzzled by Jesus' question, replied that the inscription was of the emperor. Then came the response that settled the matter: "Give therefore to the emperor the things that are the emperor's and to God the things that are God's." He had outfoxed the religious leaders again. Unfortunately, the meaning of his saying continues to puzzle us.

Responding to the Text

"Give therefore to the emperor the things that are the emperor's and to God the things that are God's." Those words have been the source of much controversy. They have been taken entirely out of the context of taxes to become the basis for the absolute separation of religion and politics. By equating the emperor's and God's due, these people argue that we must never mention matters of politics or social issues in the church, much less in the pulpit. Without a great deal of argument, let's recognize that such a use of Jesus' words is not legitimate.

Then what does this saying mean to us? The most common position is to say it urges us to make a clear distinction between our religious loyalties and those involving the state. We pay taxes. We support our nation. We involve ourselves even in political and social matters. But another kind of loyalty is due to God. Trouble is, I have never been sure what that means. After our political, national, and social debts are paid, what's left for God?

I invite you to ask yourself one question about this saying. What is there that isn't God's? Is there a loyalty to the president of the United States that has nothing to do with our loyalty to God? Consider this: If all there is, is ultimately a result of God's work of creation or redemption, is not everything due God?

> I INVITE YOU TO ASK YOURSELF ONE QUESTION ABOUT THIS SAYING. WHAT IS THERE THAT ISN'T GOD'S?

Maybe we give God part of what is God's when we pay our taxes or do such things as support a candidate for a public office. What do you think?

Dwelling with the Texts

Let's try to identify with our parishioners through recognizing some of their feelings that they will bring to worship. How might it feel to be mourning the death of a spouse with whom you have spent forty-five years? What goes on in the inner being of the divorced mother of four? If you were uncertain of your job and faced the possibility of being laid off, how would you respond to these texts? When you have finished this process of trying to identify more closely with members of the congregation, ask how they might feel toward these passages and what you intend to say about them.

TWENTY-THIRD SUNDAY AFTER PENTECOST

OCTOBER 23, 2005
THIRTIETH SUNDAY IN ORDINARY TIME /
PROPER 25

REVISED COMMON	EPISCOPAL (BCP)	ROMAN CATHOLIC
Deut. 34:1-12	Exod. 22:21-27	Exod. 22:20-26
or Lev. 19:1-2, 15-18		
Ps. 90: 1-6, 13-17	Psalm 1	Ps. 18:1-3, 46, 51
or Psalm 1		
1 Thess. 2:1-8	1 Thess. 2:1-8	1 Thess. 1:5c-10
Matt. 22:34-46	Matt. 22: 32-46	Matt. 22:34-40

Due in large part to the First Readings and the Responsive Readings, these passages ask us to wrestle with a variety of issues. It is appropriate, however, that after we have explored a number of important issues, we end up facing Jesus' declaration of the greatest of the commandments. Working on these lessons reminded me again of how fundamental love of God and others is!

FIRST READING
DEUTERONOMY 34:1-12 (RCL)

Interpreting the Text

The story of Moses' death is remarkably brief and straightforward. God shows Moses that the promise to Abraham, Isaac, and Jacob (Deut. 1:8 and 3:27) has been fulfilled; this land shall be theirs. Why can Moses not cross over into that land? Deuteronomy 3:16-17 reports that it was God's anger at Moses on account of the people. In effect, his death outside the Promised Land is sacrificial. (See also Deut. 4:21-22 and 32:52.) Moses' death is of natural causes, even though his sight was great and his energy inexhaustible. His death and burial were a private matter between him and God. The secret of the location of his grave is probably due to the fact that it has been forgotten. The

> NO MATTER WHETHER OUR LIVES HAVE BEEN OBEDIENT OR NOT, OUR DEATHS ARE PRIVATE MATTERS BETWEEN GOD AND OURSELVES.

tribute to Moses in vv. 10-12 accounts in part for the belief that a prophet like Moses would appear in the last days.

Responding to the Text

One commentator says of this lection "the death and burial of Moses was a private matter between God and Moses." It even sounds like *God buried Moses!*[1] Death is something we must do alone. No one can go through the process with us. For the first and perhaps only time in our lives we are totally isolated from others. However, God's promise to us is that we are in the arms of our Creator through the process of death. No matter whether our lives have been obedient or not, our deaths are private matters between God and ourselves.

LEVITICUS 19:1-2, 15-18 (RCL, alt.)

Interpreting the Text

"You shall be holy, for I the LORD your God am holy" (v. 2) sounds like an impossible command, yet Leviticus claims that it is required of those who worship God. While we understand that God is holy in the sense of aloofness and purity, humans can never pretend to holiness. This reading makes clear, however, that those who would be holy imitate God—try to be like God in any way possible.

Our reading includes the commandment not to "render an unjust judgment" and prohibitions against slander and profiting from a neighbor's blood. Holiness then is not some sort of purity that results from a disengagement from life; it is not a solitary monk's life. Rather, it entails practicing justice and dealing with others without partiality. Verses 17-18 appropriately provide the climax of the reading, and they are comprised of a number of injunctions regarding one's relationship with neighbors. The summation of the whole of the holiness legislation is in v. 18b: "You shall love your neighbor as yourself: I am the LORD." In a remarkably terse statement, this command says it all.

Responding to the Text

Do you know someone you would call "holy"? We are normally hesitant to claim that a human is holy. That is due, in large part, to our concept of holiness. We have the impression that the only way one could become holy would be to live in isolation, away from other people and from all the difficult problems in life.

IRONICALLY, THEN, YOU CANNOT PRACTICE HOLINESS UNLESS YOU ARE IMMERSED IN REAL LIFE.

However, this reading takes a different approach to holiness. One becomes holy not by withdrawing from life but by living in a certain way.

Ironically, then, you cannot practice holiness unless you are immersed in real life. Someone sent me by e-mail a little cartoon entitled "Tweety's Advice." The little yellow bird, Tweety, stands looking up toward heaven and says to God: "Dear Lord, so far today, I'm doing all right. I have not gossiped, lost my temper, been greedy, grumpy, nasty, selfish, or self-indulgent. I have not whined, complained, cursed, or eaten any chocolate. I have charged nothing on my credit card. . . . But I will be getting out of bed in a minute, and I think that I will really need your help then."

Granted, we need all the help we can get, but holiness is saved for those who try—those who dive in and trust that God will forgive our blunders.

EXODUS 22:21-27 (BCP);
EXODUS 22:20-26 (RC)

Interpreting the Text

This reading comes from the collection of laws found in Exodus 21–22. Each of them follows a similar pattern, first describing a situation ("when/if such and such happens") and then prescribing a just response of the situation ("then such and such will be done"). This formulation was ordinary among the ancient Near Eastern peoples. Our reading dips into this collection and pulls out three laws. The first and the third both have to do with slave owners and their treatment of their slaves. The second focuses on injury brought on a pregnant woman. In the conclusion of the second law (vv. 23-25), we find the infamous regulation, "an eye for an eye, tooth for a tooth."

The only merit in this sample of law is that it shows us something important about Hebraic law in general. The law developed so as to provide guidance in nearly every imaginable situation, including common conditions in which people are called to make judgments. Its intent was to demonstrate that obedience to God was called for in daily, ordinary circumstances.

Responding to the Text

None of us likes laws. Laws exist only because they are important to preserve order. Without traffic laws, for instance, our highways would be a mess—even worse than they are now! The law we find in our Old Testament was formulated to guide people in their effort to be obedient. We Christians, however, now find that law performs a different (or another) function. The full force of the law drives us to the

THE FULL FORCE OF THE LAW DRIVES US TO THE CONCLUSION THAT WE CANNOT OBEY THE REGULATIONS, SO THAT WE ARE NEVER WORTHY TO STAND BEFORE GOD.

conclusion that we cannot obey the regulations, so that we are never worthy to stand before God. Then we are ready to hear the Gospel message that God declares us worthy in spite of our failure to obey.

RESPONSIVE READING
PSALM 90:1-6, 13-17 (RCL)

This psalm begins with a sobering comparison of human life and God (vv. 1-6). We humans are finite and bound to time, while God is "everlasting" beyond time. The mortality of human existence is contrasted with the eternal nature of God. The reading then skips vv. 7-12, which include life under the wrath of God. Verses 3-17 are a prayer asking God to rescue humans from their plight. In v. 13 we find the standard complaint to God to relieve the community from its suffering: "How long?" The petitions ask God to have compassion on humans, to satisfy them with love, and to pour divine favor on them. The psalm ends with a repeated plea, "Prosper [or establish] the work of our hands" (v. 17).

"Turn back, you mortals!" This psalm paints a foreboding picture of the difference between God and humanity. We stand before God as small, limited, and time-bound creatures. Before the one whom we believe to be eternal and beyond time, we seem but specks in the universe, destined to annihilation. God is so radically different from us that we wonder how the divine is ever expected to hear our pleas.

> BEING REMINDED OF THE VAST GULF BETWEEN OURSELVES AND GOD MAKES US WONDER ALL THE MORE THAT OUR CREATOR CARES FOR US AND GRANTS US FAVOR.

Being reminded of the vast gulf between ourselves and God is beneficial, for it makes us wonder all the more that our Creator cares for us and grants us favor.

PSALM 1 (BCP; RCL, alt.)

This favorite psalm presents us with two different ways of going through life. First, it describes the "happy" life (the life aware of God and God's care—vv. 2-3). This is the way of those who cherish God's will expressed in the law and who find themselves renewed by God's care. The second part, vv. 4-6, pictures another way of life, one undertaken without concern for God or the divine law. Those who live this way are blown away by the difficulties of life. While God keeps watch over those who are righteous, the unrighteous perish.

The sentence that concludes v. 3 is instructive: "In all that they do, they prosper." This psalm is premised on the ancient Hebraic belief that those who are righteous prosper and those who are wicked "perish" (v. 6). We know the matter is not that simple, for Christ suffered death on a cross for having lived a righteous and obedient life. At this point ,the psalm rests on a faulty premise.

In the NRSV, this psalm is titled, "The Two Ways." It pictures humanity standing at a crossroads, wondering which path to take. It is a decision we make not once in a lifetime but again and again throughout life. Each time we face a new situation, we are forced to decide. The psalm, of course, oversimplifies the matter. It is not easy to know which is the path of sinners and which the way of the righteous. Life is far too complicated for that. Our hope to take the right way hinges on the community that supports and guides us. We do not have to travel life by ourselves, because we have one another as traveling companions.

PSALM 18:1-3, 46, 51 (RC)

This psalm purports to be the song that a king might sing after winning a victory. (See 2 Samuel 22 for another record of this psalm.) Verses 1-4 declare that God alone is one's defense in battle, and to invoke God's presence is to be assured of victory and be released from entanglement with death. Verse 46 declares that God lives and is the king's salvation. The final verse credits God for what the king has done.

Like the foundation of a building, our foundations in life are most important. This psalm praises God as the king's foundation and celebrates the victory the king has won. The difficulty with foundations is that you may not know how well built they are until they are threatened, say, by a storm. Our psalm grew out of a warrior's success, and he credits God as the basis of his endeavor. When we are engaged in one of the battles of life, we may learn that our foundation is not as secure as we thought. The death of a loved one, the

> WHEN WE ARE ENGAGED IN ONE OF THE BATTLES OF LIFE, WE MAY LEARN THAT OUR FOUNDATION IS NOT AS SECURE AS WE THOUGHT.

destruction of a home in a flood or storm, a divorce, engagement in war, or joblessness are tests of the underpinnings on which we have built our lives. We should not, however, feel ashamed if our foundations are not what we thought they were. Instead, we should seek help and strengthen the basis of our lives for the next test.

SECOND READING
1 THESSALONIANS 2:1-8 (RCL, BCP)

Interpreting the Text

Paul and his colleagues are careful to clarify their behavior in Thessalonica. We learn that they had suffered persecution at Philippi and likewise faced considerable opposition in Thessalonica (v. 2). Verses 3-7a are concerned to remind the readers of the purity of the apostles' motives and actions. They were not guilty of deceit, trickery, efforts to please, flattery, greed, or praise. One wonders if these denials come because of charges raised against the three of them at Thessalonica or some other city. As apostles, it seems, they might legitimately make "demands" of the people in this city. Does apostleship carry with it some authority that would authorize such demands? The contrasting figure to the demanding apostles is the nurse and "her own children" (v. 6). (In Gal. 4:19 Paul compares the pain he has experienced with the readers with that of a woman in child birth.) The point of the image of the nurse and children is the "care." The Greek word *homeiromai* suggests longing and kindly feelings. The next sentence is as profound as it is simple: "we are determined to share with you not only the gospel of God but also our own selves [lit., our own souls] because you have become very dear [or beloved] to us" (v. 8). Sharing the gospel arises out of genuine care for another and is so intimate that it entails one's deepest self.

Responding to the Text

Paul and his colleagues sound very much like a sincere pastor trying to convince a congregation that what she or he has done was genuine and sincere. The capstone of this passage, however, is that sharing the gospel with another is wrapped up with sharing yourself—your deepest self, your soul. When we ingest the gospel message of God's love and redemption, it becomes part of the deepest center of our lives. So there is no way I can talk with you about the Christian message without giving myself.

What does that mean for our witness? Witness is inevitably autobiographical. It is sharing how one's own life story becomes intertwined with the story of God's compassion for the world. That means witnessing builds on establishing a close relationship with another. One cannot simply talk about this matter without becoming intimate with another. Many of us have experienced another's sharing the gospel with us in this way. Can we now share it with others?

WITNESS IS INEVITABLY AUTOBIOGRAPHICAL. IT IS SHARING HOW ONE'S OWN LIFE STORY BECOMES INTERTWINED WITH THE STORY OF GOD'S COMPASSION FOR THE WORLD.

1 THESSALONIANS 1:5c-10 (RC)

See the discussion of 1 Thess. 1:1-20 for the Twenty-second Sunday after Pentecost.

MATTHEW 22:32-46 (RCL, BCP);
MATTHEW 22:34-40 (RC)

Interpreting the Text

Matthew submerges us in a series of encounters Jesus has with religious leaders who oppose him. First, it entails paying taxes to Caesar (22:15-22), then the question of whether or not the dead are resurrected (22: 23-32), and now it is the question of the greatest commandment. (This story is found in slightly differ-ent forms in both Mark 12:28-31 and Luke 10:25-28.) The Sadducees, who did not believe that the Torah taught the resurrection of the dead, had been "silenced" by Jesus' words, so now the Pharisees come on the field with another play in mind. "Teacher, which commandment in the law is the greatest?" asks one of the opponents who is an expert in the Torah. We are told that he seeks to "test" Jesus (v. 35), and this is a word Matthew uses only of this "lawyer" and the devil (e.g., 4:1, 3). However, the lawyer's motive is not clear. It could be that he is trying to force Jesus to favor either the ceremonial or the moral law of the other. Or some, but not all, rabbis of the time apparently insisted that all the commandments of the Torah are of equal importance.

In v. 37 Jesus answers the question by quoting what became the *Shema*, namely, Deut. 6:4-5 (without the preface that affirms God's oneness). These two—love God and your neighbor—are presented as

> THESE TWO—LOVE GOD AND YOUR NEIGHBOR—ARE PRESENTED AS EQUALLY IMPORTANT AND HENCE AS THE KEY TO INTERPRET ALL SCRIPTURE

equally important and hence as the key to interpret all Scripture (v. 40). It may be important to note that the word for "love" in this case, both in reference to God and the neighbor, is *agapaō* and not *phileō*, usually associated with relationships with other people.

Responding to the Text

Years ago an Episcopal priest friend and I used to argue about which of these two is most important. Is it our love of God that is the source of our love for others? I would argue the primacy of neighborly love, and Sam would argue that love of God is first and neighborly love is derived from it. My question would always be, How do we love God except by loving our neighbor?

As interesting as these discussions were, I can now see how these two are so commingled that it is foolish to try to separate one from the other. It is like try-ing to separate the human heart from the mind. We love God by loving others.

What is commanded is a life of love in which both are loved equally and in a multitude of ways.

However, one striking thing about this commandment to love God and others is that it specifies a certain kind of love. As most of you know, there are two biblical Greek words for love, *agapē* and *philia*. Usually, but not always, *philia* refers to friendship love among humans and *agapē* means the self-sacrificing love that is characteristic of God's love of us in Christ. If that distinction is true, the commandment shocks us by asking that we love both God and others in such a way as to give ourselves entirely to them.

Dwelling with the Texts

Preaching on a passage such as this Gospel lesson always makes me feel uncomfortable. Frankly, I feel guilty of hypocrisy, and how can I possibly suggest that others do as I do not do, even as I cannot do? I think other preachers sometimes wrestle with this nagging sense of not practicing what we preach, not walking the walk as well as talking the talk. And that's okay! Because we dare not allow ourselves to think that we have arrived! In the case of this greatest of all the commandments, I have to focus on the fact that God has already and always does love me in a complete way and forgives any inability I may have in loving others.

Note

1. Peter C. Craigie, *The Book of Deuteronomy,* The New International Commentary on the Old Testament (Grand Rapids: Eerdmans, 1976), 405.

TWENTY-FOURTH SUNDAY
AFTER PENTECOST

OCTOBER 30, 2005
THIRTY-FIRST SUNDAY IN ORDINARY TIME /
PROPER 26

REVISED COMMON	EPISCOPAL (BCP)	ROMAN CATHOLIC
Josh. 3:7-17	Mic. 3:5-12	Mal. 1:14b—2:2, 8-10
or Mic. 3:5-12		
Ps. 107:1-7, 33-37	Psalm 43	Ps. 131:1, 2, 3
or Psalm 43		
1 Thess. 2:9-13	1 Thess. 2:9-13, 17-20	1 Thess. 2:7b-9, 13
Matt. 23:1-12	Matt. 23:1-12	Matt. 23:1-12

These readings cluster around themes of worship and morality. They speak of those responsible for worship, of the relationship between justice and worship, of greed that influences worship, and other related subjects.

FIRST READING
JOSHUA 3:7-17 (RCL)

Interpreting the Text

Here we have the dramatic story of Israel's crossing the Jordan to enter (finally) into the land promised to them. The first six verses of the chapter tell of the preparation for the crossing and the solidification of Joshua's leadership. The story itself begins in v. 7 with God's commissioning of Joshua, in which he receives the promise that God will be with him as God was with Moses. With that promise in mind, he then hears his concrete instructions. Joshua immediately reiterates the commands to the Israelites (vv. 9-13). This dramatic passing through the Jordan serves to remind the people of God's promise to them and assures them that God will drive out the inhabitants of the land. The wonder of the event is accented by the fact that at this time of year, the Jordan would probably not be fordable. But God provides a dam so that the waters "[stand] still" (v. 16). Verse 17 summarizes the event and conclusion to the story.

Responding to the Text

Who is going to believe such a story as this one? A little boy came home from Sunday school, and his mother asked him what he had learned that day. The little boy responded, "The Jews were trying to cross the sea. But the Palestinians stopped them. Then the Jews ordered in an air strike. It worked, and the Jews were able to cross over to the other side." His mother, of course, was horrified and said, "Are you sure that's what you learned in Sunday school?" "Well, not really," the little boy confessed. "But you wouldn't believe the version of the story our teacher told us."

God fulfills the promise to the people and brings them into the Promised Land. But this is no ordinary crossing of the Jordan River. Now the story may not have happened just this way, but the telling of the story reflects the fact that the people believed it was God's doing and not their own. Isn't it often the case that we cannot share exactly what happened when we think God was present in our lives?

MICAH 3:5-12 (RCL, alt.; BCP)

Interpreting the Text

This portion of Micah comes as a kind of summary of the message found in the earlier chapters. The nation is in moral decay, first of all, because of its religious leaders. Micah strikes out at these prophets who say what they think the people want to hear and by doing so assure themselves of an ample living. The false prophets cause a darkness that engulfs the people (vv. 6-7) in contrast to the true prophet who speaks in v. 8. At v. 9 the prophet addresses the rulers of the people—the second cause of the nation's condition. One of Micah's favorite themes is God's abhorrence of injustice and inequality (vv. 9-10). Verse 11 suggests the way in which greed determines the behavior of the rulers, the priest, and the prophets. While they will do most anything for money, they still believe that God sides with them. The summary of this condensed condemnation of the people comes in v. 12. The holy city of Jerusalem will become a heap of ruins in a plowed field.

Responding to the Text

Micah has always fascinated me. I suppose I am attracted to him because I come from the same kind of background as he did. He was a common working man from the rural area south of Jerusalem and thought the big city was the nest of all evil. He seems to have refused to swallow the

MICAH WILL NOT ALLOW US TO BELIEVE THAT OUR WEALTH AND SUCCESS, OUR NATION'S STATUS, OR ANY OF THESE THINGS WILL PROTECT US FROM GOD'S ATTACK ON INJUSTICE AND GREED.

tradition that the sacred city of Jerusalem was invulnerable and that God would protect it against harm. His message defended the poor farmers and shepherds of the area who were victims of the greed of the city dwellers.

More important is that Micah will not allow us to believe that our wealth and success, our nation's status, or any of these things will protect us from God's attack on injustice and greed. We are the richest nation in the world. As individuals we have made it primarily because we live in this haven of Western culture. Like those who thought that Jerusalem was the pinnacle of success and righteousness, we are tempted to think that way about our nation. Micah's message, however, is simple: put away greed and treat others with justice and love.

MALACHI 1:13b—2:2, 8-10 (RC)

Interpreting the Text

Malachi was active after the temple was rededicated (516/515 B.C.E.) and was again functioning since the return from exile. The prophet must have himself been a priest or at least one who valued the temple and its worship (see 2:4-6). "Malachi" may not be a name but a function, "my messenger."

The reading drops us down in the middle of Malachi's second oracle (1:6—2:9), which is an attack on the practices of the priests and sacrificial worship. The priests are accused of presenting lame, sick, and blemished animals for sacrifice (1:13b-14). The oracle that begins at 2:1 is the longest uninterrupted word from God found in the book. The priests' blessings shall be made curses, and God will put them out of the temple. God commands them to keep the covenant with Levi, which was "a covenant of life and well-being" (v. 5). Levi is praised for being a genuine priest who brought many truly to worship God and is "the messenger of the LORD of hosts" (v. 7). However, the priests now have caused people to stumble. They have shown partiality to some and have corrupted the covenant with Levi. For that reason, God declares that they will be despised and stripped of all authority. Some scholars have claimed that this whole reading is patterned after the priestly blessing in Num. 6:24-26.[1]

Responding to the Text

Christians have, for the most part, dropped the whole tradition of temple sacrifice and worship. So we may find Malachi entirely out of step with our needs and emphases today. However, there is at least one thing about this reading that speaks to us. Malachi wants the people to overcome the separation of worship and their moral lives. Did you notice that the last line of the reading accused the priests of showing "partiality" in their teachings? To worship God means to practice impartiality and justice. It's like walking along the peak of a roof. To your right is sloping roof that would take you to the ground. To your left is the same thing. Either way you might turn, you would fall. The only way is to walk the peak of the roof. Likewise, we must value worship and moral living and practice both sincere worship and genuine care for others.

RESPONSIVE READING
PSALM 107:1-7, 33-37 (RCL)

Psalm 107 is a thanksgiving song expressing gratitude to God for rescuing us when we were in danger. It begins with a general introduction encouraging thanksgiving (vv. 1-3). Those who know the redemption are called together, and then the psalm describes the first of four situations of peril (vv. 4-5). In each of vv. 4-5, 10-12, 17-18, and 23-27, someone is pictured in peril, cries out to God, and is rescued.[2] Each then gives thanks to God.

The second part of the reading is made up of vv. 33-37, which begin with a description of how God creates disaster for those who are wicked. Then vv. 35-38 speak of how God provides water and transforms deserts so that they produce food for those in need.

"Thank you!" becomes an immediate and spontaneous response to a clerk who gives good service, a doctor who helps our healing, or a friend who remembers our birthday. For such an easy and spontaneous expression, it is interesting that sometimes we are hesitant to say thank you to God and Christ. The problem comes in not knowing for what we owe God. There are enough times when we thank God for what really is only an accident or a chance occasion. (E.g., we thank God that we avoided a collision with that car this afternoon, when it is doubtful that God really had anything to do with it.) Nonetheless, we are indebted to God for far more important things—love, friendship, hope, grace, and much, much more. For those daily realities, we do give thanks.

PSALM 43 (RCL, alt.; BCP)

A good many scholars believe that Psalms 42 and 43 are really two parts of what was the original psalm. In both cases, the form is the individual in discussion with her or his soul.[3] This psalm has several discernible parts and themes. In the first, the psalmist prays for God's vindication before his or her enemies (v. 1), and the second has to do with the sense that God has deserted the psalmist (v. 2). Verses 3-4 reflect a quite different mood, although they appear to be a promise to worship the God who seems absent. Finally, there comes the address to the soul with words of encouragement (v. 5). The emotional process of the psalm then moves from anger at enemies to a sense of alienation from God, to a commitment, and finally to encouragement.

Are you ever accused of talking to yourself? Of course, it is okay to talk to yourself as long as you don't answer—or so the story goes. Actually, in the Bible there are a number of incidents of talking to oneself. Think, for instance, of the rich fool in Jesus' parable who tries to reassure himself: "Soul, you have ample goods laid up for many years; relax, eat, drink, be merry" (Luke 12:19). In our psalm for today, the psalmist tries to encourage him/herself by speaking to his/her soul.

A dialogue with our deepest self often has a positive result. Addressing our souls enables us to back off from ourselves for a minute and suppose that we are distinct from our souls. It is a kind of dialogue that furthers our religious and spiritual strength. In the case of the psalmist, the discussion with the soul quiets anxiety and puts hope foremost.

> IN THE CASE OF THE PSALMIST, THE DISCUSSION WITH THE SOUL QUIETS ANXIETY AND PUTS HOPE FOREMOST.

PSALM 131:1-3 (RC)

This is an exemplary and simple prayer expressing humility and trust. It is one of the "Psalms of Ascent" (120-134) that may have been used by pilgrims on their way to Jerusalem. In the first verse the psalmist assures God (and herself or himself) that he does not aspire to that which is beyond her capacity. "Great" and "marvelous" are adjectives generally used for God's actions, so the psalmist says he does not pretend to be God. Verse 2 may indicate that the psalm is spoken by a mother. "Like a weaned child" perhaps refers to children who once fed at their mothers' breasts and now return to their mothers' embrace strictly for comfort and security (v. 2). The image of children held in a loving embrace is Israel's hope now and always (v. 3).[4]

> How do I love thee? Let me count the ways.
> I love thee to the depth and breadth and height
> My soul can reach . . .[5]

So the great poet Elizabeth Barrett Browning sought words to convey her deep love for her husband, Robert Browning. Like most poets who deal with love, Elizabeth Browning searched for language to express and convey the depth of her love. Poets seek metaphors (striking comparisons) to give expression to their thoughts and emotions.

We Christians are like poets when it comes to finding language to express God's love for us and ours for God. One comparison we have perhaps not used enough is that of a mother's love as a way of understanding God's love. Our psalm paints a vivid and unforgettable image of God's love as a mother's love. Our language needs all the help we can get to say what is so precious to us.

SECOND READING
1 THESSALONIANS 2:9-13 (RCL);
1 THESSALONIANS 2:9-13, 17-20 (BCP);
1 THESSALONIANS 2:7b-9, 13 (RC)

Interpreting the Text

The authors continue in 2:1a discussion of their ministry in Thessalonica. They seem concerned to correct any misconception of their motives and purpose. Verse 9 probably indicates that at this time the Christian missionaries, including Paul, worked to support themselves so that they were not a "burden" to those they came to serve. The image of the relationship of a father to his children emphasizes the role of the missionaries' care and concerns for those they sought to win over. Verse 12 suggests that the readers are obliged to live moral lives because they have been called into God's kingdom. What the Thessalonians received was not a "human word" but "God's word" (v. 13). Paul had a number of struggles with those who claimed he preached only his own message.

Verses 17-20 address the separation of the missionaries and their new congregation. The separation was not one of hearts, as v. 17 asserts, and it was one the missionaries sought to overcome (v. 18). Paul claims that "Satan" kept them away from Thessalonica. In all likelihood, the title is used here to refer to political forces that worked against the efforts of Paul and his associates to return to the city. The reference to the "coming" (*parousia*) of Jesus anticipates a theme that figures prominently in 2 Thessalonians. The term was used both for the revealing of a god and for the visit of a royal official. The lesson ends with the authors asserting that the readers are the authors' "hope or joy or crown of boasting before our Lord Jesus" (v. 19). The "crown of boasting" was the wreath awarded to a winning athlete.

> NOTE THE NUMBER OF IMAGES PAUL AND HIS ASSOCIATES USE THAT ARE DRAWN FROM THE FAMILY.

Note the number of images Paul and his associates use that are drawn from the family. The authors call the readers "brothers and sisters" (v. 9) and compare themselves as a nurse-mother (v. 7) and fathers caring for children (v. 11). In v. 17, the writers say they became "orphans" when separated from the Thessalonian Christians. This use of parental care underlines the imagery of psalm 131.

One reason for the omission of vv. 14-16 is likely the harsh words about the Jews in v. 15, which some scholars believe could not be from Paul's pen, since his expressed attitude toward the Jews is far different (see Rom. 9:3).

Paul commends the Thessalonians for receiving the Christian message not as human words but as God's word. How do we differentiate these two today? When we hear someone say that this or that is God's word, how do we know it is truly a divine word?

In the period of Lent in 2004, Mel Gibson's movie *The Passion of the Christ* caused a great deal of controversy. Several features of the film were the cause of the debates, but perhaps the most important one had to do with the portrayal of the Jews as those totally responsible for Jesus' death. Gibson claimed he was not anti-Semitic and had no intention of degrading the Jewish people. Some of us had to admit that the Gospel of John on which Gibson depended for his retelling the passion story does sound anti-Jewish, but we insisted that this was not part of the authoritative message of the Gospels but an unfortunate feature having to do with the historical setting of the story. People then had to decide. Were the anti-Jewish themes the word of God or the words of humans? Christians were divided. How were we to tell the difference? For some of us, it was fairly simple. Is the condemnation of the Jewish people something that our God would endorse? The answer then was relatively easy.

For additional discussion of 1 Thess. 2:7b-8, see the Twenty-second and Twenty-third Sundays after Pentecost, above.

THE GOSPEL
MATTHEW 23:1-12 (RCL, BCP, RC)

Interpreting the Text

David E. Garland offers us three important points to keep in mind as we read and preach on this passage. First, these words are part of a "family row" between the earliest Christians and the Jews. The tone of the language is that of fighting with those who are closest to you. Second, the language is modeled after prophetic oracles against a "stubborn people." The discourse is also the Christian explanation for why the Jewish revolt of the sixties failed and Jerusalem

> THE PROPER HEARING OF THIS READING IS NOT IN TERMS OF WHAT IT MEANT FOR THE SCRIBES AND PHARISEES BUT HOW WE OURSELVES ARE GUILTY OF THE SAME SINS.

was sacked. Third, notice who the audience is. The discourse is clearly addressed to the disciples and not those it condemns (see 23:1, 8-12). Jesus uses the scribes and the Pharisees as examples of what threatened the disciples. The proper hearing of this reading therefore is not in terms of what it meant for the scribes and Pharisees but how we ourselves are guilty of the same sins.[6]

The reading is only the first part of an extended discourse in Matthew 25 about the religious leaders, the rest of which are readings for the remaining Sundays after Pentecost. Jesus speaks specifically about the "scribes and Pharisees." Remember that the Pharisees were a lay movement in Judaism at the time of Jesus designed to enable them to be more obedient to God's law. The scribes are best thought of as "secretaries" who by the first century had become experts in Judaism; hence in Jerusalem they may have been low-level officials.

Jesus charges them, first, with failing to practice what they taught (vv. 2-3), then of creating burdensome regulations for the people (which they themselves ignore, v. 4). The "seats in the synagogue" was probably a metaphor for the positions of teaching and ruling (v. 2). Next, in vv. 5-7 he condemns them for loving the spotlight and being "seen by others." "Phylacteries" (v. 5) were the symbolic small boxes (containing Scripture passages) males wore on their foreheads at prayer. In vv. 8-10, Jesus warns his disciples about taking titles for themselves: rabbi ("my lord"), father ("abba"), and instructor ("master"). Matthew seems to be describing a community in which all are equal and none superior. This would have been a natural tendency for the Christian communities in the early years of the church. Authority is found in humility and service and not in station (see Matt. 20:25-27).

Responding to the Text

These harsh words are meant for you and me, and not the religious leaders of two thousand years ago. The story is told of the janitor in a large office building who was responsible for the furnace. All the important people worked in the offices above him. One day as he was burning garbage, a mouse jumped out of the basket. The little fellow huddled against the wall shivering in fright. "Please, please," the mouse said, "don't throw me in the fire." Well, a talking mouse! Wanting to have some fun, the janitor asked, "What can you do for me that would make it worth my while not to burn you?" "If you will not throw me in the fire," the mouse answered, "I'll give you your greatest wish." The janitor thought and then carefully said, "I wish that I could be like the people in offices over me." "Very well," the mouse said, "so it shall be."

The next day the janitor came to work and was ushered into a lovely office on the first floor of the building. However, he soon learned that he had to obey all the orders that were sent down from those on the floors above him. So he ran down to the basement and found the mouse. "Mouse! You make me like those who have authority on the floors above me, or I'll throw you into the furnace." "Very well," said the mouse, "so be it."

Well, the next day the same thing happened. He moved up one story but still had to obey those above him, and he insisted that the mouse promote him again.

The same thing happen several more times until the janitor found himself in the office of the CEO of the company and was sending down orders to all those on the lower floors. He loved it. He had reached his goal.

However, one day when he came to work, the rain was pouring down and the thunder rumbling. He had a golf date that day, so he went to the roof and ordered it to stop raining. But, of course, the rain continued. He then angrily went down to the basement and again ordered the mouse, "Make me as powerful with all the authority over whoever it is who is now still over me." The mouse smiled and said, "So it will be!"

The next day the janitor came to work and found himself in the basement tending the furnace.[7]

"The greatest among you will be your servant. All who exalt themselves will be humbled and all who humble themselves will be exalted."

Dwelling with the Texts

Select one of the lessons for this Sunday. Read it out loud and then ask yourself simply, "What does this passage have to say to me about my Christian life and faith?"

Notes

1. See Eileen M. Schuller, O.S.U., *The Book of Malachi: Introduction, Commentary, and Reflections,* The New Interpreter's Bible (Nashville: Abingdon, 1996), 7:861.

2. Patrick D. Miller, "Psalms," *The HarperCollins Study Bible* (New York: Harpercollins, 1993), 902.

3. See Sigmund Mowinckel's classic study, *The Psalms in Israel's Worship,* trans. D. R. A.-Thomas, 2 vols. (Oxford: Blackwell, 1962).

4. J. Clint McCann Jr., *Psalms: Introduction, Commentary, and Reflections,* The New Interpreter's Bible (Nashville: Abingdon, 1996), 4:1176–77, 1208.

5. Elizabeth Barrett Browning, "Sonnet 43," *Sonnets from the Portuguese.* Quoted from *The Literature of England: An Anthology and a History*, ed. George B. Woods, Homer A. Watt, and George K. Anderson, 3rd ed., 2 vols. (Chicago: Scott, Foresman, 1948), 2:714–15.

6. David E. Garland, *Reading Matthew: A Literary and Theological Commentary on the First Gospel* (New York: Crossroad, 1995), 227–29.

7. I have not been able to trace this story to its original source. It seems to be one of those stories for preaching that is passed from pastor to pastor.

REFORMATION DAY

OCTOBER 31, 2005
(OR TRANSFERRED TO OCTOBER 30, 2005)

REVISED COMMON
Jer. 31:31-34
Psalm 46
Rom. 3:19-28
John 8:31-36

Reformation Sunday has become a time to celebrate the great themes of the Reformers and the ongoing challenges of reforming the church. For too long this day was an occasion to condemn the Roman Catholic Church and to stress the differences between it and Protestant traditions. Fortunately, that practice is ended and now we can rejoice in a universal church that essentially shares the same faith.

FIRST READING
JEREMIAH 31:31-34

Interpreting the Text

Jeremiah walked a thin line between his message of doom and judgment, on the one hand, and his words of hope for restoration, on the other. He was active before and just after the first exile in 587. On the occasion of the exile, it appears he remained in Jerusalem to assist those left there. Consequently, Jeremiah includes some passages that are pessimistic about Judah's future (e.g., 6:1-30) and others that are hopeful and come from the time when Judah has been exiled.

Chapter 31 speaks of the redemption of Judah by God's endless love. Verses 31–34 promise that God will make a new agreement (lit. "cut" a new covenant) with the people—an agreement they will be empowered to keep. The new covenant will include both Israel and Judah (and presumably mend the break between them). It is a *new* covenant, unlike the old one the people had broken. The important features of the new covenant include the promise that God would implant the law in the people's hearts, which means that everyone will have an inner knowledge of the law and education will be unnecessary. The law was exterior but now will be within the hearts of the people. They will all "know" the Lord, not just in the sense of intellectual knowledge but intimate relationship. (The same Hebrew word translated "know" here is used in Gen. 4:1, where we are told that Adam "knew" Eve and she bore a son.) Perhaps the most important feature of this new covenant, however, is that it is based on God's forgiveness (v. 34).

Responding to the Text

As a child, I remember trying to turn a somersault to show off for some visitors in our home. Unfortunately, I was no more limber then than I am now, and my attempts were all failures. However, after each one, I would declare something like, "Wait! I wasn't ready! I'll do it this time!" Not only did I get a second turn but a third, fourth, and fifth until Mom and Dad and their guests grew restless and wandered away.

There are some things we learn only very slowly, if at all. So we need countless "turns" until we "get it right." It is not surprising that the Hebrew people failed in their efforts to be faithful to the law and needed a fresh try at it. However, note that God does not promise a *new law* but a *new covenant*. God supplies a new basis for the law—an obedient heart with the whole of the law written on it. The whole promise is built, however, on the last words of the reading: "for I will forgive their iniquity, and remember their sin no more." Forgiveness means a fresh start, another turn in spite of our ineptitude.

RESPONSIVE READING
PSALM 46

Interpreting the Text

These are words of encouragement and trust that still anxiety and eradicate fear. It is a psalm concerning Jerusalem and the city's special place in God's plan. The structure of the poem goes something like this: first, a general affirmation of God's power and the strength that affirmation brings (vv. 1-5); second, God's protection of Jerusalem (vv. 6-7); and finally, an invitation to trust God in the midst of all threatening situations (vv. 8-11).

Powerful images supply the essentials of the statement. It begins with a basic affirmation that sets the tone for the whole psalm. God is always there to help us. Verse 2 pictures an earthquake of the worst kind—"though the earth should change." Notice the picture of God's presence in the city in vv. 4-7. In v. 8, the river appears as a metaphor for the self-renewing source of blessing. Yet even there the psalmists are not sticking their heads into the sands, for the situation is bleak. Again, the reason for survival is God's presence. In fact, in confidence in the presence of God, we find our strength and assurance. The psalm is dotted with assertions of God's nearness. God is always "present," a fortress in crises (v. 1), an immovable proximity in the city (v. 5), and a closeness of peace and quiet. All that is necessary is that we quiet the noise around us and in us so that we can concentrate on that divine presence.

Responding to the Text

Reading this psalm on a Reformation Sunday brings Luther's great hymn "A Mighty Fortress Is Our God" to mind. Luther and his followers needed often to remind themselves of God's presence in the midst of trouble. However, so too do our own circumstances evoke the confidence of this psalm. All we have to do is insert some of our world's specific troubles into the language of this poem. "The nations are in an uproar, the kingdoms totter; he utters his voice, the earth melts." Most important of all, perhaps, is our desperate need to practice the discipline of stillness and quiet confidence.

> GOD IS ALWAYS "PRESENT," A FORTRESS IN CRISES (V. 1), AN IMMOVABLE PROXIMITY IN THE CITY (V. 5), AND A CLOSENESS OF PEACE AND QUIET. ALL THAT IS NECESSARY IS THAT WE QUIET THE NOISE AROUND US AND IN US, SO THAT WE CAN CONCENTRATE ON THAT DIVINE PRESENCE.

However, perhaps the stillness the psalmist has in mind is more than the elimination of the endless noise all around us. I don't know about you, but when I am under pressure of some kind, when I need to concentrate, most of the noise I must silence is the noise within myself: the doubting voices, the screaming muscles, the steady rumble of my own lack of confidence. If I am to "know" God is the Lord, I must quiet all the blasts, the roars, and the murmurs within me.

On one occasion, I was preparing a sermon on the "still small voice" mentioned in 1 Kings 19:12. I wrote an eloquent analysis of the noise in our society and our desperate need for silence. As I sat back and reread that part of the sermon, it finally struck me. The whole time I had been thinking about silence, writing about it, and planning to plead for more periods of silence, I had the stereo on playing music. The irony is, of course, that we sometimes are not at all conscious of all the sensations seeking their way into our minds and hearts. "Be still, and know that I am God!"

SECOND READING

ROMANS 3:19-28

Interpreting the Text

Surely this is one of the key passages for most of us. In chapter 1 through the beginning of this reading, Paul is trying to convince the readers of the universality of sin and its effects. Our reading is the transition from the problem, as Paul sees it, to the solution. His whole point is to bring us to a sense of our responsibility for our sins and the realization that we cannot rescue ourselves. Consequently, he brings us to a desperate dependence on God. Paul was convinced that there was no other way out of the human predicament than Christ. As he understands it, the law only makes us aware of our plight, or it brings us "the knowledge of sin."

Verses 21–31 are the climax of the argument. They are set off from all that has come before these words with a simple "but now" (*nyni de*). The section has a number of different and essential ideas. First, God's own righteousness has been made known in Christ, and faith is the only way of responding to it (vv. 21-22). Second, summarizing his earlier argument, all humans are alienated from God and are responsible for their situation. Third, God's new act is to pass judgment on us—a "not guilty" judgment. He borrows the word "justify" from the legal court systems of the day. The verdict is an out and out gift ("grace") without any qualifying merit. It is "justification by grace." Fourth, exactly what the phrase "whom [Jesus] God put forward as a sacrifice of atonement by his blood, effective through faith" is probably hopelessly ambiguous except to say that it invokes the classic cultic language for atonement. The point is that God is the righteous One who can make us righteous. Finally, the closing verses of the reading (vv. 27-28) make what seems an

> GOD'S NEW ACT IS TO PASS JUDGMENT ON US— A "NOT GUILTY" JUDGMENT.

obvious point, namely, that we have nothing to boast about, for it is God's righteousness, not our own, that saves us.

Responding to the Text

Have you ever known people who stubbornly refused to believe an idea in spite of all the evidence and arguments presented to them? After a while, it dawns on you that lack of evidence or logic was not the issue. The issue in those cases is that the idea was so personally threatening that no discussion was going to break through. In other words, the idea in some way seemed to annihilate a precious unchangeable feature of a personality.

I have come to the conclusion that this is the case with Paul's radical idea of justification by grace. Evidence, arguments, insights, and so on, are not going to change us so that we can easily accommodate this radical idea. Most of us have been soaked for years in the fluids of accomplishment, work, and goodness. Before we had a religious thought in our tiny brains, our parents were telling us that if we were good girls or boys we would be rewarded. If we were "naughty," there will, however, be no dessert, no television, and so on. In the workplace, the atmosphere is saturated by the accomplishment ethic (we accomplish things because we work hard). You can always pull yourself up by your bootstraps. Imagine a boss who tells you that you cannot get promoted by working hard and accomplishing the company's goals. Promotions will be done by grace!

This is, I think, the fundamental problem we face today in modern Western society. There's no free lunch, as we like to say. Paul and Luther had the same problem. The truth is that justification by grace is not an idea. It is a way of life. Learning a way of life takes time and perseverance. For that reason, we are never done preaching and teaching justification by grace. Sure, they've heard it before, but they need to hear it again. No! Wait! *I* need to hear it again.

THE GOSPEL
JOHN 8:31-36

Interpreting the Text

This is the only reading in the RCL taken from John 8. There is good reason for that apparent neglect, given the polemic nature of the language of the chapter and the dangerous possibility of some taking the references to the "Jews" as meaning the Jewish people as a whole. Our passage is a reading for Reformation Sunday because it speaks of the freedom the believer has in justification by grace.

We may want to check out the meanings of some of the key words in the Johannine passage before preaching on it. "Truth" in the Fourth Gospel refers consistently to the revelation of God in Christ; the truth about who God is and the divine plan of salvation. In that sense, it is synonymous with Jesus' "word." Freedom in this case has to do with having the possibility of living as God intended humans to live. A disciple in the Fourth Gospel is one who believes and does not refer exclusively to the circle of the Twelve (see 6:66-67). "Sin" most often refers to unbelief rather than moral error.

The Jews who believed in Jesus are confused by Jesus' declaration in v. 32 because they "have never been slaves to anyone." (They say this in spite of the fact that the history of the people of Israel includes periods of slavery.) Jesus, of course, is speaking of the slavery of one's quest of genuine life.

FREEDOM IN THIS CASE HAS TO DO WITH HAVING THE POS-
SIBILITY OF LIVING AS GOD INTENDED HUMANS TO LIVE.

The metaphor of the son and the slave in the household is clear, but its use then to speak again of making believers free doesn't seem to follow. The question becomes what it means to be a child of Abraham and a child of God, and the tone of the conversation becomes more and more hostile (see especially 8:44).

"Ya' know!" That expression has become a standard filler in a conversation in which you don't know what to say. For instance, a professional athlete is interviewed just after losing an important game and says something like this: "Well, ya' know! They played very good. Ya' know! We just couldn't get our game goin'. Ya' know! Tomorrow's another day. Ya' know!" The word "ah" used to be the sound we made to fill up the silence in the spaces between our words, but now increasingly it is "ya' know." It fills the gaps of our speech like putty fills the cracks in a wall.

The use of the word "know" is interesting in this slang, but it is equally important in this Gospel lesson. Discipleship is defined as "knowing the truth." Now surely, knowing in this sense is not simply the acquaintance with some facts, some theory, or some other information. Jesus speaks of a knowing that changes human life. Know the truth, and you are freed. Now some of us know the truth about Christ, but we are not free as a result of knowing it. Knowing is sometimes not knowing. So what does it mean to know in this passage?

Maybe it is like a teenage boy who falls madly in love with the neatest girl in the freshman class. He carefully gathers the information. She smiles at him when they pass in the halls. At lunch she makes sure she sits at the same table as he does. He knows she likes him. But to know is not always to know! And so he takes that gigantic leap—he asks her out on a date. *He acts on what he knows.* He takes risks on the basis of what he knows. He lives what he knows.

Know the truth, and you will be free.

Dwelling with the Texts

The lessons hammer away at the fact that we humans are not able to change our lives in significant ways. The Hebrew people needed the law written on their hearts or they could not obey. Romans points out that we cannot make ourselves righteous, and now John suggests that knowing is more than comprehension—it is a basis for living. Reformation Sunday rescues us each year from our temptation to "be religious" and implants a confidence in God's work on our behalf.

ALL SAINTS DAY

November 1, 2005
(or transferred to November 6, 2005)

Revised Common	Episcopal (BCP)	Roman Catholic
Rev. 7:9-17	Ecclesiasticus 44:1-10, 13-14 or Ecclesiasticus 2:(1-6) 7-11	Rev. 7:2-4, 9-14
Ps. 34:1-10, 22	Psalm 149	Ps. 24:1-2, 3-4, 5-6
1 John 3:1-3	Rev. 7:2-4, 9-17 or Eph. 1:(11-14) 15-23	1 John 3:1-3
Matt. 5:1-12	Matt. 5:1-12 or Luke 6:20-26 (27-36)	Matt. 5:1-12a

All Saints Sunday is one of the most important of the special days in the Sundays after Pentecost, but it may also be the most misunderstood. Our readings will aid our reflection on this day and lead us to a sense of communion with those Christians who have gone before us.

FIRST READING

REVELATION 7:9-17 (RCL);
REVELATION 7:2-4, 9-14 (RC)

These two readings and the second reading in the Episcopal lectionary, Revelation 7:2-4, 9-17, can be treated together without violating their differences.

Interpreting the Text

Revelation provides some rich passages for consideration on this day but also offers more than its share of obscurity. Chapter 7 is the interlude between the seven seals (6:1—8:10) and the seven trumpets (8:1—11:19). John often overlaps the first and the seventh of his series of sevens. Chapter 7 is the vision of the Israelites whom God had "sealed." The essence of vv. 2-4 is the command that the "servants" of God be "marked . . . with a seal on their foreheads" before the angels could damage the earth and sea. That is, they are to be protected so that their souls would not be destroyed in the disasters of the end time. "Sealed" may be a reference to baptism (see 2 Cor. 1:21-22). The precise number of those to be sealed is one hundred forty-four thousand, a number that has haunted interpreters for centuries. It is no accident that that total is gained by multiplying twelve by twelve. Here the number seems to be the whole people of God, but in chapter 14 it identifies only the martyrs. John's symbols should not be forced into rigid meaning, for they are far more flexible than that.

Verses 9-17 introduce a crowd too large to be counted. In this case, their identity is made clear. They are the martyrs of the "great ordeal," who "have washed their robes and made them white in the blood of the Lamb" (v. 14). The enigmatic symbol of robes washed in the blood of the Lamb suggests the way in which God rescues and purifies the faithful, even though

> THE ENIGMATIC SYMBOL OF ROBES WASHED IN THE BLOOD OF THE LAMB SUGGESTS THE WAY IN WHICH GOD RESCUES AND PURIFIES THE FAITHFUL, EVEN THOUGH THEY SUFFER PHYSICAL HARM.

they suffer physical harm. Now physical harm cannot touch them. They cannot hunger or be stricken. This description anticipates the grand finale of Revelation in 21:1-4.

Responding to the Text

Revelation is a like an epic poem, written in startling imagery that at times is gruesome and at other times beautiful. It is never easy to interpret poetry of this kind, and we are always walking the edge of violating the language by trying to make it literal. One way to let the poetry of Revelation influence us (as it was probably meant to do) is to *hear* it read rather than reading it. When we listen to this passage, we imagine a heavenly community gathered around God and free to be who they are. However, we also hear how it is they got there! Sealed and marked by God, they survived the horrors of harassment and persecution without surrendering their faith.

God does not promise us life without threats and without pain. Note that this heavenly community of faith has had their robes washed in blood. We would like to think that baptism and Christian life somehow protect us from harm, but we know that is not true. Why else does that dear saintly widow suffer still more on her deathbed? No, the security of faith is found in having something that is lasting and eternal even while all else is crumbling around us. We don't have to separate our souls from our physical bodies to embrace this idea. We know, don't we, that physical suffering tears at our souls as well? It is not a matter of soul and body but of that which is most important in life and that which is less important.

ECCLESIASTICUS 44:1-10, 13-14 (BCP);
ECCLESIASTICUS 2:(1-6) 7-11 (BCP, alt.)

Interpreting the Text

The book of Ecclesiasticus goes unnoticed most of the time but on this occasion offers us some insights into the "saintly" life. It is also and perhaps better known as "The Wisdom of Jesus, Son of Sirach" and most likely is rooted in the teachings of a sage who lived in Jerusalem soon after 200 B.C.E. His work was included in the Greek translation of the Hebrew Scriptures ("the Septuagint") that originated in the third through the first centuries B.C.E. It is a typical wisdom book, comprised of pithy sayings that express profound truths. Chapter 2 is comprised of three poems, each of which contributes to the effort to obey God. Chapters 44–51, on the other hand, are a long eulogy in honor of our religious ancestors. The assigned reading comes from what might be called the introduction and praises all those who have contributed to our religious heritage.

Responding to the Text

All Saints Day is given over to recalling in appreciation the lives of those who have influenced us in positive ways. Many of the world religions give ancestors a pivotal role, and some (like Buddhism) pray to ancestors and make offerings to them. In our culture today, there seems to be less and less appreciation of the past and those who were part of it. A survey of a group of early teens resulted in the startling awareness that the Vietnam War is an unknown entity for many of these youth. This is not to criticize young people, but it is to recognize that, with the speed of change in our culture and the ever-renewed promise of the future, the past may not play as important a role as it should. Perhaps this day is to remember those in the past whose influence lives on even in our own lives. In doing so, we honor our saints.

RESPONSIVE READING
PSALM 34:1-10, 22 (RCL)

This is a psalm of thanksgiving that begins with an affirmation and commitment along with an invitation to join in the song (vv. 1-3). There follows descriptions of times of fear, shame, and trouble in which we learn of God's faithfulness (vv. 4-7) and concludes with another affirmation and invitation in vv. 8-10. While the poem moves freely without linear structure, it touches on those experiences in which we need and have divine help.

A former teacher of mine seemed to me to be without weakness or need. He was filled with self-confidence, masterfully successful in his career, and inexhaustible in his energies. Some years later, I learned that he had suddenly and prematurely died. Within that strong and energetic body of his, there lay a deadly disease that took his life.

The psalmist speaks of the "young lions" who "suffer want and hunger." The image is that of the strongest, most self-sufficient creature in nature. Who would ever think that young lions suffer want for anything? Yet they do. I realize now that my beloved teacher was not as strong as I had thought. Yet the psalmist promises that even those who seem to be without want and still seek God "lack no good thing."

PSALM 24:1-2, 3-4, 5-6 (RC)

This psalm is one of the "entrance" hymns, intended to be sung as the people enter the temple. The first six verses focus on the worshipers and their worthiness, while the last half of the psalm shifts attention to the door to the sanctuary. Verses 1-2 describe the God we have come to worship. Then, vv. 3-4 ask and then answer the question of who is worthy to approach God. Worshipers will receive both blessing and vindication, according to v. 3, and the final verse is a summary/conclusion.

Most of us have known people who seemed especially gifted and whose lives some how influenced ours. We each have our secret list of *our* saints. They need not be paragons of morality. They need not be without their own weaknesses and blind spots. But they offered us strength in a crucial time, or forgiveness when there seemed to be none, or guidance when there was no way to go. God makes saints of us all by offering us love and forgiveness that we can pass on to others.

PSALM 149 (BCP)

This reading celebrates God's relationship with the people and prepares for an eventual victory over others. As elsewhere in the Pss., the situation requires a "new song" (e.g., 33:3 and 40:3), since God is continually doing new things. God "adorns the humble with victory" (v. 4) because humility is the mark of the faithful. Note that the faithful people "execute vengeance on the nation and punishment on the peoples," bind the rulers (v. 8), and bring them to justice (vv. 7-9). This is the "glory" of the humble.

When we call to mind some of the saintly people we have known, how often they are self-defacing, unassuming and unpretentious. They are seldom (but sometimes) great and prominent leaders. When it is read on All Saints' Day, this psalm is striking because it describes a humble people who go on to victory over their neighbors. It is difficult to think of those we found saintly going to battle to "execute vengeance on the nations." (I think of a quiet, gentleman who suffered and died from bone cancer,) Yet on another level, we believe in their lives we glimpse another world in which justice and righteousness reign. It is that same surprise we found in the beatitudes!

Second Reading
1 JOHN 3:1-3 (rcl, rc)

Interpreting the Text

These verses are a tiny piece of a document whose precise form is unclear. While we often speak of the Johannine "Epistles," it is not at all clear that 1 John should be thought of as a letter. It seeks to offer comfort and guidance to a congregation or group of congregations who had recently suffered a schism. Chapter 3 comes amid part of the author's assurances that the remaining portion of the congregation(s) is correct in its stand against the separatists and true to their faith. Their confidence is founded on the experience of God's love (cf. 1:1-3) that has made them children of God, a title the author uses six times for the readers. The world (which represents opposition and oppression) may not acknowledge our identity, but it does not know God's love as we do. What God has in mind for the children of God in the end time is not known, but the author is sure that we who have God's love will in the end become more like Christ himself. Verse 2 implies that for now we do not know Christ fully, but with his final

WHAT THIS AUTHOR HAS EXACTLY RIGHT IS THE RELATIONSHIP BETWEEN GOD'S LOVE AND OUR DESIRE FOR PURITY FROM SIN.

appearance, we will see him as he is. Both the fact of the love of God in the present and the promise of the future are the basis for an exhortation in v. 3. Since we will become like Christ, we should now try to "purify" ourselves. The word "purify" is related to and synonymous with the word "holy." However, in this context and because of the author's polemic against the separatists who falsely claim that they are without sin, here the word probably means to be free from sin (1:8-10).

Responding to the Text

There is no one who can claim to be pure of sin, but there are some who seem more successful in overcoming the rebellious and disobedient selves we all have. The author of 1 John, of course, does not pretend that any of us on our own power can rid ourselves of sin. However, what this author has exactly right is the relationship between God's love and our desire for purity from sin. The whole of the reading is framed with an assurance of God's love. What is wrong with many of the efforts to rid ourselves of sin is the notion that if we do so, God will then love us or love us more. However, the two are just reversed. We seek freedom from sin *because God already loves us*. It is like children who think they have to "be good" or Mom and Dad will not love them. On the other hand, there are some like the saints who are so confident in their parents' love that obedience comes easy.

REVELATION 7:2-4, 9-17 (BCP)

See the comments on the First Reading for this day.

EPHESIANS 1:(11-14) 15-23 (BCP, alt.)

Interpreting the Text

The author of this letter begins with a list of all the gifts God gives us in Christ (1:3-14) and then describes his prayer for his readers. It is fascinating to note what Paul prays for on behalf of the Christians at Ephesus: a spirit of wisdom and revelation; enlightened hearts to know what hope God has given them; God's glorious inheritance for them; and God's immeasurable power. After concluding his list, the author states a belief in what God has done in Christ and what the eventual outcome of that will be. Paul sees a straight line from God's raising Christ to his position above "all rule and authority and power and dominion" to God's putting "all things" under the authority of Christ and making him "the head over all things for the church." The power that raised Christ from the dead is the assurance that Christ will eventually rule all.

Responding to the Text

Inheritance is very important these days, as it has been for centuries. My own parents were relatively poor, and there simply was no inheritance for their three children. I have sometimes felt jealous of the young couples who used an inheritance as a down payment on their first house. However, as a pastor, I have experienced a good many situations and families in which the inheritance was like dynamite that blew the family apart. Suddenly, siblings, cousins, nephews, nieces, uncles, and aunts were alienated from each other, all because of an inheritance. It forces me to realize how a beautiful gift like an inheritance can be turned into poison in the hands of sinful human beings.

Still, the promise of an inheritance is a marvelous metaphor for the gifts God has promised us in Christ. Earlier in Ephesians 1, Paul says simply, "In Christ we have also obtained an inheritance" (v. 11). As members of Christ's body, the church, we receive still additional inheritances. Each of the saints who has touched our lives leaves us an inheritance. It is not about money, of course, but it makes us rich nonetheless. Today we remember all those who have gone ahead of us and left us their inheritance in Christ.

THE GOSPEL
MATTHEW 5:1-12 (RCL, BCP);
MATTHEW 5:1-12a (RC);
LUKE 6:20-26 (27-36) (BCP, alt.)

Interpreting the Text

Both of the Gospel lections for today include the Beatitudes. Granted, there are some significant differences between Matthew and Luke on these gifts, and we should remind ourselves of those similarities and differences (e.g., Luke has only three beatitudes but also three woes; Matthew includes nine beatitudes and no woes). However, it would be legitimate to focus on the idea of beatitude in general as part of this All Saints Day.

The word "blessed" holds all the beatitudes together—Matthean and Lukan. The pronouncements of blessedness are not the sole property of the Hebrew-Christian faiths, but rather were quite common and may be found in Egyptian as well as Greek and Jewish literature. The Greek and Hebrew words may be translated in a number of ways, such as, "happy," "fortunate," and the best of the different translations "favored by God." The idea of the pronouncement of beatitudes arose from the fact that language was considered powerful in bringing into reality what is spoken.

The focus of the beatitudes in Matthew is either eschatological or ethical. For instance, the blessing of the meek points toward a future time when ownership will change; and the blessing of peacemakers endorses an ethical action. In contrast, the three beatitudes in Luke are all eschatological and have to do with eventual reward. On All Saints Day, we acknowledge both kinds of beatitudes, but clearly we celebrate the blessed conditions in which the saints now live.

Responding to the Texts

Who's blessed? We talk a great deal these days about "blessings." The kids are a blessing to us; we've been blessed with good health; we are blessed to have been born in this nation. We take seriously the words of the old hymn, "Count your many blessings, name them one by one."

In the light of this common cultural understanding of blessedness, our Gospel lesson is disturbing. The words of Jesus clash with our understanding of blessedness. The conditions he calls blessed are just the opposite of what we think it means. Look at them. In nearly every case, Jesus' blessing is on those who are actually the reverse of our culture's view. Those who are aggressive, strong, and self-reliant seem the blessed ones, not the poor in spirit. As someone once said, if the meek do inherit the earth, you've got to wonder if they will have the courage to claim it.

The beatitudes pose a radically different set of values from those that bombard us most of our lives. They ring out like alien voices in our culture. Didn't he know that "the nice gals and guys finish last"? Or, as Ziggy would say, they finish last if they finish at all. Jesus articulates the divine values in distinction to the common sense of our world, the foolishness of God judged by the wisdom of the world. The result is that the beatitudes give us a glimpse of the radical inversion of the human condition

> JESUS ARTICULATES THE DIVINE VALUES IN DISTINCTION TO THE COMMON SENSE OF OUR WORLD, THE FOOLISHNESS OF GOD JUDGED BY THE WISDOM OF THE WORLD.

for those who find themselves without worldly blessedness. They declare the promise of God to those we think are without blessing.

It may be good for us to count our blessings once in a while. However, it is better for us to remember that we are blessed because Christ brings the rule of God into are lives. So, who's blessed?

Dwelling with the Texts

As we allow our minds to wander over the memories of those who proved to be saints in our own lives, we soon realize there are too many to name. One single life like ours has been strengthened by so many different people, it is hard to separate them out. Soon we realize that we are surrounded by a community of saints, including both those alive now and those whose lives are precious memories. The All Saints sermon might be easier for us if we would first scan the long list of saints for whom we ourselves are thankful.

TWENTY-FIFTH SUNDAY AFTER PENTECOST

NOVEMBER 6, 2005
THIRTY-SECOND SUNDAY IN ORDINARY TIME /
PROPER 27

REVISED COMMON	EPISCOPAL (BCP)	ROMAN CATHOLIC
Josh. 24:1-3a, 14-25	Amos 5:18-24	Wisd. of Sol. 6:12-16
or Amos 5:18-24		
or Wisd. of Sol. 6:12-16		
Ps. 78:1-7	Psalm 70	Ps. 63:2, 3-4, 5-6, 7-8
or Wisd. of Sol. 6:17-20		
or Psalm 70		
1 Thess. 4:13-18	1 Thess. 4:13-18	Thess. 4:13-18
		or 4:13-14
Matt. 25:1-13	Matt. 25:1-13	Matt. 25:1-13

What does God have planned for creation? Most of these readings focus on that final "Day of Lord," what it will bring, and what we are asked to do in the interim.

FIRST READING
JOSHUA 24:1-3a, 14-25 (RCL)

Interpreting the Text

The conclusion of the book of Joshua is the creation of a new covenant between the people and Yahweh at Shechem. The covenant is based simply on all that God has done in freeing the people from slavery and leading them into their new land, and Joshua summarizes that history in vv. 3-13. In the light of that history, he calls the people to decide whom they will serve. This passage indicates that there was already a tendency for the people to abandon loyalty to Yahweh for the Baalim of Canaan and possibly, too, that new groups from the indigenous people who on this occasion were incorporated into the people of Israel. This covenant is premised on the belief that Yahweh was not willing to share the rank of deity with the other gods (v. 19). The people's pledge is represented in a large stone that serves as a witness to the covenant making.

Joshua calls the people to decision. Not many of those gathered at Shechem that day, or their ancestors, had made a decision to trust Yahweh and follow where their leaders took them. Now, however, they stood at a pivotal point in their nation's history, and Joshua was calling them to make a new decision.

One of the misunderstandings of decision in the act of faith is that once made it endures for one's entire life. The history of the people of Israel suggests otherwise. They were now facing a new future—a radical cultural change in their new homeland. Joshua insists that this is an occasion for a new covenant between the people and their God. The same is true for us as individuals and as a congregation. There are times in our history when we need to pause and reassess our commitment.

> JOSHUA INSISTS THAT THIS IS AN OCCASION FOR A NEW COVENANT BETWEEN THE PEOPLE AND THEIR GOD. THE SAME IS TRUE FOR US AS INDIVIDUALS AND AS A CONGREGATION. THERE ARE TIMES IN OUR HISTORY WHEN WE NEED TO PAUSE AND REASSESS OUR COMMITMENT.

AMOS 5:18-24 (RCL, alt.; BCP)

Interpreting the Text

Amos, the eighth-century prophet who was a shepherd from Tekoa (1:1), for the most part preached a message of doom and judgment for Israel. The little tidbit of Amos in our First Reading is no exception. Here Amos seems to want to dissuade people of the notion that the "day of the LORD" would bring them prosperity and good fortune (a view of the day as a "day of light"). The opposite is the case, Amos insists. It is a time of judgment (a view of the day as a "day of darkness"), and the people of Israel will not fare well. He uses the powerful image of one who runs from a lion only to encounter a bear or escapes only to be bitten by a snake. Judah will not be able to escape the judgment. In the final verses, Amos insists that Israel's worship is of no value because it is not accompanied by righteous and just living.

Responding to the Text

We are indeed our own worse enemies. Our own self-confidence blinds us sometimes to the true nature of our lives and our society. It is interesting that Amos doesn't single out individuals but speaks of the society of Israel as a whole. It is cultural smugness that makes our lives hollow and pointless. Amos warns us first to beware of hypocrisy—believing too

> AMOS DOESN'T SINGLE OUT INDIVIDUALS BUT SPEAKS OF THE SOCIETY OF ISRAEL AS A WHOLE. IT IS CULTURAL SMUGNESS THAT MAKES OUR LIVES HOLLOW AND POINTLESS.

much in our own ability to please God. He then offers us a simple antidote: let your lives be filled with justice (fair legal proceedings) and righteousness (relationships of mutual concern). In a day in which we can easily become taken up in an ever-increasing affluence and world domination, we need to take note of both Amos's warning and prescription.

WISDOM OF SOLOMON
6:12-16 (RCL, alt.; RC)

Interpreting the Text

This document was written in Greek sometime between 250 B.C.E. and 50 B.C.E. and demonstrates a breakdown in the relationship of Judaism to the Hellenistic culture. This author calls for the Jews to disassociate themselves from Greeks and Egyptians. In the postexilic period, Wisdom became personified in the figure of a woman—*Sophia* or "Woman Wisdom." That process is evident already in Proverbs (e.g., 1:20-33) and Job (e.g., 28:12-28). The use of *logos* ("word") as a synonym for Wisdom (18:15) provides a background for its use in the New Testament.

The reading is a plea for us to adopt and follow the ways of Wisdom. Verses 12-14 have to do with the ready availability of Wisdom. The author claims that Wisdom is easily found, and she is eager to aid all who seek her. Verse 15 summarizes all that is to be gained by those who adhere to the ways of Wisdom: "perfect understanding" and freedom "from care." The final verse of the reading returns to the theme of Wisdom's presence and eagerness to be sought.

Responding to the Text

How do you picture God? Remember as a child trying to draw a picture of God or imagining what God might look like? Of course, God evades all our efforts to put the divine in a box or package the divine for easy travel. I was serving a predominantly white, small, downtown church in an area populated almost exclusively by Hispanics and African Americans. We offered an after-school program for the children of the area as a way to witness to the church's commitment to the neighborhood. One little African American boy was led into the church for the program by his mother. He immediately ran over to where I was standing (and wearing my clerical collar) and, looking up at me, asked, "Are you God?" His mother had spoken of the church as God's house, and he thought finally he could meet God! I had to disappoint him!

During the period just before the beginnings of Christianity, the Jewish people developed a means of speaking of God that helped them to continue to think of God as beyond our conception but still acknowledge God's effort to be known in the world. They thought of God or one facet of God as Wisdom. Our lesson emphasizes how God is immediately available to us through the presence of Wisdom, and we are justified to think of the Jewish Wisdom as synonymous with our Christ.

Responsive Reading

PSALM 78:1-7 (RCL)

Psalm 78 is one of the so-called historical psalms because it recites the major events of Israel's journey and (more importantly) how they influence the present and future of the people. This particular psalm sketches the history up to the time of David and the establishment of the southern kingdom as the home of the faith. The psalmist speaks of "parables" and "dark sayings" (or riddles), meaning that there is a hidden theme in this history, most probably the fact that Israel kept rebelling against God. Teaching the next generation is the means by which the tradition is kept alive and made lively. Verses 5-8 raise the concern that those in the next generation will repeat the errors of their ancestors—a common point on the part of wisdom teachers. (Verse 8 is the completion of v. 7 and therefore might be treated as part of the reading.)

One commentator has said of this psalm that it is a reminder that "knowledge does not guarantee faithfulness; however, it insists that knowing the story is the foundation for faith and hope and life."[1] As a church, we are commissioned to pass the faith on to the next generation and nurture them in both understanding and behavior. Among other things, our task is to help our children avoid the mistakes we have made in our Christian lives. This kind of education isn't an elective; it is a requirement.

> "KNOWLEDGE DOES NOT GUARANTEE FAITHFULNESS; HOWEVER, IT INSISTS THAT KNOWING THE STORY IS THE FOUNDATION FOR FAITH AND HOPE AND LIFE."

However, this psalm is also the articulation of a fundamental mystery in Israel's history, what the psalmist calls a "parable" or a "dark saying" (i.e., a "riddle"). It is the mysterious way in which God chose and guided a people through their history, never abandoning or deserting them. Hence, the history we teach is not like the history classes in high school or college. It is a history permeated with divine purpose.[2]

PSALM 70 (BCP; RCL, alt.)

This psalm is found a second time in our Psalter as part of 40:13-17. It is a moving prayer for God's help and freedom from one's enemies. The psalmist begs for deliverance from unnamed opponents with the hope that God will cause them shame. The shame and honor theme here indicates how important in Hebraic culture was one's status in one's own eyes and in the eyes of others. In v. 5 the supplicant speaks of her or himself as "poor and needy." We cannot discern if these are adjectives used of one who is physically and economically poor or whether they refer to spiritual need and want. Or could it be that both are the case? However, these words indicate how the Hebrew people believed that any-one should come to the feeling of poverty and need when standing in the pres-ence of God.

The Psalms have been at the heart of Christian (as well as Jewish) life and faith for centuries. One of the reasons for their continued use is the fact that nearly all of us at one time or another find that a psalm seems to have been written just for us and just for that moment. Like all great literature, the Psalms speak for com-mon daily experiences. This one is no different. Lots of us have felt the way this psalmist did about some enemies or opponents. We may not be honest enough to acknowledge it even to ourselves, much less to others, but the truth is that most of us have had strong emotions about others who at least from our perspective seem to "desire to hurt me." Most experts today would say that emotional health is furthered by the recognition of our feelings about those who threaten us. The psalmist is honest enough to ask that God put the adversary to shame. It doesn't really matter if that is a morally correct feeling. Feelings are not moral or immoral. It does matter that we find in prayer a Friend who hears our cries for help.

PSALM 63:2, 3-4, 5-6, 7-8 (RC)

Readers are to think of the psalmist as in the sanctuary and yearning for God's defeat of the enemy (vv. 9-10). The imagery of the poem sketches the long-ing of the worshiper for intimacy with God. The authors declare that they will praise God, call on God's name, meditate on God through the night, sing for joy, and cling to God. All of these are word pictures of those who yearn for God's presence. However, these pictures of the human efforts are related to reflections on who God is. For instance, God's "steadfast love" is more valuable than life itself.

One of the most painful experiences in life is the feeling that God has aban-doned you and is nowhere to be found. Our psalm today does not explain the reasons for the psalmist's craving for God, but the craving itself is obvious. Experiences of such abandonment seem common, especially among devout people. One thing this psalm teaches (as do many others) is that feeling as if God has forsaken us is not the feeling of those who have lost their faith but of one whose faith is most important. To feel alienated from God is part of the normal spiritual life. Remember that Jesus' word of abandonment from the cross is also a quotation of a psalm: "My God, my God, why have you forsaken me?" (Mark 15:34; cf. Ps. 22:1).

SECOND READING

1 THESSALONIANS 4:13–18 (RCL, BCP, RC); 1 THESSALONIANS 4:13–14 (RC, alt.)

Interpreting the Text

These words of Paul are addressed to a fledgling Christian community in the Greco-Roman world. As such, his readers struggle with issues that seem basic to our ears. The essential problem is that the Thessalonian Christians looked forward to Christ's reappearing (*parousia*) but are worried now that their loved ones who have died will miss out on that glorious day. Paul seeks to quiet their anxiety with a vision of what that final day will involve (v. 18). Far from missing Christ's return, the dead in Christ will be the first to meet their Lord after he

> THE DEAD IN CHRIST WILL BE THE FIRST TO MEET THEIR LORD AFTER HE HAS RAISED THEM FROM THE DEAD.

has raised them from the dead. Paul sketches a picture of that final time in ways that parallel the coming of a famous ruler or commander to a Greco-Roman village. The word *parousia* itself was used for such an occasion, which included "a cry of command" and "trumpets" (v. 16). After the resurrected Christians, the living Christians will join Christ "in the air," and together they "will be with the Lord forever." This may be one of the first articulations of the Christians' hope for the final day.

Responding to the Text

When my father died, the Jehovah's Witnesses and others rushed to visit my mother like vultures descending on a corpse. One of the things they said to Mom was that after death Dad was not with God, as Mom believed, but that he would lie dead in the ground until the final resurrection. Far from consoling her, this view of life after death deeply disturbed my mother.

It is true that within the whole of the Christian church there are a variety of ways of understanding how God rescues us from the grave. They range from immortality of the soul to the resurrection of the physical body that must be buried whole and not cremated. The matter is not simply a theological puzzle to be discussed and reasoned out, for it involves deep feelings for our loved ones. Paul provides one picture of the time of resurrection and Christ's return to reassure the young Christians who fear that their deceased loved ones will be left out of the triumphant coming of Christ. His view of resurrection is part of that picture and came to represent the main Christian view.

THE GOSPEL

MATTHEW 25:1-13 (RCL, BCP, RC)

Interpreting the Text

This is the first of three parables in Matthew 25. Each has to do with Christ's reappearance at the last day, and each makes a related point. Jesus' parables consistently draw some parallel between a common experience in life and the reign of God, and in this case, as in others, it is a wedding. The point of this allegory is simply that Christians are called to active discipleship during the period before Christ's return. As one commentator writes:

> Discipleship is not passive waiting for the end time. Like the maidens, the Christians may know what is needed—oil, good deeds—but they may lose the opportunity for proper action. This is an eschatological ethic for Matthew and not simply an interim ethic.[3]

Responding to the Text

Today we hear a great deal about the belief that Christ is soon to return, that the end of the world is near, and that the Rapture will soon occur. The so-called Rapture has inspired a large series of fictional books and for some has become a constant preoccupation. The student of church history knows that this fervor over the end of the world has been continual over time. Each major event in world history is explained by some as part of the calendar of the end time. There is nothing about this faddish preoccupation that is necessarily wrong or evil, unless, of course, it becomes a reason for inactivity. If we try to use the anticipation of the end time as an excuse for not serving the needy, not attending to the alienated and the persecuted, then it has been badly misconstrued.

IF WE TRY TO USE THE ANTICIPATION OF THE END TIME AS AN EXCUSE FOR NOT SERVING THE NEEDY, NOT ATTENDING TO THE ALIENATED AND THE PERSE-CUTED, THEN IT HAS BEEN BADLY MISCONSTRUED.

It is said that a famous church leader was once asked what he would do today if he knew that Christ would return tomorrow. The leader responded, "I'd work in my garden." The point is that our Christian service is a demand on us all the time. The not-so-wise maidens did not use the bridegroom's absence to prepare for his arrival, and we too are called to be about the business of the reign of God, regardless of what God may have planned for the future.

Dwelling with the Texts

Luther preached the following words, which seem to be one way of approaching the reality of death in faith:

> Hence, one must look upon a Christian death with different eyes . . . learning to speak and think of it as the Scriptures do and not considering deceased Christians to be dead and buried people. To the five senses that is the way it appears. As far as they [our senses] can lead us, it brings only woe. Therefore go beyond them and listen to what St. Paul says here, that they are sleeping in Christ and God will bring them with Christ.[4]

Notes

1. J. Clinton McCann, *Psalms*, New Interpreter's Bible (Nashville: Abingdon, 1996), 4:993.

2. See Marvin E. Tate, *Psalms 51–100,* Word Biblical Commentary 20 (Dallas: Word Books, 1990), 295–96.

3. John R. Donahue, *The Gospel in Parable* (Minneapolis: Fortress Press), 104.

4. Martin Luther, *Luther's Works,* American Edition, 51:239–40, John W. Doberstein, ed. and trans. (Philadelphia: Fortress Press, 1959).

TWENTY-SIXTH SUNDAY AFTER PENTECOST

NOVEMBER 13, 2005
THIRTY-THIRD SUNDAY IN ORDINARY TIME /
PROPER 28

REVISED COMMON	EPISCOPAL (BCP)	ROMAN CATHOLIC
Judg. 4:1-7	Zeph. 1:7, 12-18	Prov. 31:10-13, 19-20, 30-31
or Zeph. 1:7, 12-18		
Psalm 123	Psalm 90	Ps. 128:1-2, 3, 4-5
or Ps. 90 or 90:1-8,	or 90:1-8, 12	
9-11 12		
1 Thess. 5:1-11	1 Thess. 5:1-10	1 Thess. 5:1-6
Matt. 25:14-30	Matt. 25:14-15, 19-29	Matt. 25:14-30
		or 25:14-15, 19-21

As we stand near the end of the long period of the Sundays after Pentecost, these readings offer a multitude of themes interwoven with one another. One possible common theme among them is the responsibility of Christians in the interim between Jesus' ministry and his parousia. Moreover, that responsibility is for justice.

FIRST READING
JUDGES 4:1-7 (RCL)

Interpreting the Text

This fascinating story presupposes the Deuteronomic view of history sketched in Judges 2:11-23. Israel's evil actions have brought oppression from another group; they cry out for deliverance; God raises up a judge who defeats the oppressive power; and Israel once again prospers for a time before beginning the cycle all over. The judges were charismatic leaders who ruled for an undetermined period. They would eventually be replaced with kings. The story of Deborah and Barak preserves the fact that women rose to the position of judge and prophetess. In this case, she proves to be the brave one, and the cowardly male (Barak) depends on her (v. 8). The Israelites are subject to a Canaanite king with a mighty army. Deborah's strategy is to draw the Canaanites into a trap, and Barak reluctantly agrees to it. Strangely, the reading ends with v. 7. The rest of the story is that Deborah's strategy works and the Canaanite king is eventually killed by Jael, who drives a tent peg into his temple (v. 21). The victory is celebrated in the ancient hymn we know as the Song of Deborah (Judges 5:1-31).

Responding to the Text

This story corrects the impression that women in the Old Testament are presented only as inferior creatures who are little more than property. As a judge and prophetess, no one has elected Deborah. Instead, her charisma has won her the office. Now, faced with an overwhelming enemy, Deborah has to convince her male colleague, Barak, to assist in an attack on the enemy. The attack succeeds, and the Israelites live at peace for forty years (see 5:31).

God doesn't seem to be aware of any reason why women could not serve; God calls any number of women to service. How strange it is that an ancient document like the book of Judges should be such a forward-looking and inclusive story. Now that our culture seems to have caught up with that of the time of the judges, we celebrate God's use of women in the min-

> GOD DOESN'T SEEM TO BE AWARE OF ANY REASON WHY WOMEN COULD NOT SERVE; GOD CALLS ANY NUMBER OF WOMEN TO SERVICE.

istry of the church in all the ways that once were reserved for men. Let us thank God for leading us beyond our prejudices.

ZEPHANIAH 1:7, 12-18 (BCP; RCL, alt.)

Interpreting the Text

The book of Zephaniah reflects a period in Jewish history somewhere around the mid-600s B.C.E. and later. Generally the message is one of condemnation and judgment, although there are glimmers of hope in the idea of a faithful remnant (3:12-20). The lesson includes the prophet's use of the concept of the Day of the Lord in a way similar to Amos. Like Amos, the prophet must persuade the people that the crucial intervention of God will bring them punishment and not reward. Moreover, the people had come to think that God would do neither harm nor good to them, but the prophet declares that their comfortable lives will be ended. Verse 15 itemizes the nature of the Day of the Lord. The picture in v. 18 is even more radical; the Day of the Lord will see the consuming of the whole earth.

Responding to the Text

Occasionally we still encounter a street-corner preacher announcing the coming doom. Along with television preachers, street preachers preserve the "hellfire and brimstone" preaching that was so important in the history of our nation. However, such doom and gloom is no longer typical of Christian proclamation. And for that we can be thankful.

But perhaps the church today has become too timid. In the midst of our nation's ever-increasing affluence, too often we do not seem to have a prophetic word of warning. The prophet Zephaniah is hardly anyone's favorite. Yet we need to note his harsh words for a society that had lost touch with their God. Do we see something of ourselves in these words for another time? We don't need to be frightened out of our wits by doom and gloom, but we do need to be called to responsibility for the poor, the destitute, the oppressed, and the dying in our world.

PROVERBS 31:10-13, 19-20, 30-31 (RC)

Interpreting the Text

Proverbs 31:10-31 is a poem in praise of the "capable wife" and provides an interesting link with the story of Deborah in the first lesson. Proverbs begins with a passage concerning "Woman Wisdom" (1:20-33) and concludes with praise of the good wife who incarnates Wisdom. (See the reading from the Wisdom of Solomon 6 for the Twenty-fifth Sunday after Pentecost). The wise wife provided order and meaning to the family structure. Verses 11-12 speak of her relationship with her husband, while vv. 14-19 praise her contributions to the economic life of the society. Not only is she effective as manager of her household, but she is compassionate toward the needy (v. 20). The final verses first contrast the worthy wife with one who uses charm to make her way and then admonishes fairness and justice toward her.

In fairness, we should acknowledge that, as valuable as this poem is, it praises woman for her traditional role in the society and family of the time. She is successful at providing for her husband. One commentator observes, "It is her fulfillment of the roles in the home assigned to her by society that causes her to be praised in the very gates of the city where Woman Wisdom first raised her cry."[1]

Responding to the Text

My wife has been a pastor in the Evangelical Lutheran Church in America since the early days when women were being ordained in the Lutheran Church in America. One Sunday morning she was greeting worshipers at the end of a service, when a little boy about six years old approached. "Pastor Myrna," he asked her, "can boys be pastors too?" That simple question suggests how far the church has come in incorporating women as equals in the ministry of the church.

Yet, even today, many women feel harnessed to the traditional roles they are expected to play. Our reading is a beautiful tribute to the worthy wife, but even it praises woman for serving her husband and fulfilling standard roles in society. As women in Western cultures have been freed to participate in all areas of work and service, the church has begun to see more clearly that sexism has no place in our society or worshiping communities.

RESPONSIVE READING
PSALM 123 (RCL)

This psalm is a moving prayer for divine mercy. Like one who has no other recourse, the psalmist leads us to total dependence on God's love and grace. Verses 1 and 2 give expression to that utter dependence, comparing it with human situations of reliance. In the spirit of that total reliance, the psalmist prays for mercy. Note the experience of the psalmist that surfaces in vv. 3 and 4. She or he has "had more than enough contempt" and scorn. The plea for mercy comes out of painful experiences with other people.

The news is increasingly filled with reports of children and youth who have been brought to desperation by the bullying they experience. The constant put-downs, insults, and heckling literally devastate a person's sense of self-worth. Some victims are driven to acts of anger and others to self-destruction. Suddenly bullying has become a social problem.

Maybe this is a good time for us to recognize other kinds of bullying that take place among so-called adults. Maybe it is time to acknowledge that the poor and hungry are bullied and made to feel worthless. Abused children and those who suffer spousal abuse are equally victims of such bullying.

Our psalmist this morning speaks of her or his experience of bullying—being treated with contempt and scorn. It is interesting, however, that this psalmist asks for God's mercy amid such experiences of bullying. What that mercy seems to entail in this case is a gracious presence—a sense of companionship with God. So the plea is not so much for forgiveness but for strength mercifully given.

PSALM 90 or 90:1-8, 12 (BCP);
PSALM 90:1-8, (9-11) 12 (RCL, alt.)

Verses 1-12 vividly contrast the nature of God and that of humans. They alternate between two related themes: first, the contrast of God's transcendence over time with the temporality of human life (vv. 1-6, 9-10, and 12), and second, the opposition of our fragility and divine wrath (vv. 7-8, and 11). Verses 13-17 conclude the poem with a prayer for God's redemption and presence. The effect of this alternation in the first 12 verses is to keep the reader pulling together these two pairs as a model of the human life. The prayer relieves the depression of the contrasting verses with a reliance on God.

In 2004, vivid pictures of the surface of Mars were sent back to earth by NASA's two robotic rovers. They were awesome, to say the least. To think that we are able to gain contact with another planet so far removed from our own! What will these gifted women and men who probe the unknown dimensions of our lives do next?

The wonder of human achievement in just our lifetime continues to make us curious of what, if any, are the limitations of human accomplishment. It sometimes seems that nothing is beyond the reach of the human mind. But then we read Psalm 90 and again realize our fragility and limitations when compared with God. The contrast of our lives and the reality of God is powerful. Standing before the power and timelessness of God helps us to remain humble and remember that we are human not divine. That experience does not stifle the ambitions of our search for knowledge, but it reminds us that beyond our knowledge there is Another.

> THE CONTRAST OF OUR LIVES AND THE REALITY OF GOD IS POWERFUL. STANDING BEFORE THE POWER AND TIMELESSNESS OF GOD HELPS US TO REMAIN HUMBLE AND REMEMBER THAT WE ARE HUMAN NOT DIVINE.

PSALM 128:1-2, 3, 4-5 (RC)

This psalm has three discernible sections—vv. 1-2, 3-4, and 5-6. The first is a general benediction. The second specifies how "fear of the LORD" will insure that "it shall go well with you." The third section sounds more like a priestly benediction that entails (1) the prosperity of Jerusalem, (2) living to see your grandchildren, and (3) peace for Israel.

The theme of this psalm, like others (e.g., Psalm 1), is that fearing and worshiping God brings peace and prosperity. The theme roots in the Deuteronomic ethic held that if you are faithful to God you will be blessed and if not then you will be cursed (see Judg. 2:6-23).

If you are like me, you sometimes wonder why it is that the most righteous of people seem to suffer the most hardship. We think of the saintly woman in the church who suffers a lingering death from cancer. Or of the person who devotes his life to the service of others only to be prematurely killed in an auto accident. I remember my agony when Martin Luther King Jr. and Robert Kennedy were assassinated. They represented the best of promises for our nation in a difficult period; yet they were murdered.

For these reasons, some of us have trouble with this morning's psalm. Without qualification it declares that those who fear the Lord prosper. As much as many of us would like to believe this to be true, experience teaches us something different. Moreover, the assumption that we will prosper if we are faithful to God assumes that such a selfish motive as prosperity is acceptable. Yet today we hear a good deal about "prosperity Christianity." However, the major difficulty with this view is the life and death of Jesus. The epitome of righteousness does not prosper but suffers and dies.

SECOND READING

1 THESSALONIANS 5:1-11 (RCL);
1 THESSALONIANS 5:1-10 (BCP);
1 THESSALONIANS 5:1-6 (RC)

Interpreting the Text

Following his words of instruction about the coming of the Lord in 4:13-18, Paul continues his theme in this reading by stressing a readiness for the final day, although we cannot be sure if this particular theme is one for which the Thessalonians are in need. According to some commentators, the lesson moves through three units: "(1) the day of the Lord (vv. 1-3), (2) the call for watchfulness (vv. 4-8a), (3) Christian existence (vv. 8b-10), with v. 11 forming a general conclusion to 4:13—5:10."[2]

1. "Times and seasons" opens the question of the relative importance of the present and near future but is then qualified by the fact that the Day of the Lord comes "as a thief in the night"—that is, an unknown time (see Matt. 24:43 and Luke 12:39, as well as Isa. 2:9-19 and Amos 5 18-20). Verse 3 sounds like the prophet Amos and utilizes the imagery of the expected mother.

2. Paul concludes that since Christians are "children of the day," they will not be tempted to sleep through the appearance of Christ. Since Paul is using day and night metaphorically, "belonging to the day" means that Christians are already experiencing the light of truth. This is all to emphasize that the Christians are to be watchful for the arrival of their Lord.

3. Christians need not fear the final day, for they are not "destined for wrath," and they may expect salvation (rescue) on that last day. Verse 10 seems to undercut Paul's point, for now he says in effect that it does not matter whether we are awake or asleep since we will be made alive by Christ. However, some take "awake" or "asleep" here as metaphors for "dead" or "alive," as they are used in 4:13-15. "Who died for us" is the clearest statement of the meaning of the cross in the Thessalonian letters.

Fear is one of the classic means for helping people get serious about their religious faith. In the hottest of days in Atlanta, a church sign read something like this: "If you think this is hot, just wait to see what may await you after death." A bumper sticker reads, "God is coming soon, and boy is he ticked!" Abuses of our human propensity for fear are common in religious circles.

However, this lesson invites us to think differently. Paul seems to have no interest in trying to frighten the Thessalonians into faith. He does not threaten them with the consequences of sin when the last judgment comes. To the contrary, Paul does just the opposite. He seems to say to his readers *be ready but not worried*. You are, he says, "children of the day," therefore we are already experiencing some of what is coming in the last day. God has not chosen us to suffer wrath but joy. Maybe this positive note has more and better results than the fearmongers get.

> "WHO DIED FOR US" IS THE CLEAREST STATEMENT OF THE MEANING OF THE CROSS IN THE THESSALONIAN LETTERS.

THE GOSPEL

MATTHEW 25:14-30 (RCL);
MATTHEW 25:14-15, 19-29 (BCP);
MATTHEW 25:14-30 or 25:14-15, 19-21 (RC)

Interpreting the Text

This is the second of Matthew's three parables about Christ's *parousia*. One commentator summarizes the point of this parable as "responsibility during the interim period."[3] It works on the bases of the relationship between owner and servant, as do a good number of the parables. The plot is simple and follows the threefold pattern so common in oral literature. In this case, the story line goes like this: entrustment, departure, investments, return, and judgment. "A man" prepares for a journey by entrusting his property to his servants in decreasing amounts (i.e., five, two, and one talent) depending on their capabilities. Each servant invests the man's property, except the third one who hides his. The master returns and receives his property plus what it has earned, except for the third. He condemns the third who is thrown into "outer darkness." A "talent" represented a large amount of money, the equivalent of fifteen years' wages for a common laborer.

The point of the parable is found in the dialogue between the man and the third servant upon the owner's return (vv. 24-30). The third servant makes excuses for his failure to invest his share of the man's wealth by referring to the harshness of the man and the servant's resultant fear (vv. 24-26). The man condemns the servant for his failure to invest the talent (vv. 26-27) and then punishes him by (1) taking the talent away from the servant and (2) having the servant thrown "into outer darkness, where there will be weeping and gnashing of teeth" (vv. 28-30).

The parable seems to highlight the paralyzing nature of fear and the cowardice of hiding the money. Arland J. Hultgren believes that v. 29 means that "only the person who has been tested in small matters can be entrusted with larger ones." Moreover, "wherever God's gift has already borne fruit, God gives in greater abundance; where it has been fruitless, it is lost completely."[4]

> "WHEREVER GOD'S GIFT HAS ALREADY BORNE FRUIT, GOD GIVES IN GREATER ABUNDANCE; WHERE IT HAS BEEN FRUITLESS, IT IS LOST COMPLETELY."

Responding to the Text

We have probably all learned a great deal about the stock market in the last five years. If nothing else, we have been reminded of how risky it is to invest our money. But isn't it true that life is filled with risks?

Have you ever had the joy and frustration of watching a child trying to decide how to spend the money she received for her birthday? She is given the money to spend as she likes. She studies the rows of toys, considering one row after another. She may try to buy two smaller toys only to find that they cost twenty-five cents more than she has. Finally, she makes a decision and starts up to the counter only to change her mind and go back to reconsider her selection. (We adults call it "buyer's remorse.") The process for the child may consume thirty minutes or more. With the risk involved in the investment in mind, maybe we can better understand the servant who hides his master's money rather than investing it. If we look for some reason by which we might understand his actions, we are brought to the excuse he offers the owner. "Master, I knew that you were a harsh man . . . so I was afraid, and I went and hid your talent in the ground." A harsh man? Did we miss something in the story? We are told nothing about the man. So how did the servant come to think of him as harsh? Or, are we to emphasize the other part of his excuse: "I was afraid"?

He has been given the equal of fifteen years of a laborer's salary. Fifteen years! Who among us would not be afraid? Who among us would not want to be as cautious as possible with the money?

The servant had a right to be afraid, and so might we. So might we, except for one thing. In Christ we have been given freedom to take risks. Martin Luther called it the freedom of the Christian in the gospel.[5] We do not have to be afraid of failure. We do not have to fear anyone, no matter how harsh he or she may be. In Christ we have been given our security.

Dwelling with the Texts

Part of the hymn "Lord, Speak to Us, That We May Speak," written by Frances R. Havergal (1836–1879) is appropriate for preachers to consider.

> Oh, teach us, Lord, that we may teach
> The precious truth which you impart;
> And wing our words, that they may reach
> The hidden depths of many a heart.[6]

Notes

1. Carole R. Fontaine, "Proverbs," *The Women's Bible Commentary*, ed. Carol A. Newsom and Sharon H. Ringe (Louisville: Westminster John Knox, 1992), 152.

2. The work of B. Rigaux, quoted in F. F. Bruce, *1 & 2 Thessalonians,* Word Biblical Commentary 45 (Waco: Word Books, 1982), 108.

3. Dennis C. Duling, "Matthew," *The HarperCollins Study Bible: New Revised Standard Version* (New York: HarperCollins, 1993), 1904.

4. Arland J. Hultgren, *The Parables of Jesus: A Commentary* (Grand Rapids: Eerdmans, 2000), 277.

5. Martin Luther, "The Freedom of the Christian," trans. W. A. Lambert and Harold J. Grimm; *Luther's Works,* 31:327–77.

6. *Lutheran Book of Worship* (Minneapolis: Augsburg, 1978), 403.

LAST SUNDAY AFTER PENTECOST, CHRIST THE KING

NOVEMBER 20, 2005
THIRTY-FOURTH SUNDAY IN ORDINARY TIME /
PROPER 29

REVISED COMMON	EPISCOPAL (BCP)	ROMAN CATHOLIC
Ezek. 34:11-16, 20-24	Ezek. 34:11-17	Ezek. 34:11-12, 15-17
Psalm 100 or Ps. 95:1-7a	Ps. 95:1-7	Ps. 23
Eph. 1:15-23	1 Cor. 15:20-28	1 Cor. 15:20-26, 28
Matt. 25:31-46	Matt. 25:31-46	Matt. 25:31-46

Christ the King Sunday suffers under the burden of an outdated metaphor for Christ ("the King") and one that has made many uncomfortable because of its gender exclusion. Still, if Christ be a king, what a strange king he is, as our Gospel lesson suggests.

FIRST READING
EZEKIEL 34:11-16, 20-24 (RCL);
EZEKIEL 34:11-17 (BCP);
EZEKIEL 34:11-12, 15-17 (RC)

Interpreting the Text

This passage is found in the last major portion of Ezekiel (chaps. 33–48), which has to do with the restoration of Israel. Ezekiel's period of prophecy extended from 593 until sometime while Israel was still in exile in Babylon (perhaps 571). Before Israel's exile, his message was primarily one of doom, but after the exile he promised a restoration of the people. Chapter 34 is a rather complex series of speeches concerning shepherd and sheep. Verses 1-10 are an oracle of woe against Israel's shepherds because they have failed the people. Verses 11-16 describe Yahweh as the shepherd of the people, and 17-22 address the conflicts among groups in the "flock" of Israel.

In v. 2 the word the NRSV translates "Ah" can also be rendered "woe." The shepherds Ezekiel criticizes probably include the leaders of the people as well as the kings. Verse 10 ends the attack on the false shepherds with the promise that God will "rescue my sheep."

In the second part of the reading (vv. 11-16), God becomes shepherd, seeking the lost and rescuing them from danger. The language in these verses suggests the way in which the scattered exiles are united and brought home. The third part begins with v. 17 and speaks of God's judging among the sheep and between goats and rams. Suddenly, in v. 23 God declares that David will be set over the sheep and will care for them. It is probably for that reason the reading concludes with v. 22.

The use of the imagery of sheep and shepherd is a frequent one in the Old Testament literature and a common metaphor in the ancient Near East for the people and their king.

Responding to the Text

Remember the fight that broke out in the championship baseball game between the New York Yankees and the Boston Red Sox in 2003? It is memorable in part because of the long-standing rivalry between these two teams. But I will never forget one of the coaches dashing onto the field to join the battle and then being thrown to the ground. The whole scene was depressing, and one had to wonder how coaches and managers could allow such a thing to occur.

> THE LANGUAGE IN THESE VERSES SUGGESTS THE WAY IN WHICH THE SCATTERED EXILES ARE UNITED AND BROUGHT HOME.

A crowd without guidance—supervision—can quickly become a mob. It is comparable to a flock of sheep that has no responsible shepherd. In the First Lesson, the prophet Ezekiel chastises the leaders of Israel for abdicating their role. The sheep are scattered and preyed upon by wild animals. It is a vivid portrayal of the failure of Israel's leaders, the nation's defeat at the hands of the Babylonians, and their deportation from their homeland. So outraged is Ezekiel by Israel's leadership that he declares God will become the people's shepherd.

How does God continue to shepherd the people of God today? Leaders of nations stand under the scrutiny of Ezekiel's standard for shepherds.

RESPONSIVE READING
PSALM 100 (RCL)

This psalm combines two calls to worship and praise. The first is vv. 1-3 and the second vv. 4-5. In the first, God is presented as our Creator and then as our Shepherd, and the two images spark fresh consideration of the divine. In the first, we are invited to fill the earth with "joyful noise" (v. 1), and in the second, we are asked to share our thanksgiving to God (v. 4). To worship God is to do both.

You can tell a lot from how a group of people worship. Some will worship through silence and others through liturgy, ceremony, and ritual. African American Christian worship is often filled with singing, clapping, and sometimes even dancing. The sermon is a lecture in some tradition and in others a rousing motivational presentation. In each case, the form of worship betrays the kind of God we worship.

This psalm calls us to worship. It provides an entrance into the divine presence. How we worship, however, is defined by who God is. Notice that in each of the summons there is attached a statement about God. In the first, we are asked to know that the Lord is God, our Creator and our Shepherd. In the second, God is good, faithful, and loving.

PSALM 95:1-7 (BCP); PSALM 95:1-7a (RCL, alt.)

Scholars believe this psalm originated as a hymn recited (or sung) in the procession into the temple. The psalmist begins with a declaration of God's kingship and universal rule. The divine hands hold both the heights and the depths of the creation. With v. 6 the theme changes from that of God as king (v. 3) to that of shepherd. God is not only the Lord of the created order but of human life as well. The king was often called the shepherd both in Israel and other of the nations of the ancient Near East. Verses 8-11 were perhaps a priestly admonition in preparation for the reading of Torah.

How do we dare to describe God? Any of our language seems puny and weak over against the creator God who transcends our world of time and space. Because of the difficulty in speaking of God, it is interesting how the psalmist undertakes the task. The psalm confronts us with our God through use of two very different images or metaphors. Note that early in the psalm, God is described as the great King who is above and beyond any others who pretend to be gods. However, toward the end of this portion of the psalm, the picture changes. Now the great King is spoken of as Shepherd and we are the people of the Shepherd. Shepherd-King. King-Shepherd. Neither is adequate by itself, but together they capture something of our experience of the divine.

PSALM 23 (RC)

This beloved psalm is a perfect fit with the reading from Ezekiel. The psalmist begins by speaking of God as a shepherd (vv. 1-4) and then shifts the imagery to that of a host in whose house we dine (vv. 5-6). Equally important are the experiences the psalmist describes. While the shepherd leads the people to safety and supplies all their needs, suddenly in v. 3 the worshiper speaks of journeying through the shadows of death. When God hosts us at a meal (v. 5), it is with our enemies. God is a faithful shepherd and a caring host, but life is still filled with dangers and conflict.

For many of us, the image of that weird little creature we call ET made a lasting impression on us. Who would have guessed that in the days of monsters and unimaginably evil creatures, little ET would find his way into our hearts? The

---

GOD IS A FAITHFUL SHEPHERD AND A CARING HOST, BUT
LIFE IS STILL FILLED WITH DANGERS AND CONFLICT.

---

remarkable thing about ET is the way he participated in the lives of human beings and became identified with little children. Among the first words ET learns during his sojourn here on earth is the word "Ouch!" When he finally returns to his home, he shares the same "ouch" his dear friends experience at the moment of separation.

The peculiar feature of our God-shepherd-host is similar. Our God identifies with the pains and sorrows of human life. He accompanies us through dark shadows and sits at table with us in the presence of our enemies. The good shepherd, you see, does not abandon us to the painful dimensions of life but shares them with us.

SECOND READING
EPHESIANS 1:15-23 (RCL)

See the discussion of the Second Lesson for All Saints Day.

1 CORINTHIANS 15:20-28 (BCP);
1 CORINTHIANS 15:20-26, 28 (RC)

Interpreting the Text

First Corinthians 15 contains Paul's lengthy discussion of the resurrection of the dead in the light of Christ's resurrection. In connection with Christ's resurrection, Paul is brought to a depiction of Christ's ascension and assumption of heavenly power. In the verses prior to this reading, he lists some of the reasons for believing that Christians will be raised from the dead, and one of them is the fact that Christ was raised. So, in our lesson, he speaks of Christ as the "first fruits," meaning the first harvesting of the ripe fruit (v. 20). However, that leads him into one of the several places he discusses Christ and Adam (see also Rom. 5:12-21). Verses 21-22 assume what seems to have been a Jewish understanding of how death came into the world. One person, Adam, sinned and hence died; henceforth all humans die. In a comparable way to how Adam brought death into human experience, so one person, Christ, has brought life. (Paul returns to this theme in vv. 45-49 of this chapter.) Those brought to life after Christ (the first fruits) are those who "belong to Christ."

Verse 24 marks Paul's move from Christ's resurrection to the "end" time. As ascended Lord, Christ defeats all the heavenly powers thought to inhabit the sky. The three words, "ruler," "authority," and "power" appear elsewhere in Paul's letters (e.g., Rom. 8:38) and identify the cosmic forces of evil that are also at work in earthly kingdoms. "Death" is still another of these cosmic powers,

> "DEATH" IS STILL ANOTHER OF THESE COSMIC POWERS, AND IT IS THE LAST OF THE HEAVENLY EVILS CHRIST WILL OVERCOME.

and it is the last of the heavenly evils Christ will overcome. Paul's thought is interrupted briefly at v. 27 when he quotes Ps. 8:6 and then explains that this does not include Christ, who is "the one who put all things in subjection under him." The reading concludes with the final goal of all of time: "God will be all in all." This seems to suggest that the reality now is that God shares authority and power with forces of evil but in the end will be the total reality.

Responding to the Text

One morning soon after we moved to Atlanta, I was on my way to the university when, out of the corner of my eye, I saw a billboard that announced, "The Bull is taking charge." I was busy with the traffic but wondered immediately what the sign could mean. What Bull? How is it taking charge? My mind was filled with possibilities, none of which I wanted to believe was true. Later that day on the way home, I saw the sign again and was able to read the whole of it. It was an advertisement for a beer, which they called "the bull"! That hardly

> IF CHAOS SEEMS TO RULE NOW, IN THE END CHAOS WILL BE OVERCOME AND GOD WILL BE IN CHARGE. WITH THAT HOPE AND THAT PROMISE WE LIVE.

calmed my anxiety, for now I had to ask how a beer takes charge!

Who's in charge? Or, is there anyone or anything in charge? Some times there seems to be no one in charge of our world, as we wander from one crisis to another. Is life without an ultimate rule or a final order? Absolute disorder? Anarchy? Chaos? We need to know who's in charge, if anyone.

Paul speaks of Christ's resurrection and how he will eventually take charge of the whole of the universe—conquering all the enemies of truth and order and putting all things in subjection to one will, the divine will. Even he—Christ himself—is subjected to God so that, as Paul writes, "God may be all in all." That's the hope and the promise we have as Christians. God, not the bull, is in charge and will eventually *take charge*. If chaos seems to rule now, in the end chaos will be overcome and God will be in charge. With that hope and that promise we live.

The Gospel
MATTHEW 25:31-46 (RCL, BCP, RC)

Interpreting the Text

The vision of the final judgment on the occasion of Christ's *parousia* is the last of the three parables in Matthew 25, and—more important—the last of Jesus' teachings before the beginning of the passion story in chapter 26. In a sense, however, 25:31-46 is not a parable in the strict sense. Yes, this is a story that shatters our assumptions about the world as do the parables, but this passage has been more appropriately called an "apocalyptic vision." One thing is certain: the first evangelist situates this story so that it serves as a capstone to all of Jesus' teachings and prepares us for the passion story.

> THE FIRST EVANGELIST SITUATES THIS STORY SO THAT IT SERVES AS A CAPSTONE TO ALL OF JESUS' TEACHINGS AND PREPARES US FOR THE PASSION STORY.

The opening image is that of a king seated on a throne before all the nations of the world. The belief that God would judge the whole of humanity at the end of time is scattered throughout the Hebrews Scriptures, but Dan. 7:13-16 may be the closest parallel to Matthew's picture. "Nations" translates *ethnē*, which is sometimes taken to mean "Gentiles." Sheep were sometimes valued more highly than goats, but both were used in sacrificial worship.

With the judgment of the "righteous," vv. 34-36 define the criteria for the judgment: serving the Son of Man when one finds him in need. What is startling about this story is that neither the righteous nor the "accursed" have any recollection of having seen the king in need. Both ask in amazement, "Lord, when did we see you hungry . . . ?" The king's response is equally surprising and is the key issue in the interpretation of this passage. He says of their serving "just as you did it (or did not do it) to one of the least of these who are members of my family (*adelphoi*), you did it to me." The story shocks us since the king is identified with "the least."

Among others, the important interpretative question is who are the *adelphoi*? Matthew seems to use this term for any believer (particularly the vulnerable missionaries) and not for unconverted Gentiles. The argument has been between those who understand "the least of these" as Christian missionaries in the Gentile world and those who read it as a "universal" reference to the needy. Some argue that the original meaning of the expression was Jesus' family of believers but that it is logical to extend the title to mean all those who are among the "least."[1]

The point that shakes the foundations of our religious assumptions is that the righteous and the unrighteous have no idea that they did or did not serve the King incarnated in the needy. The righteous are righteous for what they did with-out thought of reward or goodness but only because they encounter the "least." In other words, righteous behavior is done for the simple reason that others are in need without thought of what is right or wrong and what is rewarding and what is not.

> THE RIGHTEOUS AND THE UNRIGHTEOUS HAVE NO IDEA THAT THEY DID OR DID NOT SERVE THE KING INCARNATED IN THE NEEDY.

Responding to the Text

There are some things that have been so drilled into us that we hardly know where they came from. For instance, have you ever thought about why we smile? It seems that, from the first time the baby curls the corners of her mouth up, the parents are filled with joy, praise the child, and encourage her. There are those old cynics who say that the first facial expression we identify as a smile may be nothing more that the baby's reaction to gas.

Another thing that we are conditioned to believe is simply that, if you are good, you will be rewarded and, if you are bad, you will be punished. So this strange parable knocks our socks off! The so-called sheep had no idea they were doing anything good or righteous when they fed the hungry, gave the thirsty a drink, welcomed a stranger, gave the naked clothing, took care of the sick, or vis-ited prisoners. They are utterly shocked when Jesus tells them that when they did these things they *were doing it to him*. Likewise, the goats never thought that they had neglected Jesus when they failed to do these things.

Righteous behavior is not done for the sake of its reward. The sheep aren't aiming at heaven or thinking, "Ah, here's a chance for another star in my crown." They are not conscious that they have served Christ, *because they're not keeping records of their deeds*. They served the needy because there was a need to fill!

What all this leads us to is the simple fact that with this King of ours, we can-not secure our eternal destiny; we cannot nail down our eternal future. Conse-quently, we must depend on God's merciful grace.

Dwelling with the Texts

The Gospel lesson urges us to think about those times we may have or will meet Christ disguised as a needy person. Given that fact, we would do well to think about all the people we encountered this day who were in some sort of need (and who isn't?). How can we learn to be more sensitive to others and their needs?

Note

1. See, for example, Eugene M. Boring, *The Gospel of Matthew* (New Interpreter's Bible; Nashville: Abingdon, 1995), 8:456.

MARCH 2005

Sunday	Monday	Tuesday	Wednesday	Thursday	Friday	Saturday
		1	2	3	4	5
6	7	8	9	10	11	12
13	14	15	16	17	18	19
20	21	22	23	24	25	26
27 Easter Day	28 Easter Monday	29	30	31	Good Friday	

APRIL 2005

Sunday	Monday	Tuesday	Wednesday	Thursday	Friday	Saturday
					1	2
3 2 Easter	4	5	6	7	8	9
10 3 Easter	11	12	13	14	15	16
17 4 Easter	18	19	20	21	22	23
24 5 Easter	25	26	27	28	29	30

MAY 2005

Sunday	Monday	Tuesday	Wednesday	Thursday	Friday	Saturday
1	2	3	4	5	6	7
8 Mother's Day 7 Easter	9 6 Easter	10	11	12	13	14
15 Pentecost	16	17	18	19	20	21
22 1 Pentecost	23	24	25	26	27	28
29 2 Pentecost	30 Memorial Day	31				

JUNE 2005

Sunday	Monday	Tuesday	Wednesday	Thursday	Friday	Saturday
			1	2	3	4
5 3 Pentecost	6	7	8	9	10	11
12 4 Pentecost	13	14	15	16	17	18
19 5 Pentecost Father's Day	20	21	22	23	24	25
26 6 Pentecost	27	28	29	30		

JULY 2005

Sunday	Monday	Tuesday	Wednesday	Thursday	Friday	Saturday
					1	2
3 7 Pentecost	4 Independence Day	5	6	7	8	9
10 8 Pentecost	11	12	13	14	15	16
17 9 Pentecost	18	19	20	21	22	23
24 10 Pentecost	25	26	27	28	29	30
30 11 Pentecost						

AUGUST 2005

Sunday	Monday	Tuesday	Wednesday	Thursday	Friday	Saturday
	1	2	3	4	5	6
7	8	9	10	11	12	13
12 Pentecost	15	16	17	18	19	20
14	22	23	24	25	26	27
13 Pentecost	29	30	31			
21						
14 Pentecost						
28						
15 Pentecost						

SEPTEMBER 2005

Sunday	Monday	Tuesday	Wednesday	Thursday	Friday	Saturday
				1	2	3
4 16 Pentecost	5 Labor Day	6	7	8	9	10
11 17 Pentecost	12	13	14	15	16	17
18 18 Pentecost	19	20	21	22	23	24
25 19 Pentecost	26	27	28	29	30	

OCTOBER 2005

Sunday	Monday	Tuesday	Wednesday	Thursday	Friday	Saturday
						1
2	3	4	5	6	7	8
20 Pentecost						
9	10	11	12	13	14	15
21 Pentecost						
16	17	18	19	20	21	22
22 Pentecost						
23	24	25	26	27	28	29
23 Pentecost						
30	31					
24 Pentecost						

NOVEMBER 2005

Sunday	Monday	Tuesday	Wednesday	Thursday	Friday	Saturday
		1	2	3	4	5
6 25 Pentecost	7	8	9	10	11 Veteran's Day	12
13 26 Pentecost	14	15	16	17	18	19
20 Last Pentecost	21	22	23	24 Thanksgiving Day	25	26
27	28	29	30			